Reimagining Culture

BERG

Ethnicity and Identity

SERIES

ISSN: 1354-3628

General Editors:
Shirley Ardener, *Founding Director, Centre for Cross-Cultural Research on Women, University of Oxford*

Tamara Dragadze, *School of Slavonic and East European Studies, University of London*

Jonathan Webber, *Institute of Social and Cultural Anthropology, University of Oxford*

Books previously published in the Series

Sharon Macdonald (ed.), *Inside European Identities: Ethnography in Western Europe*

Martin Stokes (ed.), *Ethnicity, Identity and Music: The Musical Construction of Place*

Joanne Eicher (ed.), *Dress and Ethnicity*

Simone Abram, Jackie Waldren and Donald Macleod (eds), *Tourists and Tourism: Identifying with People and Places*

Jeremy MacClancy (ed.), *Sport, Identity and Ethnicity*

Reimagining Culture

Histories, Identities and the
Gaelic Renaissance

Sharon Macdonald

Oxford • New York

First published in 1997 by
Berg
Editorial offices:
150 Cowley Road, Oxford, OX4 1JJ, UK
70 Washington Square South, New York, NY 10012, USA

Berg is the imprint of Oxford International Publishers Ltd.

Library of Congress Cataloging-in-Publication Data

A catalogue record for this book is available from the Library of Congress.

British Library Cataloguing-in-Publication Data

A catalogue record for this book is available from the British Library.

ISBN   1 85973 980 6 (Cloth)
1 85973 985 7 (Paper)

Typeset by JS Typesetting, Wellingborough, Northants.
Printed in the United Kingdom by WBC Book Manufacturers, Bridgend,
Mid Glamorgan.

For Mike

Is thubhairt mo thuigse ri mo ghaol:
cha dhuinn an dùbailteachd:
tha'n coimeasgadh 'sa' ghaol.
(Somhairle Mac Gilleain, from 'A Chiall 's a Ghraidh')

Contents

List of Illustrations

Acknowledgments

Over the long course of completing this book, I have amassed immense practical and intellectual debts which are far too extensive to deal with at all adequately here. My first and immeasurable debt is to the people of Carnan, who so generously offered me hospitality and friendship, and who put up with my hanging around and my questions. 'Carnan' is a pseudonym, as are the names given to all individuals here, in order to try to lessen to some small extent the intrusion that a study such as this may be. In some cases I have also altered minor factual details in order to try to protect individual identities. I consider myself exceptionally fortunate to have been able to come to know, to some extent at least, so many in Carnan; and I think perhaps that part of the reason for my tardiness in letting this book inch its way towards publication is a fear of transforming relationships, formed over many years now, which have become very dear to me. I am aware that this book may seem odd and perhaps not as expected; but, full of shortcomings though it certainly is, it is my best and most honest attempt to understand life in Carnan, and I offer it as a perverse gift to those among whom I lived.

To fully name individuals here would run counter to the attempt to disguise those who helped me in my research, and indeed there are too many people in Carnan who showed me kindness to name individually. However, I would like to extend especial thanks to those who offered me accommodation, to Peggy and especially to Murdina for giving me my first and enduring real sense of the complexity of questions of Highland identity, for help with my faltering Gaelic, and for comments on some parts of this manuscript; to Christina, Robert, John, and especially the late Robert, who, perhaps more than anybody, showed me a radical and positive view of the Highland past and the vital place of jokes and wry humour in Hebrideans' outlook. I also thank Peggy and Lachy, and particularly Lachy, for so much valuable talk in and about Gaelic, and about local life. 'Dollag' has provided a very treasured friendship and letters which at various points have helped me clarify points which were puzzling me. Gratitude is also due to the teachers and pupils of Carnan school, and to all those who provided me with information about Gaelic education. Margaret deserves a particular mention not only for her friendship but also for reading and commenting on this manuscript, so saving me from a number of possible inadvertent offences and errors. Those that remain, of course, are entirely my own responsibility.

Funding for this research has come from the Economic and Social Research Council, the Sir John Rhŷs Bequest for Celtic Studies (University of Oxford), St Catherine's College, Oxford, and Keele University. I extend gratitude to these organisations and to the colleagues with whom I have worked over the years who so often have made me think again about my research. I also thank staff at Comunn na Gàidhlig, Highland Enterprise and the School of Scottish Studies and Jonathan MacDonald, Skye Museum of Island Life for the assistance that they have given me. I am grateful to Canongate Books Ltd (14 High Street, Edinburgh, EH1 1TE) for permission to quote from Sorley MacLean's poem 'A Chfàll 'sa Ghraidh' originally published in *Spring Tide and Neap Tide: Selected Poems 1932–72*; and to Shirley Ardener for permission to reproduce two diagrams by E.W. Ardener (Figures 9.1 and 9.2).

Intellectually, I have a particular debt to the late Edwin Ardener, the supervisor until his untimely death of the doctoral thesis on which this book is based. Edwin not only gave me my first lessons in Gaelic at his kitchen table, he also generously shared ideas and insights on matters Hebridean as well as anthropological. I am also fortunate to have benefited from comments on all or part of various versions of this book from the following: Mike Beaney, Edward Condry, Jeanette Edwards, D. Ellis Evans, Michael Gilsenan, Richard Jenkins, Màiri MacArthur, John MacInnes, Maryon McDonald, John McLeod, Catherine Shoupe and especially Susan Parman. I may not have always done justice to their comments but they have all helped me to make this a better book than it would have been. I am also grateful for support and interest from Shirley Ardener, Ruth Finnegan, Ronnie Frankenberg, Kirsten Hastrup, Wendy James, John Law, and Ken MacKinnon; and to all those who have commented on my work in seminars and discussions. At Berg, Kathryn Earle's encouragement and enthusiasm have been important in helping this book see the light of day; as has Judy Mabro's thorough copy-editing. Some debts, of course, reach much further back, and I would like to acknowledge my gratitude to my mother, Brenda Macdonald, and to my late father with whose ghost parts of this book have sometimes been a conversation.

My sister, Julie White, has drawn the pictures which grace these pages, so helping resolve two dilemmas, one concerning the poor quality of many of my photographs and the other of wishing to include illustrations while preserving anonymity as far as possible. I thank her for doing such a beautiful job.

Mike Beaney, my husband, has played an enormous role in the research at all its stages. He deserves special thanks for the hard drinking and days of lugging sheep about that he did in Carnan for the sake of my fieldwork, and for the help and vision he has given during the long labour of producing this book. I also thank our children, Thomas, Harriet, and particularly our eldest daughter, Tara Catriona, for being wonderful field-work assistants. Their observations have often made me stop and look and think again. And their evident love for Carnan and desire to return have also made me acknowledge better some of my own feelings and profitably complicate further, to some extent at least, my account here.

Preface

In Scotland during the 1980s, cultural identity and the Gaelic language were the subject of much – and sometimes heated – debate. After years of decline, there were signs that Gaelic culture was undergoing a renaissance. Gaelic language policies flourished: Gaelic playgroups, Gaelic learners' societies, bilingual and Gaelic medium education were established, and the Gaelic media expanded. In other domains too – Gaelic arts, local and oral history, community cooperatives, crofting politics – there seemed to be evidence of a renewed energy and interest in the *Gàidhealtachd* throughout Scotland.

This book is an ethnographic study of cultural identity and language in a community which I call Carnan. Situated on the Isle of Skye, an Inner Hebridean island lying off the north-west coast of Scotland, Carnan was widely regarded as a symbolically important 'test-case' of the Gaelic renaissance. Here I look at ways in which local people express their senses of belonging, and in particular at their responses to Gaelic language policies. Few local people had played much direct part in creating those policies, though at the time of my main fieldwork in the mid-1980s Gaelic cultural developments were finding their way into more and more areas of their lives and local people were increasingly drawn in to implementing them. As such, this research could be seen as an anthropological study of the impact of the outside world on local people. However, the case is complicated by the ambiguity of the boundaries (*is* Scotland the outside world?) and by the fact that the 'Gaelic culture' being projected onto the contemporary Highlands is often assumed to have been there in the first place. This is not then another account of 'acculturation' but a story of a kind of 're-culturation' – the reimagining of Gaelic culture.

My use of the term 'reimagining' in the title of this book is intended to evoke both the sense of 'return' – of resurrection – that is contained in ideas of cultural 'renaissance' and 'revival', as well as of the creativity of culture production. The idea of return suffuses much discourse of development in the Highlands, though this is not to say that renaissance developments are only preoccupied with a return to the past; on the contrary, theirs is an attempt to negotiate between the 'new' and the paradoxically 'old again'. It is with these negotiations that I am concerned. I also use the terms 'imagining' and 'reimagining' as part of my own analytical perspective to indicate that identities and culture always entail particular ways of seeing, and that they may be subject to alternative perceptions and objectifications, and to reworking.[1] This is not meant to imply that imaginings are somehow 'unreal' or 'imaginary': on the contrary, they are an important constitutive part of social life (cf. Anderson 1983; Jenkins 1996). Through the term '*re*imagining', my intention is to particularly emphasise that identities and culture are not imagined once and for all but must constantly be recreated (cf. Lerner 1993). This is a process in which previous imaginings come into play but may find themselves reshaped: it is a process at once creative and constrained.

To tell a story of the reimagining of Gaelic culture – and to understand local responses to Gaelic language policies – this book reaches both back in time and out beyond the spatial boundaries of the local community. Many of the sources for reimagining Gaelic culture lie in history; and many of the technologies for imagining – literature about the Highlands, educational policies, economic initiatives – have their origins or impetus elsewhere. The Gaelic renaissance is part of Scottish national identity and part of the wider movements of ethnonationalism within the established nation-states of Europe. How it is experienced locally needs to be understood at least partly in this light. This, then, is a *situated ethnography*. It argues that we cannot properly understand the local as synchronically and diachronically sealed. It also argues that, without the 'inside' perspectives that ethnography provides, our own categories of analysis may not be challenged and we risk simply projecting ready-made assumptions as 'explanations' of the local (and its responses). This ethnography, then, is intended as a challenge to academic and popular quests to find 'cultural identity' and the forms in which such identity is usually thought to be revealed.

There are, of course, always other stories that could, and perhaps should, be told. One of these concerns the identity of the ethnographer. In reflecting on the birth of my own interest in the subjects of this book – identity, language and Scotland – it is difficult, however, to know which autobiographical fragments to choose here. Not all those who lived in the Highland locality where I carried out my fieldwork would have sympathy with my uncertainty, however. On one occasion when I went to talk with one of Carnan's knowledgeable elderly men, Donald Murdo, he turned the tables – as happened not infrequently – to ask about my own identity. When it turned out that not only had I no knowledge of where 'my people' might have come from beyond the level of my grandparents, but that I had not even attempted to trace my family tree further back, he frowned and announced sternly: 'You should begin at the beginning'.

I still am not able to begin with the distant genealogy that he considered a proper beginning. And I continued with my presumption to explore issues of identity and history in Carnan without having clarified my own in the manner he thought fit. However, I accept his implication that my own identity is not irrelevant to my explorations here and that, although I am concerned in this book to draw the scope of 'reflexivity' much wider than personal autobiography, it is right to include information which might help readers know where I 'am coming from' should they wish to do so.

The nearest that I can get to the proper beginning that Donald Murdo requested is to tell of such tenuous Scottish affinities that I have. I was not born in Scotland and nor, except for the duration of my fieldwork, have I lived in Scotland. I am, it would seem, an example of what Hansen (1952) has called 'third generation return' – the first generation lives in the place, the second leaves, the third has a hankering to return (and perhaps does so). My paternal grandfather was born and brought up near Inverness, but then left to work overseas, returning in later life to Elgin, on the North East coast, where he was heavily involved in running the local football club. My father, born in Singapore, but later brought up in Scotland, left in early adulthood to train and work in England. A sculptor, his departure was, as he saw it, an escape from the grey small-town parochialism of the Scottish North East. He would, however, wear a Scottishness on such occasions as suited him: playing records of Scottish dance music when we had American visitors; saying a tremulous Scots grace for the entertainment of his children; and taking photographs of the Callanish stones on Lewis as part of a group of Edinburgh-based 'Scottish artists' in the early 1980s. He told us that we were Macdonalds of Glencoe and my sisters and I would pore over clan maps, copying out the Macdonald of Glencoe coat-of-arms. Even as teenagers, we were only mildly reluctant and embarrassed when our strongly Scottish Nationalist Hong-Kong-born grandmother (of Italian parentage) cajoled us to watch the television programme 'Andy's Party' (a jolly studio *ceilidh* full of wailing bagpipes and Highland flings) or persuaded her second husband to wear full dress tartan for strolls in our Derbyshire village. Summer holidays were frequently spent in Elgin but I remember that even as a child I felt frustrated that we did not visit the 'real Scotland' of which I had read – wild, bekilted, mist-encircled Highland Scotland. It was a place of the imagination to which I thought I might be able to 'return'.

This must clearly be a very inadequate account by Donald Murdo's standards, and perhaps by anybody's. I tell it, however, not to establish any right to speak on the subject of Scotland or identity – for it clearly does not do that – but to acknowledge that my own interest in the subject before I began my research was indubitably infused with a particularly kitsch romanticism, though perhaps also with a glimmer of alternative perceptions and realities. It gives some hints at a dimension of my own confused starting point when I began this research, before I had the privilege of living for any period of time in the Scottish Highlands.

I have some misgivings about beginning my account with this sketch of autobiography – and not only because it is so unflattering. To begin with any threads of personal connection with Scotland (absurdly inadequate though mine clearly are) might imply that I agree with the position so frequently maintained with regard to Scottish identity (and indeed many other identities, particularly those of so-called minorities) that it is necessary to be a *bona fide* Scot to say anything on the matter. I do not agree, however. Although the participant-observation method in social anthropology does entail attempting to see things from 'the native's points of view' (Malinowski 1922: 25), it does not necessitate being a native. Crucial to social anthropology is not only trying to present the picture 'from the inside', but also trying to throw that picture into relief, highlighting cultural specificities which insiders – by the very fact that they are insiders – easily take for granted. In other words, anthropology is not just about 'telling it as it is' (which can only ever be an aspiration, of course) but about telling how it might be otherwise. To do this we bring to bear, implicitly or explicitly, both theoretical concepts from our discipline and ideas about cultural alternatives in other times and places derived from reading and experience.

Donald Murdo's idea that the proper place to begin is with kinship and history is one with which many involved with the subject of identity would have sympathy, though it is necessarily a culturally specific one. His injunction to me bears the imprint, I think, of concerns which we might count as traditional to Gaelic culture – genealogy being a main theme of the Gaelic poetry of the fifteenth to the seventeenth centuries, for example (Thomson 1974: ch.1) – but also of the much more recent and widespread popular movement to trace family genealogies. There are many other, often less obvious ways in which identities can be articulated, however, as I try to show in this book. Like genealogy, these may, to greater and lesser extents, themselves draw their impetus from the particularities of Highland history, or from a wider cultural domain.

One question about my identity in relation to my research that I am often asked concerns my surname: 'Did it help being a Macdonald?' This question, which I have never been asked by Highlanders, carries a cultural assumption that a surname might indicate a kinship relation and that this in turn might mean that I would be 'more accepted' or even that people might feel some sort of obligation towards me. This idea, I think, may also bear the inflection of an assumption of 'clannishness' among Highlanders. As to whether my name did make any difference, I am unsure. Certainly, as I try to acknowledge above, I was treated with a great deal of kindness and generosity. However, this was not, I think, based on any imagined kinship via naming. Local people were well aware that visitors to the island sometimes assumed on the basis of their surnames (or even on the basis of the often rather fanciful 'translations' of surnames into 'clan' equivalents that are used to sell all kinds of tartan paraphernalia) that they had some kind of special relationship with local people, but this was laughingly dismissed in anecdotes told amongst Carnan folk. Moreover, a name like 'Macdonald' was so common as to be unremarkable (about half of the children in the primary school shared my surname) and most people referred to me simply as 'Sharon'. Indeed, when on leaving I came to give my address to various friends I was surprised to find that some (including one MacDonald family who I thought had perhaps been especially kind to me partly on the basis of an imagined kinship) were not even aware of, or had forgotten, my surname. Nevertheless, in an inverse move, my name could be used to account for and substantiate existing relationships and perceptions of me. For example, one man remarked: 'Aye, well, if you're a Macdonald I suppose your people were Highlanders way back and maybe that's why we get on as we do'. Fortunately too, for my fieldwork and also for local social relations, being a Macdonald does not engender any hostility from those with surnames from clans which were once enemies of Macdonalds (which on Skye refers especially to MacLeods, the second most common surname in Carnan). Instead of reading identities off from a single marker such as a name, identities in Carnan – including my own – were defined through much more complex and often subtle social relations, in ways which could, and did, change and develop over time.

Notes

1. The term 'reimagining' has been formulated in light of Benedict Anderson's *Imagined Communities* (1983) which has been influential in the development of a number of my arguments here. Where Anderson uses 'imagining' to highlight the non-inevitable nature of conceptualising the nation, and the need for particular technologies to do so, my aim here is to emphasise too that nation/community building is a continuing process of reworking (cf. Ringrose and Lerner 1993; especially Lerner 1993).

1

'A Quest for Culture': On Anthropology, Authenticity and Ambivalence

O n one of my first evenings in Carnan, in the Summer of 1983, Màiri, the Gaelic teacher with whom I was staying, took me for a walk along the dramatic cliffs near her home. Màiri was well-practised in catering for visitors with an interest in Gaelic and traditional culture and as we walked she told me Gaelic names for the landmarks we passed and local stories about them. It was a weaving together of place and significance, of local accounts, such as the Indian woman who was said to have been blown off the cliffs when a sudden gust of wind caught her sari, and more temporally distant folklore, such as the meaning of a small hillock – Dun Dearg – named after a red-haired warrior. Her talk then turned to strange beliefs about *soluis bioraich*, inexplicable ghostly lights seen by the older people of the townships – lights which portended doom, or even drew people towards it. In a serious tone she began to tell me of an elderly crofter who had followed a light one night and had never been seen again. However, she was evidently finding it hard to keep a straight face and soon we were laughing. The vision she had been trying to conjure up for the naive anthropologist was somehow out of keeping with that bright and calm evening. She knew too, as she told me as we laughed, that had her mother known what she was telling me, she would have shaken her head and told her not to be 'so foolish'.

Summoning up exaggerated or exotic images of Gaelic culture and rural life for outsiders is a game which many local people liked to play. They shared many jokes about outsiders' views of Highlanders as uneducated, untravelled rustics – jokes in which the Highlanders' superior wit, learning and cosmopolitanism invariably triumph. However, the triumph is subtly

1

achieved: it mostly entails an apparent acquiescence with the outside vision until the tables are turned in the punch line. The jokes show local people confronting externally-produced imagery; and remind us both that such imagery is part of the reality with which they deal, and that all is not what it seems.

This play with images is one of the means by which local people define themselves. Yet although it may mean highlighting aspects of the traditional as fictional, it does not mean that they necessarily reject all aspects of what they see as distinctive or traditional in their culture. Màiri, with her university-training, fashion-sense and frenetic life-style could easily have made herself at home on the mainland. However, she, like others, had chosen to return to the Island; like the majority of people over thirty, Gaelic was the language she spoke at home with her mother and that she spoke with most of her peers in the local townships; she listened regularly to the Gaelic radio and took a keen interest in Gaelic events; like most others of her age she attended a local church, knew most of the people of the area and to whom they were related. Her world was both local and cosmopolitan.

It is not surprising that Màiri, like other Highlanders, should be acutely aware of outsiders' images of Gaelic culture. The Scottish Highlands have long been the subject of others' romantic imaginings. The Isle of Skye, with its legendary mists, imposing mountains, and abundant history, is perhaps the most romanticised of all. It is the seat of the Lords of the Isles, home of Flora MacDonald, place of escape for Bonnie Prince Charlie, and home of the ancient MacCrimmon pipers. Thousands of tourists arrive each year apparently in search of the cultural authenticity and refuge from the heartless processes of modern society that the tourist brochures and enormous literature on the Highlands seem to promise. Those who are referred to as 'incomers' or – in a colonial idiom which is increasingly taken for granted rather than accompanied by an amused smile – 'white settlers', also arrive to live out what they expect to be a more wholesome, healthy life. In this escape from the haste, change and anonymity of modern society, Gaelic culture is imagined as a place of traditional community. Its geographical marginality, empty spaces, lack of urbanisation, the Gaelic language, Highland hospitality, crofting, the apparent relatedness and closeness of the inhabitants, and the alleged slowness of everyday existence are all taken as evidence of a way of life which modernisation has largely passed by.

The Highlands have not, however, been untouched by modern developments. At one level this is obvious and many tourists and incomers lament the ubiquity of *Mother's Pride*, corn flakes, fish fingers, Ford Escorts, polyester clothes, *Neighbours* and 'kit' bungalows. More than this, however, many of the features which give rise to the appearance of 'backwardness' – crofting, depopulation, the poor public transport system, the lack of other facilities – are consequences of the workings of capitalism, urbanisation and market forces (cf. Ennew 1980; Parman 1990). Although there clearly are longstanding elements in contemporary 'Gaelic culture', much of what is now regarded as distinctive about the Highlands was formed not outside, but as part of, the development of the nation-state and modern society (Chapters 2 and 3 below). And the renaissance of 'traditional' culture, witnessed, for example, in the more up-market tourist souvenirs such as hand-knitted 'Icelandic' jumpers, Celtic jewellery, and yellowed maps with Gaelic place-names, is also thoroughly part of wider social and cultural developments.

Tradition, Modernity and Authenticity

Identifying some aspects of Gaelic culture as traditional or authentic and dismissing others as 'foreign' imports is typical of writings about the Highlands. However, the complex history of appropriation and imagining Gaelic culture makes such categorisation extremely difficult and clearly a matter for which we need a more subtle classification than one of authentic/inauthentic or traditional/modern. For example, how would we label the Norse importations into the Gaelic language, the nineteenth century introduction of sheep, Hebridean psalm intonation or recent 'revival' of waulking songs? Although this book charts the historical development of various aspects of contemporary Gaelic culture my aim is not to adjudicate on what is or is not authentic. I am, however, interested in the classifications of 'authentic' and 'traditional' and the effects that they have.

If it is only the traditional which is described as 'authentic', Màiri's cultural identity is likely to be perceived as at least to some extent inauthentic or alienated. For although she speaks Gaelic (one of the prime markers of authenticity) at home, she mostly speaks English with her colleagues in the High School staff room, she is a fan of *Coronation Street*, enjoys Jean Rook's column in the *Daily Mail*, and would feel stranded without her car.

In many ways, this quest after the authentic – and the kinds of locations in which it is thought to be found – can itself be seen as 'modern' (MacCannell 1989). That 'tradition' and 'community' are perceived as 'authentic' is only possible in light of a contrast with something posited as inauthentic, namely 'the modern' and 'society'. In its way, then, 'tradition' as a semantically conspicuous category is itself a product of modern society. That the Scottish Highlands have so frequently been described as 'traditional' and regarded as a potential source of authentic cultural identities is not evidence that they have been left out of modernity's equations. On the contrary, it is a part they play within them. In this ethnography, although much of what I describe is at one level specific to the Highlands, this is not a case for regarding them as 'non-modern'. Rather, it is an argument for seeing modernity as more heterogeneous, and more characterised by tensions and ambivalences, than it is sometimes depicted as being.[1] This book is a description of a particular kind of experience of modernity: that of an area which has been cast as 'traditional' and 'remote' within it.[2]

Seeing modernity as heterogeneous and ambivalent runs counter to modernity's own self-image. The modernist 'quest for order' (Bauman 1991: 1) propels attempts to segregate the traditional and the modern, and to judge between authentic and inauthentic. 'Cultures', 'communities' and 'identities' – all conceived as properly bounded, singular and distinctive – are modernist products. This is not just to say that cultures, communities and identities are 'individuated' within modernity. As Charles Taylor has written in his analysis of the development of 'the modernist [personal] identity', individuals come to be conceived not merely as different or distinct, but as endowed with 'inner depths' and a kind of 'calling' to express their individuality:

> Just the notion of individual difference is, of course, not new . . . . What is new is that this really makes a difference to how we're called on to live. The differences are not just unimportant variations within the same basic human nature; or else moral differences between good and bad individuals. Rather they entail that each one of us has an original path which we ought to tread; they lay the obligation on each of us to live up to our originality . . . . Expressive individuation has become one of the cornerstones of modern culture. (1989: 375–6)

This notion of 'expressive individuation' is formulated particularly clearly in relation to nations which project themselves as 'communities' (cf. Anderson 1983) with their own distinctive 'culture' and 'identity'.[3]

One of the principal means through which modernist conceptions discount alternatives is through categorising them as pathological. Ambivalence becomes a scandal (Bauman 1991: 18). Cultures whose elements do not 'cohere' appear dysfunctional; communities in change are depicted as 'dying'.[4] Identities which are not unified and singular – identities which cannot express that which is authentically *self* – are medicalised as 'split', 'repressed', or 'schizophrenic'.[5] This can readily be seen in discussions of Highland and of Scottish identity, where, as McCrone notes, 'psychiatric disorders are a . . . speciality' (1992: 176). The overwhelming concern with a possibly ailing identity and culture in the Scottish context is sourced in particular by Scotland's peculiar political and cultural position as a 'stateless nation' (ibid.) and the fact that this 'nation' consists of at least two historically and linguistically distinct 'cultures' (or nations) – Lowland and Highland.[6]

In many ways, the fact that Gaelic culture has furnished so many of the most visible symbols of Scottishness – tartan, bag-pipes, whisky – is puzzling. Until, and in many quarters long after, Highland culture began to be romanticised in the latter half of the eighteenth century, Highlanders were mostly regarded by their Lowland neighbours as something near a different race with nothing culturally to recommend them whatsoever. Tartan, bag-pipes and whisky have all, at various times, been banned by Lowland authorities. However, the same cultural conspicuousness which could lead to their outlawing, was also a potent marker of difference which, once domesticated, could be appropriated as a symbol of *Scottish* distinctiveness. If any part of Scotland was different from England – that niggling 'Other' – the Highlands surely were. The symbolic appropriation of Highland culture could, however, only take place once the substantive social barriers that the symbols formerly marked had receded into the past: i.e. once the Highlands had ceased to be a threat to the Lowlands (cf. Lynch 1992: 363).

Part of the attractiveness of Gaelic cultural symbols seems to be the imagery of the Highlands as a 'whole' and socially cohesive society – one with a sure sense of its own difference and a willingness to patrol its boundaries. A distinctive language, romanticised as a nation's 'collective treasure, the source of its social wisdom and communal self-respect' (Herder, in Barnard 1969: 165) in the expressive individuation of nations, was a clear, though problematic, symbol of the qualities of nationhood which the Highlanders seemed to possess. Historians have argued, however, that 'Gaeldom' was never internally cohesive and that antipathy within the Highlands was always as great as that with outsiders (e.g. Smout 1969: 20). Nevertheless the myth of a unified 'close' or 'clannish' society provides a reservoir for borrowing such an idea for Scotland as a whole.

However, the Highlands – which have not remained 'untouched' and 'traditional' – often do not live up to the symbolic role which they have been accorded. The myth of a whole society and a singular, unified identity and culture constantly creates a sense of disappointment and failure about the present. Not only is this medicalised, it is also (as illness often is, of course) moralised. The 'decline' of Gaelic culture is taken not only as evidence of 'illness' it is also seen as a moral failure – though there is sometimes ambiguity as to where responsibility lies. In perhaps the majority of histories, the moral failure is located outside the Highlands. Decline is a result of a history in which Highlanders are victim to external forces. Yet this view of history as something which 'arrives like a ship' (Sahlins 1987) from outside deletes any agency which Highlanders may have had. They become flotsam and jetsam tossed up on the externally driven wave of history. While this may accurately characterise some periods of history, it ignores the subtle ways in which local people appropriate and shape the developments which face them. It is an approach which renders them passive. Yet, the dominant alternative in discourses about the Highlands – an alternative which does accord local people agency – tends to go to the other extreme by attributing decline to Highlanders' own failure to 'look after' their culture and support the initiatives taken to save it. This is a view which often surfaces in discussions among exasperated policy-makers (see especially Part III), particularly in relation to the Gaelic renaissance developments. Both of these alternatives effectively subscribe to a view of 'real' culture and identity lying only in the 'traditional' – the authentic is that which has been, or is in danger of being, lost.

Gaelic Renaissance

The Gaelic renaissance refers to the growth of interest in the Gaelic language and Gaelic culture in Scotland, especially since the early 1980s.[7] It is not, however, an unprecedented phenomenon, being in some ways a continuation of the appropriation of Gaelic culture into Scottish identity which began in the late eighteenth century. Indeed, there are two periods which stand out in the shifts to a more positive evaluation of Gaelic culture and language within Scotland, both of which can be seen as of particular significance in the articulation of Scottish national identity and its place in Britain and Europe more widely. The first is the Romantic movement of the late eighteenth century, a period during which nation-states were being formed throughout Western Europe and during which there was a good deal of 'tradition invention' as nations sought to declare their inevitability through writing themselves back in history.[8] These developments, and the Romantic movement itself, were thoroughly modern.[9] The second is the more recent Gaelic renaissance, whose beginnings are largely outside the Highlands, during the 1960s, and which has come to be translated into policies affecting Highland populations more directly during the 1970s and especially since the 1980s. This is a period of ethnic revival and ethnonationalism throughout Western Europe, a time of challenge to the claims of those earlier nation-states to represent the identities of all their inhabitants, and a period of fostering cultural difference in anticipation of greater integration within the European Community.

The more recent renaissance has been characterised by a flourishing of policies aimed at reversing the decline of numbers of people speaking Gaelic; a decline which saw less than 2 per cent (1.71) of the Scottish population reporting as Gaelic-speaking in the 1981 Census (and only 1.37 per cent in the 1991 Census). These policies have included the establishment of Gaelic arts, bilingual and Gaelic education schemes, Gaelic playgroups and Gaelic media (see Table 2.1). At the point when I carried out my main research, between 1983 and 1986, many of these schemes were first being put into place in Carnan. Bilingual-medium primary education was in its early days, proposals for Gaelic-medium primary education in the area were emerging, a Gaelic-medium playgroup was established, a *co-chomunn* (community cooperative) had just been set up, and the first Summer Shielings – a project which involved bringing schoolchildren from the mainland to learn Gaelic with Carnan's families – was held in 1983; and a Gaelic festival in 1986. The first Gaelic road signs had recently sprung up; and more, with Gaelic names sometimes surprising to local people, seemed to appear by the week; a local history society was established and a small museum was opened. There was also much local talk of Gaelic developments elsewhere, especially developments in the South of Skye, instigated principally at the initiative of Iain Noble, a merchant banker from Edinburgh. These included a Gaelic College (Sabhal Mòr Ostaig), opened in 1972, which began in the 1980s to teach subjects such as business studies to students in Gaelic; and a number of local industrial developments – a hotel, a whisky business, a knitting mill and shop, a farm, a general trading company and a partnership in a fish-farming company – all of which were intended to employ Gaelic speakers (*Cor na Gàidhlig* 1982: 32). The 1980s also saw new development initiatives directed at crofting and 'crofting communities' (e.g. grants for housing and land improvements) which, while not specifically concerned with the Gaelic language, have more generally been concerned with maintaining and strengthening what is sometimes called 'the cultural base' of Gaelic. Funding for these developments has largely come from the state, though there have been significant inputs from private finance (as in the case of Iain Noble's Gaelic projects) and from the European Commission.[10]

These schemes were being established against a backdrop of more than a hundred years of falling numbers of reported Gaelic speakers – from 231,694 when the first Census figures were taken to 80,978 in the 1961 Census – and a surprise 9.8 per cent upturn in the 1971 Census. This upturn (which has not been maintained) was widely reported in the media as evidence of a genuine increase in numbers of Gaelic speakers and, as such, as evidence of a halt to the gradual disappearance of Gaelic culture. However, the upturn may have been partly an artefact of the nature of the Census question put: the 1971 Census was the first in which the Gaelic-speaking question was more clearly about *ability* to speak Gaelic ('*can speak* Gaelic') rather than use ('*speaks* Gaelic'). Moreover, as discussed further in Chapter 8, closer analysis reveals a more complex picture than one of straightforward increase in numbers of people actually speaking Gaelic. Insofar as the increase may have been one of an increased willingness to report as Gaelic-speaking, the upturn was, I suggest, evidence of a more widespread interest in Gaelic language and culture in Scotland as a whole, and of a new twist in the incorporation of Gaelic distinctiveness into *Scottish* national identity.

Anthropology, Community and Identity

Anthropologists, through their close study of cultural difference, are well-placed to counter easy assumptions of homogeneity. The ethnographic study of Europe has illuminated extensive diversity within nation-states, highlighting the importance of locality and of localised cultural idioms in many people's lives.[11] While much of this work could be regarded as illuminating the variability of modernity 'on the ground', or even of resistances to aspects of it, it has not often been conceptualised this way. Especially in the earlier ethnography of Europe, localities studied by anthropologists have been portrayed as 'traditional' and therefore as 'outside' or 'left behind by' the changes elsewhere in modern society (cf. Boissevain and Friedl 1975; Davis 1977). This reified dichotomies between Society and Community (*Gesellschaft* and *Gemeinschaft* in Tönnies' famous formulation), and Modern and Traditional, rather than investigated them.

The focus on *communities* as temporally and spatially sealed played a large part in this. Without an understanding of history or of wider political, economic and cultural relations, it was easy to assume that anything apparently unfamiliar was original, distinctive and longstanding to that locality, and to screen off the less exotic as newly arrived foreign importations. More recent work, which has made much more sustained attempts to incorporate history and that wider context has vividly demonstrated, amongst other things, that the apparently ancient might be relatively recent, that the supposedly indigenous might be appropriated, and that the 'foreign' might be a locus for articulating the local.[12]

Community ethnographic studies have generally presented each community as having its own distinctive identity. Anthony Cohen has suggested that this is a matter of Britain's 'rich cultural heterogeneity' (1982: 2), 'the enormous significance with which people invest their cultural distinctiveness' (ibid.), and 'a populist tendency to cultural "localism"' (ibid.: 1). While he argues that this highlights the existence of *diversity*, we might also argue that the apparent ubiquity of the emphasis on 'cultural distinctiveness' highlights a cultural commonality. Marilyn Strathern makes the same argument when she writes: 'the idea that "rural communities" . . . are somehow peripheral ones effectively blocks our understanding of the way their self acknowledged differences draw on common British ideas about difference' (1987: 32); and Jane Nadel-Klein has argued that localism is not so much 'anathema to the logic of modern political economy' as 'a consequence of it' (1991: 502). The expressive individuation of localities has, perhaps, become as taken-for-granted as parallel ideas about persons. Again, however, we need to consider the implications of our disciplinary approach, for the expressive individuation of cultures is fundamental to anthropology (cf. Handler 1988). Our methods and theories are premised upon the identification of difference between cultures and, in many forms of social and cultural anthropology, some kind of unity and integration within cultures (Wagner 1991; Strathern 1991, 1992). This emphasis on cultures as expressively individuated is, however, in its way a non-relativising one, for it does not acknowledge the possibility of people conceptualising themselves in other ways.

Given the widespread connotations of communities as having singular integrated identities, the community focus is especially likely to produce assumption of localism and expressive individuation. However, attempting to go 'beyond the community' just by avoiding working in such locations in many ways fails to tackle assumptions about them, and they often remain – as in so much theorising of modernity – as an unchallenged utopic other. In my own work my aim is not to take 'community' as an analytical unit but to look at it as a field to be investigated; and, like 'tradition', to show it as created within a modern dialogue rather than a fossil from the past. The geographically defined 'community' of Carnan constitutes not the boundaries and limits of my investigation but the position from which to begin, and through which to focus, the discussion.

Much anthropological work on the Scottish Highlands has emphasised the long history of romanticization and ways in which features of contemporary Highland life have been shaped by their relationship with wider British society. Malcolm Chapman, on the basis of textual analysis, has argued that Gaelic culture is an artefact created by an 'urban intellectual educated' elite, based largely outside the Highlands. The Gael has 'served . . . as a figure of opposition, a mythical alter-ego' (1978 : 129) in that elite's attempts to define its own world as 'ordered, rational, civilised and right' (ibid.). Chapman's work is important in showing how and why the Highlands have persistently been defined as a location of the traditional. Although his focus is principally upon the literary, such definition has had its effects upon very material dimensions of life in the Hebrides as other ethnographers have shown (Condry 1980; Ennew 1980; Parman 1972, 1990).

Chapman's work raises questions about the general assumption that 'cultures' belong to, or are the product of, those who 'live' them and whose name they take. His work makes clear that much of what we classify as 'Gaelic culture' was not locally made. However, this does not necessarily mean that local people should be regarded as 'alienated' or subject to 'false-consciousness' if they adopt or participate in aspects of that culture. To do so would be, yet again, to cast local people as passive recipients of outsiders' imaginings, and as culturally inauthentic. It is an equally modernist move: an inverse romanticism. Màiri's interest in seeing Highland step-dancing revived, her following of certain Gaelic singers, her keeping of a cow on the croft, her burning of peat on the fire, would all be liable to be seen as affectations, fostered by an outside world which wants to keep the Highlands traditional for its own self-definitions and self-satisfaction. Yet, as I hope Màiri's self-aware and good-humoured irony in teasing me shows, it would be a mistake to see local people as easily duped by outsiders. So too, it would be a mistake to impute meanings to cultural practices solely on the basis of outside classifications.

This Study: Ambivalence and Analytic Models

It was people like Màiri, their ambivalences and ironies, which led me to question some of the modernist assumptions about identity as singular and unified. While I had expected to find differences between individuals, I found myself surprised by an apparent contrariness within individuals, who would sometimes espouse what seemed to me contradictory views about their culture and language. Within the same conversation an individual might castigate young people for not speaking Gaelic and complain about attempts to encourage them to do so; they might talk positively of the warmth and closeness of the local community while later saying that there was no life in the Highlands today; they might talk wistfully of the past as though sorry to leave it, and thankfully of the present, happy to have left the past behind; they might embrace aspects of both 'traditional' and 'modern' culture.

Such ambivalences are not, however, simply a matter of individual contrariety. Nor are they a symptom of a pathological identity. Rather, they express different currents within the repertoire on which local people draw in negotiating and expressing their senses of belonging and difference. They are, to some extent at least, a specific realisation of a wider modern dialogue and of contradictions which provide part of the motive force of local social life.

In this study, then, I try to incorporate rather than exclude ambivalence. This is not, however, to incorporate it as unexplicated inevitability. On the contrary, my aim is, through history and the contemporary ethnography, to try to situate it. Given the intertwining of anthropological and lay models of culture and identity in the contexts which I describe, a note on those which I employ here is necessary.

McCrone observes that the idea of 'society' used by sociologists is often, rather unreflectively, coterminous with the nation-state (1992: 1). More generally, sociological and anthropological models of 'society' and 'culture' as bounded entities with internal coherence, are part of modernist conceptions of the expressive individuation of identity. Given the importance of language in such conceptions, it is not surprising that many ethnic groups have been identified and named by outsiders, especially European colonists, on the basis of linguistic specificity (Ardener 1989, especially ch.3). For allied reasons, perhaps, language has also assumed an important role in theorising about the nature of society and culture. Although the ideas of Saussure are particularly associated with Lévi-Straussian structuralism, they have many parallels with ideas in earlier British social anthropology, especially those of Radcliffe-Brown and Evans-Pritchard (Ardener 1989: 19). Their salience for modelling society in the romantic nationalist mode lies in the notion of *langue* – a bounded, patterned, internally-coherent system underpinning the more variable actualities of speech, *parole*.

One of the most important features of Saussurean structuralism is that of *relationality*: the sense of any linguistic sign cannot be understood in isolation but only in terms of all the other signs in the system. Identity is not inherent to the sign but relational – a matter of absences as much as presences, a matter of positioning rather than essence. This important insight about identity and relationality can, however, be preserved without assuming such a tightly-knit and bounded system. Indeed, this is part of the drive of Edwin Ardener's interpretation of Saussure (1971; 1989: ch.1) and one reason for his characterisation of Saussure's position as 'socio-linguistic' (1989: 17). Sociolinguistic theorising, which has largely defined itself against a conception of 'linguistic theory as concerned only with an ideal speaker-hearer in a perfectly homogeneous community' (Hymes 1974: 48),[13] attempts to retain the idea that we cannot understand the meaning of any one term or inflection in isolation, while allowing us to begin from a much more modest, specific and perhaps untidy focus and to work outwards from this. There is no necessary homogeneous community in sociolinguistic analyses – on the contrary, analysis typically focuses upon linguistic practice, variation and change (e.g. changes in accents, 'registers' and 'codes', and 'switching').[14] These generate a repertoire of possibilities – of different idioms – with different degrees of overlap and spread, which may be variously drawn upon and realised. The possibilities within the repertoire are themselves not bound in so tight a relationality as in the Saussurean system, but characterised by different degrees of 'partial connection' (Strathern 1991). A change in one element will have consequences but will not necessarily reconfigure the meaning of all of the other pieces in the game. And the repertoire itself is not fixed and bounded (as is *langue*) but is a notional set to which new elements can be added with further studies. By contrast with structural approaches, sociolinguistics focuses upon *variety* and *change*. Who the speakers and hearers are, their social positioning, and the manner of utterance and context become crucial; and this, in turn, means that questions of methods, the researcher and power assume a new importance.

In this study my aim is not to attempt to capture the essence of 'Highland identity', but to describe what seemed on the basis of my fieldwork to be some of the most significant ways in which identities were conceptualised and enacted. Rather than tie these into a neat and coherent system, I present them as a repertoire of sources for imagining identities. These sources may offer up contradictory possibilities: this is part of the dynamic of social life. My argument is not, therefore, that individuals can design their identities just as they choose. Although it may be the case that global developments are making it increasingly possible for individuals to reflex-ively create identities disembedded from their local contexts,[15] there still exists in any particular context a repertoire of sources for imagining which enable and constrain the possibilities. Moreover, ideas of what is entailed in 'having an identity' and 'having a culture' (Handler 1988) have themselves become particularly salient and uniform global sources for imagining. They are part of 'an international political model that people all over the globe use to construct images of others and of themselves' (Handler and Linnekin 1984: 287). These models privilege ideas of coherence and overt cultural markers, particularly language. However, there are other, outwardly less visible, and seemingly more messy, means through which belonging is articulated in everyday life. In relation to the dominant international political models of identity, these other ways of identifying are relatively 'muted' (Ardener 1975). This is not to say that they are, therefore, somehow more 'real' or 'authentic' than the dominant articulations. Nor need we think of 'mutedness' and 'dominance' as fixed or exclusive characteristics (cf. Ardener 1989: 131): Rather, what we are dealing with here is a relativity of mutedness, and the capacity of individuals to articulate themselves in a mix of relatively muted and relatively dominant forms. This idea is captured by the sociolinguistic emphasis on *varieties* of language, differentially exercised according in part to context and social position (e.g. Hudson 1980: ch.2). Instead of understanding these different modes of articulation as relating to distinct world-views, or to different 'levels', the sociolinguistic model suggests instead a repertoire of overlapping possibilities, capable of expansion and of incorporating ambivalence. This makes it better able to recognise the interrelatedness of local and global articulations, through whose interweavings the local is made cosmopolitan, and larger identities, such as the ethnic and the national, may be brought 'home'.

The Fieldwork and the Place

As part of my research I travelled quite widely in the Highlands and also to key places on the Scottish mainland, such as Inverness and Edinburgh, and spoke with many people involved in various ways in the Gaelic renaissance – including, for example, Gaelic teachers and education coordinators in the Outer Isles, organisers of *Feis Bharraidh* (the Gaelic cultural festival on the Isle of Barra), tourist officials, and staff at the Highlands and Islands Development Board (as it then was) and the School of Scottish Studies. However, I decided to focus my work within one particular locality and to spend most of my time there, in order to know better those who do not normally express themselves in books, on the media or through policy-statements. In other words, the aim of participant-observation fieldwork was to focus on those who were central to the Gaelic renaissance but whose voices seemed rarely to be directly heard within it.

My choice of Carnan on Skye as the location for my detailed fieldwork was partly fortuitous, having through various contacts originally gone there in the Summer of 1983 to stay with a Gaelic teacher to learn Gaelic. It seemed, however, a good place to return to, for a number of reasons. First, there were many Gaelic developments going on, and Carnan was widely seen as a kind of 'last bastion' of Gaelic on Skye. Lying not in the more inaccessible Outer Hebrides but in a part of Skye popular with tourists and close to the Island's capital, Portree, Carnan seemed to have retained its Gaelic against the odds and to be embracing the Gaelic language policies. It also had a relatively young age structure; and as such, was often taken as a 'good example' of a Gaelic community, and as symbolic of the potential of the Gaelic renaissance to hold off and even reverse the encroachments of Anglicisation.

Carnan was, and is, to my eyes and to those of many others who visit, extremely beautiful with its pebbled and sandy beaches, heather-covered moor land, cliffs and striking rock formations. Yet, like many Highland and Island localities, it does not entirely conform to outsiders' expectations of what 'a community' should look like. It consists of eighteen inhabited townships (some with only one or two dwellings), housing a population of around 600, strung out along about eight miles of road slicing between the sea and the basalt spine towering to the rear of the moor land behind the croft houses. Townships themselves are not nucleated – there is no central pub or village green or even post-office – and the area as a whole is not strongly so (and insofar as it is, this is very recent – see Chapter 7). Indeed, especially in Winter (referred to in Gaelic as *an Dùbhlachd*), when there are only a few hours of daylight this far North, and when gales and rain sweep the Island, the area can seem bleak, and the houses, which are commonly separated by several hundreds of metres of croft land, locked into isolation. Yet in the Summer, when most visitors come, it is easier to perceive community and a rural way of life. If the weather is fine, in the long light evenings, when many have returned from work, there will be individuals or small groups out on their crofts stacking hay or up on the moor turning peat.

The houses themselves are mostly two storey stone or white painted houses which are often referred to today as 'traditional' and tend to be regarded as rather quaint by visitors (though Frank Fraser Darling in 1955 regarded them as an unseemly 'modern' introduction); or 'kit' houses (so-called because you choose them from a catalogue and they do indeed arrive on a lorry in kit form for local assembly) which are usually either brown or grey pebbledash bungalows and box-shaped houses (generally loathed by visitors) or Scandinavian style, with steep roofs and external

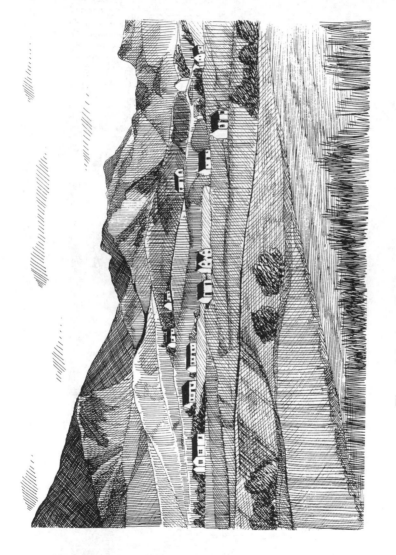

Figure 1.1. A crofting township (by Julie White)

Figure 1.2. A 'traditional' Highland house (by Julie White)

wooden panelling (which for some reason are thought especially appropriate to the Highlands). Sometimes, there will be a new kit house alongside an older white house, or even an older still ruined 'black-house' – a low, stone-built, thatched cottage, built prior to the twentieth century, now preserved mainly in Skye's folklife museums. Some people cultivate small gardens (which involves quite a battle against the sea wind and the sheep which so often seem to manage to slip through the gates or holes in the fence), growing flowers such as roses and edible plants such as rhubarb, though many houses are surrounded by uncultivated croft land – coarse grass and, especially towards the sea, clumps of reeds – and sheep often graze right up to the door. Peat is the most common form of fuel for burning on the open fires and in the Rayburns that are ubiquitous in Carnan homes; and most houses have a peat-stack, protected by tarpaulin or heavy poly-thene, standing near to the back door; and there is always the distinctive smell of burning peat in the air. Even though few people in Carnan croft on a large scale, many keep a cow or two, a few sheep and chickens; and almost all seem to have one or more collies. Some people fish a little during the Summer, mostly for home consumption. In addition to a small fenced garden, then, a croft house might be surrounded by various out-buildings (for housing feedstuff or chickens), agricultural and fishing implements (maybe a tractor or a spare wheel for one, a plough, a boat, some creels, half a dozen crates, a reel of rope, a barrel or two), and other items which have come to the end of their life or may come in useful (hulks of old cars for storing feedstuff or housing chickens, Rayburns, washing machines, baths, mangles). There might be a residential caravan parked to one side, with electricity lines running from the house, which may have been the living quarters of the family while they built the house, or is the home of young relatives who cannot afford a 'proper place' of their own, or is rented out, or is the Summer living space of the house owners while they rent out their own house to holidaymakers.

One difficulty of fieldwork in the Highlands, and indeed in many other areas of Britain, is that much social life goes on behind the closed (though in the Hebrides, generally unlocked) doors of family homes. There are, of course, some collective venues, which in Carnan included schools, hotel bars, churches, shops, some agricultural activities, and various clubs and meetings. I participated in as many of these as possible and learned such diverse skills during my fieldwork as country dancing and sheep branding. I also visited people in their homes, initially on a kind of snowballing basis of being sent to people who I was told would be suitable for my study, being either 'good on the Gaelic' or 'good on history'. Although knocking on doors of people I had never met before constantly filled me

Figure 1.3. 'Kit' house with peat stack (by Julie White)

with anxiety, word rapidly spread about a 'student interested in the Gaelic' and I was generally welcomed. Indeed, such was the help that I received that I have often wondered how it is possible to do fieldwork anywhere else. Many of the people I visited became friends and I returned many times, sometimes to have a *crac* (talk, gossip) over a cup of tea, other times perhaps to help bring in the hay or cut the peat. However, I was concerned that the people to whom I was sent might not represent the breadth of opinion in the locality and I also wanted to hear from people who were not 'good on the Gaelic' or on history. Of course, I met such people through my general contacts but to make sure I also decided to undertake a household survey and questionnaire in all of the households in the central townships of Carnan. This incorporated a life-history element and was also intended to provide socio-demographic data about such matters as place of upbringing, birth-place of parents, time away from the island and patterns of work, as well as views on specific Gaelic issues. Most of the figures that I give in this book about Carnan's population are derived from this survey, as I note in each case. The number of households covered was around fifty, incorporating a population of just over one hundred.

Because Highlanders have long been much subject to the gaze of the outside world, they have become adept at dealing with 'visitors' and officials. Màiri's stories of ghostly lights were just one example of the kind of teasing to which gullible 'strangers' might be subject. On other occasions, as letters pages to the local press from aggrieved tourists reveal, local people may behave in an abrupt and taciturn way to those seeking Highland hospitality. They may also give short shrift to those with bureau-cratic paperwork to be filled out. I myself certainly experienced both the teasing playing up of Highland stereotypes and the gruff disruption of them, particularly in my early days of fieldwork. Indeed, such responses to stereotypes are part of my study. Time, however, meant that I came to be related to not only as someone 'here today and gone tomorrow'; and by the time that I came to carry out my survey, I think I was sufficiently well-known not to seem too much like some kind of official, though even so women in particular often initially protested that they were somehow unqualified to answer my questions. However, I also carried it out rather informally – the whole process usually taking several hours of chatting over cups of tea, with many digressions and interruptions – so there was opportunity to relax, expand upon questions, and to return to them.[16]

I usually explained my research as being interested in 'Gaelic and what is going on around it' and sometimes more generally in terms of 'what it is like to live here' and sometimes in terms of more specific aspects of my research, such as how important were relations or how people felt about community developments, when I was looking at such matters as kinship and the community cooperative. Having a student studying Gaelic or the local area was not at all unfamiliar to local people, and many seemed to have experience of some young relative or other doing such a 'project'. This experience was one which reinforced the idea of Carnan as a place which was worthy of scholarly and outside interest; though many seemed to assume that only the past – a time when Gaelic was stronger and, it was said, people visited each other in their homes rather than staying in watching television – was deserving of real attention. The fact that I had learnt some Gaelic implied that I was particularly 'for the Gaelic', for who else but a Gaelic enthusiast or activist would go to the trouble of learning a language when they could communicate equally (or more) efficiently in English? After all, even though some older people (and a few very young children) were more fluent in Gaelic than English, there were no Gaelic monoglots in Carnan. Because I was interested in the full range of possible responses to Gaelic and community developments in Carnan, I tried to avoid making judgmental statements about these myself and did not press my use of Gaelic where those I was talking with seemed more comfortable in using English.[17] Nevertheless, the kinds of statements which people made to me about Gaelic are likely to have been shaped in part by their perception of me as 'for the Gaelic'; though as will be clear from the account below this did not mean that they all provided me with the sorts of accounts that an enthusiast would want to hear.[18] Moreover, particularly as I had a child during my fieldwork, I was certainly not *only* seen as a student of Gaelic; and there were undoubtedly many who (to some extent rightly) saw my return to Skye with my daughter and husband as really an excuse to live on the Island.[19] (As one woman said of my continued 'project' *'Tha e a' cuir seachad an tìde, co-dhiù'* – 'It passes the time anyway'.) As with most anthropological fieldwork, then, my account below is based upon my direct experience of day-to-day life in Carnan, on responses to questions that I asked either in the course of more formal interviews or less formal conversations, on responses in which I would be seen primarily as a researcher and in others in which I would be seen more as another mother, wife or neighbour in the locality. Disentangling these is impossible.[20] Indeed, it is this mix of sources and contexts, together with the potential to reshape directions and questions, to follow up unexpected suggestions and look out for further examples over time, to be surprised and have space to allow cultural assumptions and initial research agendas to be challenged, that is the particular contribution – and particular kind of validity – of anthropological fieldwork.

The Structure of this Book

The book is divided into three connected parts: Histories, Identities and Cultural Renaissance. My aim through this is to situate the local reception of Gaelic renaissance developments and to show how histories and identities both promote and are produced by these developments.

In Part I – Histories – my intention is not to provide an uncontested 'background' to the present but to highlight different strands and possibilities in 'the Past' and its various interpretations. This is related throughout to contemporary perceptions and 'repertoires for imagining' in order to show how the past and ideas about the past are produced by those involved in the Gaelic renaissance as well as others, and also how versions of 'the Past' may inform social relations and responses to the Gaelic renaissance today. My concern in this part of the book is to show how accounts of the past are used to imagine and reimagine a Gaelic 'people' and a Gaelic culture today.

Chapter 2 begins from a dominant Gaelic revivalist conception of the history of Gaelic language and culture – one which conceptualises Gaelic as the language of Scotland, looks back to a Golden Age when language, culture and identity were homogeneous and untouched by Anglicisation, and links Gaelic to a wider Celtic heritage. The chapter explores the historical emergence of such a conception; and in particular, the way in which the *Gàidhealtachd* came to be seen as 'a culture', the processes of 'expressive individuation' involved in this, and the centrality accorded to language as a vestibule of identity. This chapter is largely an account of processes of identity making largely located outside the Highlands, and of the ways in which ideas of Gaelic culture have been embroiled in the development of this dominant Western discourse. As such this chapter is important for setting the background against which identity variations and alternatives discussed in later chapters can be seen.

Chapter 3 focuses on crofting and church history – both of which are frequently invoked in accounts of Highland identity. The chapter explores different currents in these histories in order to highlight the ambivalent possibilities that the past offers as a source for contemporary identity-definition as well as different possible definitions of 'community' and Gaelic 'peoplehood'. As I show, these enmesh, though only partially, with the identity definitions outlined in Chapter 2. I consider here too debates about Highland history among academic historians in order to show the way in which history is mobilised in contemporary identity projects, and especially in the revival of Gaelic community and language.

Part II – Identities – looks at the ways that Carnan people articulate their senses of distinctiveness, belonging and social relations in their day-to-day lives. It is about their everyday identity imaginings and reimaginings. My focus here is not only upon the more general ethnic and cultural identities of 'Highlander' and 'Scot' but also upon other classifications brought into play in everyday interaction through which those 'larger' cultural identities are articulated and realised. These include classifications of gender, of 'locals' and 'incomers', of 'the people' and 'the powers-that-be', and of different categories of church membership. My argument here is that 'identity' – what it means to have a sense of belonging – is not necessarily focused (only) on the more widely recognised markers of 'having an identity' and 'having a culture' (e.g. a distinctive language and a single history) but is also concerned with more apparently mundane and trivial matters, such as ideas about how animals should be treated, ways of talking about relatives, attitudes towards rubbish, and jokes. It is, I suggest, through the overlap and 'mapping' of these different identities – an overlap which works because of shared but rather unspecific idioms for imagining – that more 'distant' identities can be brought directly 'home'.

Chapter 4 is concerned with the significance of crofting and 'traditional Highland culture' in articulating identities. The chapter considers further local ways of understanding the history discussed in Chapter 3, and how that history shapes contemporary social life and informs visions of 'the crofting community'. It looks too at performances of traditional culture, its symbolic importance, and local people's awareness of, and tactics for dealing with, outsiders' visions. This is discussed further in Chapter 5 which deals with the expression of belonging through idioms of place and kinship. I argue that these are distinct from romanticised conceptions of place and kinship that are often associated with the Highlands. The chapter also discusses the salient local notions of 'exile', 'home' and 'away', 'locals' and 'incomers', and gender divisions, to show how these enmesh with ideas about 'the people', egalitarianism and hierarchy. Different repertoires for conceptualising identity are discussed here, together with the ambivalences which may arise.

The Highland churches, especially the Free and Free Presbyterian churches, discussed in Chapter 6, are often seen as at odds with romantic visions of Gaelic culture; and yet can also be articulated to the idea of 'the people' (Chapter 3). This chapter looks at this ambivalent potential and the way in which divisions between the churches, and distinctions between church 'Members' and 'the Elect', are played out in daily life. The chapter considers the ways in which the churches may invoke notions such as 'tradition' and 'Highland culture'; and the implications this has for the repertoire of local identity possibilities.

The final part of the book – Cultural Renaissance – focuses more directly on a number of development projects in Carnan associated with attempts to regenerate Gaelic culture. It draws on the previous parts of the book to show why the developments were often ambivalently received; and why there were sometimes misunderstandings between outside agencies involved in the revival and local people. It also shows the ways in which some local people appropriated the possibilities offered by the renaissance developments; and became themselves involved in reimagining Gaelic culture.

Chapter 7 looks at a number of community regeneration projects in Carnan which, while not directly concerned with Gaelic language revival, were associated with the Gaelic renaissance. The chapter explores various ideas about communities (e.g. as authentic 'grass-roots' organisations) in relation to the local experience of community development. It shows how the idea of 'community' was mobilised as a resource for acquiring better local amenities; and looks at the competing interests – and conceptions of 'community', 'tradition' and the state – involved in this. It discusses too the expectations that many local people had about the role of agencies such as the Highlands and Islands Development Board, expectations which were often informed by past historical experience and notions of the relationship between 'the people' and 'the powers-that-be.'

Chapter 8 focuses on a number of Gaelic revival developments in Carnan, particularly the Gaelic playgroup and bilingual-medium education. It draws upon earlier chapters to explain ambivalence about these developments; and to show how some revivalist (and more longstanding romantic nationalist) ideas about the central importance of language to cultural identity were often not fully shared by local people. It also suggests that a younger generation in Carnan may be reconceptualising their identity, and the place of language, within it. Throughout these chapters my aim is to show how ideas like 'tradition,' 'community' and 'Gaelic revival' are locally perceived and enacted. These are matters in which local people are frequently highly reflexive. The process of reimagining Gaelic culture is a dynamic and ongoing one in which they are active, though not all-powerful, players.

This discussion is extended in the final chapter, 'Reflections on Reimagining', to some of the more recent Gaelic renaissance developments within Scotland in general and Carnan in particular. This highlights the importance of acknowledging the *situatedness* of the ethnography – its particular moment in time – though also the enduring, though not static, nature of repertoires for imagining described here. I also return in this final chapter directly to some of the central theoretical themes of the book and consider their implications for the ways in which we address questions of culture and identity.

Notes

1. There is a growing number of ethnographies which address and describe variations within modernity and postmodernity. See especially, Handler 1988; Dorst 1989; Rogers 1991; Miller 1994 and Stewart 1996.
2. Cf. Clifford on Northwest coast native American communities: 'theirs were different, not separate, paths through modernity (no one escapes the market, technology and the nation-state' (1991: 212). For further discussion of the idea of 'remote areas' see Ardener 1989: ch.14. His piece, which is influential in my account here, deals with the Scottish Hebrides. See also Nadel-Klein 1995 and 1997 for discussion of the representation of Scotland in anthropology and other discourses, particularly in relation to urban-rural imagery and the Highland Line.
3. Cf. Taylor 1989: 376. The formulation is especially clear (and influential) in the writings of the German Romantic nationalists, particularly Herder (1744–1803) (see Barnard 1969; Berlin 1976; Kedourie 1993; Hobsbawm 1990; Llobera 1994).
4. For critiques of functionalist problems with dealing with the 'dysfunctional,' see, for example, Kuper 1996; Marcus and Fischer 1986. I discuss 'community' further in Macdonald 1993; see also Cohen 1985 and Marcus 1992.
5. This is a major theme in social psychological discussions of identity, particularly since Erikson 1968. Ethnic identity is a particular subject of concern, identity crises often understood as emanating from 'uprooting', a lack of clear cultural context and individuals finding themselves 'stranded between two identities'.
6. The notion of 'sourcing' is taken from Taylor (1989). 'Nation' is sometimes used as synonymous with 'nation-state' but at others, as here, it refers to an 'ethnie' (Smith 1986) or 'ethnic group' (Barth 1969). Barth makes the crucial point that the key feature of ethnic groups/nations is self-ascription and ascription by others – i.e. ethnicity is a symbolic, definitional matter rather than a question of objective features of cultural distinctiveness. However, in the modern world

'nation', 'ethnicity' and 'culture' (among others) have become terms to be 'pirated' (cf. Anderson 1983: 66), and the dominant model of what it is to be an ethnically distinct group is (increasingly) based upon a fairly standardised set of criteria.

7. The term 'Gaelic renaissance' seems to have first been used in the 1970s to refer to twentieth-century Gaelic poetry, some of it from the early decades of the century (Thomson 1974: ch.7). As a term to refer to the revival of Gaelic language and culture more generally, it has come into widespread usage towards the late 1980s. There is no clear marker of the 'beginning' of this development, though a document produced in 1996 by the Gaelic promotion organisation Comunn na Gàidhlig notes: 'The big revival started just over a dozen years ago, heralded by the founding of the first Gaelic playgroups' (1996: 9).

8. I do not mean by this that it was a matter of arbitrary invention by nationalists for conscious social engineering. Rather, it is a more complex process (cf. Kapferer 1988) which 'arises out of the need to make sense of complex social and political arrangements' (Breuilly 1982: 343).

9. The definition of modernity only in relation to its Enlightenment heritage is part of a modernist denial of ambivalence. Romanticism was not an alternative to modernity but an integral part of it (cf. Solomon 1988, Cranstone 1994).

10. In Skye the first European Commission funding came in the form of the Agricultural Development Programme beginning in 1987, which as its name implies, was directed at agricultural matters. See Hunter 1991. While in the 1980s few Gaelic-language projects received European funding, there was much speculation that this might become available and some of the state funding seems to have been provided in anticipation of attracting further funding from the European Commission later (which, especially into the 1990s has occurred to some extent).

11. For some overviews see, for example, Cohen 1982 and 1986; *American Ethnologist* 1991; Macdonald 1993; Godard, Llobera and Shore 1994.

12. There are a lot of examples which could now be given. Specifically on the Hebrides the works of Condry (1980) and Parman (1990) are excellent examples. More widely in European ethnography these points are particularly well-made in Cowan (1990), Herzfeld (1991) and Rogers (1991).

13. This is generally conceived by contrast with a Saussurean and a Chomskian legacy, though there are important variations in sociolinguistics, some of which are noted in the following footnote.

Post-structuralist theory has also developed Saussurean notions of the arbitrary nature of the signifier-signified relationship and of relationality to argue for the indeterminacy of meaning (e.g. Attridge 1989), though this seems to me to lead to too great a degree of indeterminacy at least in respect of the material here.

14. It should be acknowledged, however, that some approaches within sociolinguistics do nevertheless strive for, and produce, a neatly segmented speech community and leave little scope for change, flexibility or variety within their analyses. In effect, these are structural-functional analyses. My attempt here is to borrow some of the potential as I see it within sociolinguistics without falling into either the overly taxonomic, static analyses of some sociolinguistics, or those which emphasize individual creativity and micro-scale interactions at the expense of awareness of constraints and power differentials. See Martin-Jones 1989 for a useful account which also suggests that anthropological and sociological work on bilingualism in Europe is forging such perspectives.

15. This is an argument being made by various social theorists. See especially Melucci 1989, Giddens 1991, King 1991, Lash and Friedman 1992 and Lash and Urry 1994. For some relevant discussion of the cross-cultural dimensions – and perhaps alternatives – of these developments see Friedman 1994, Gewertz and Errington 1991, Hannerz 1992 and essays in Fardon 1995.

16. As many of those who I interviewed seemed uncomfortable with being tape recorded I generally took notes instead. Also, I found in some of my recorded interviews that respondents seemed to be more likely to give me the kind of responses that they would have regarded as appropriate for broadcasting on Gaelic radio. One woman, for example, told me on tape that Gaelic was the only language that was used in her home. I knew, however, that her sons were barely fluent in the language but when I digressed to ask about them she was very flustered: she had, after all, given the sort of response which I should have wanted. Note taking – about which I was open though often relied on making notes of 'key words' which I wrote up more fully afterwards – seemed not to produce the same effect.

17. Although I had learnt a fair amount of Gaelic before I began fieldwork proper, I suffered the inhibition in becoming fully fluent that it was always possible to switch to English when conversation became more sophisticated. Sensitive to the possibility that certain things might perhaps only be uttered in one language, I wanted as far as possible not to determine the language spoken and although my presence must

clearly have influenced language choice in many situations I tried to follow whatever language was being used by others, though sometimes switched into Gaelic myself if I felt that English was being used specially for me. Because, in a bilingual situation, no single language can be regarded as a 'system', both constitute a repertoire of codes and registers not all of which will be used or even known by all individuals in the locality (see Dorian 1981: 84). Here, then, I sometimes give Gaelic terms, sometimes English ones, and often both, depending upon what I heard used, or upon translations that I was given. Not everybody within 'the community' will, however, be familiar with all the terms used here.

18. There seems to be no reason why respondents should only produce the responses that those researching would want to hear as sometimes seems to be assumed. Likewise, it seems to me naive and even arrogant to regard fieldwork as merely a projection by the researcher: those being researched have agendas, minds and bodies of their own. There is, however, a problem when research is constituted without sufficient conceptual space to be able to allow for unexpected responses. Anthropological fieldwork is valuable precisely because of its relative conceptual openness; though this same flexibility potentially creates more intricate ethical dilemmas.

19. I returned to Oxford for the birth of my daughter in September 1984 to spend some time writing and teaching before returning to Skye. The main part of my fieldwork in Carnan, then, was two stays of around seven months each – January until August 1984, and July 1985 until January 1986 – both interrupted for short visits to mainland Scotland and England. I have also made many return visits since. During fieldwork, then, I personally underwent a social transition from being a single young woman associated particularly with one local family, to being a mother and wife in a household of my own.

20. There are, of course, also moral questions here. I have undoubtedly included material in this book which was derived from encounters in which I was not being related to primarily as a researcher. This, I think, is probably inevitable in anthropological fieldwork. I have, however, sought to disguise the identities of those about whom I write and hope to have avoided anything which might be harmful to any individual.

Part I
Histories

'Every thing in those countries has its history'. Dr Johnson, speaking of the Highlands at Armadale in Skye in 1773 (Johnson and Boswell 1924: 44)

The Scottish Highlands are often thought of as being particularly rich in history. Although this is not a new perception, *pace* Dr Johnson, it is today an important dimension of the way in which many 'minorities' are thought about, and a key aspect of 'having' an identity. Having an identity entails 'having a past'. In this part of the book I am concerned with the development of some of these ideas as they relate to the Scottish Highlands. This is not intended as a comprehensive history – impossible though such an enterprise would be, of course. Rather, each chapter takes an aspect of Highland history which has been mobilised in the Gaelic renaissance, and attempts to explore assumptions about the nature of identity and peoplehood that these entail. These assumptions are also traced back through other writings, partly in order to highlight their specificity by way of illustrating alternative imaginings.

One important contribution of anthropology to debates about history has been illustration of how the past may be constructed in light of contemporary interests.[1] This is one of my concerns here too. It is not one history that I deal with here, however, but a number of alternatives – alternatives which are not equally audible in the present or equally likely to be sustained into the future. This variability depends upon the politics, social relations and technologies in which they are enmeshed.

I am also concerned, however, to show how the past – particular ways of thinking or material arrangements forged in specific historical periods – may shape the present. The past *informs* the present; it adds to and shapes the repertoire of contemporary possibilities. Moreover, the past cannot simply be constructed as we please, either by those 'on the ground' or by historians and anthropologists. 'The past' is not infinitely plastic. Just as in ethnographic fieldwork when we find ourselves being surprised by an event or remark and having to rethink our account of what is going on, so too may historical records challenge our preconceptions; and my accounts here have certainly been reformulated many times in the light of reading in and about history.

A note is necessary on the peculiar, and probably to historians rather scandalous, approach to history that I take here. I move between past and present, between rather enormous stretches of time and space, and much more specific and localised ones, focusing in on particular documents and events. Much that I might have written about, and much that is undoubtedly important, is ignored; though none that I have thought challenges my main anthropological arguments. The particular selections and juxtapositions that I have made are intended not to provide a comprehensive historical narrative but to illustrate patterns in the formations of ideas of identity and peoplehood, and the alternatives which the past can offer.

Note

1. Particularly relevant to my thinking about the relationship between anthropology and history are Ardener 1989a; Silverman and Gulliver 1992; and Hastrup 1985, 1992.

2

'Our Language, Our Heritage': Imagining Gaelic Culture

I met Duncan during the Gaelic festival week on one of the Outer Hebridean islands. He was running a mobile book and leaflet van, dealing with Gaelic literature. It was a quiet day and he seemed pleased that somebody had come to browse. '*Se latha math a th'ann*' ('It's a fine day') he ventured and I agreed in Gaelic. He went on to ask me where I was from and when I said 'England' seemed surprised (perhaps as much at the bluntness of my 'confession' as the location). I explained that I had learnt my Gaelic in Skye; and that, yes, although I was from England, my father was from Scotland, though I had no Gaelic-speaking relatives. He was relieved and rather cheered for he too was a learner. His father was from Tiree – 'and there's really good Gaelic there, you should go' – but Duncan had been brought up in Glasgow and had only come to learn of, and appreciate, his 'cultural heritage' by his own endeavours. His father, a policeman, did not seem to be all that interested. We switched into English as the conversation got more complex and confidential. Duncan told me how Summer holiday visits to Tiree had always given him an interest in the place and he had started learning Gaelic with his grandfather when he was quite young; but it was not until he was at University that he really began to get interested in 'you know, the Celts and the history and all that'. He felt annoyed with his father for not telling him about these things, especially the Clearances. 'That's what's wrong with that generation', he told me, 'I think they feel inferior somehow and so they just repress it all. But you've got to have a cultural identity and it does you no good to pretend you haven't'. It was especially important, he told me, not to 'let the language die. Because if that goes, everything goes – you might as well pack your bags and forget it'. And it was 'a tragedy' if the language did die because it had been around for 'thousands and thousands of years'. What was more, he said, picking up a pamphlet produced by An Comunn Gàidhealach (The Gaelic Association), Gaelic was 'The Lion's Tongue'. That meant, he explained, that it was 'the language of *Scotland* not just the Gaels'. Once it was spoken right across the country and should, therefore, really be at the centre of Scottish education today instead of all that English history and should be given better recognition and funding. What was more, 'there's a whole Celtic heritage there', tying Scotland in with the Welsh and Irish, though they seemed to do better on the language front he thought. However, he hoped that Gaelic was back 'on the way up'. 'That is why learners like us are crucial really', for we showed that, even if we had not been brought up in the Hebrides, the language still mattered to us, that it was part of 'our heritage'. That was also why Duncan was running this book van, even though few locals had looked in all week and it had been 'tourists and teachers mostly' and sometimes 'a bit tedious'.

Duncan's views about cultural identity, the centrality of language within it, Gaelic as the language of Scotland, and a shared 'Celtic heritage', are part of a constellation of ideas widely shared in Gaelic renaissance circles. These ideas are supported by a particular account of history; and they themselves have a history. It is these histories that this chapter explores. My intention here is anthropological: to highlight the culturally specific and located nature of ideas that are commonly taken for granted, to explore their assumptions and their effects. I am interested in processes of selection and condensation in the formation of particular knowledges, and in the way in which certain identity categories themselves arise and may be projected back.

In this chapter, I explore the nature and emergence of accounts such as Duncan's. This entails consideration not just of the Gaelic renaissance of the 1970s and 1980s, and the broader Scottish nationalism and ethno-nationalism with which the flourishing of interest in Gaelic was linked, but also involves attention to earlier periods, particularly late eighteenth-century romantic nationalism which provides many of the categories on which the Gaelic renaissance and ethnonationalism draw. The chapter, then, is concerned not just with some of the various 'imaginings' that we have seen of 'Gaelic culture', but with some of the tools and processes involved in that imagining.

Duncan's account is a compelling one; and one which, moreover, is increasingly articulated by people who, unlike Duncan, are not actively involved in Gaelic promotion. In 'denaturalising' the account, my intention is not to deny its validity as a form of cultural expression. Highlighting the 'invention' of certain traditions or historical accounts, particularly in relation to national and ethnonational pasts, has become commonplace but as Kapferer observes all 'traditions' may be said to be invented in some sense (1988: 210). My aim, however, is to highlight the cultural specificity of the notions of identity and culture that are part of certain ways of constructing histories. This form of denaturalisation is necessary, then, in order to make space for seeing cultural alternatives.

The Lion's Tongue?

The leaflet which Duncan handed to me – one of several others which I also picked up in his van – was called 'An Comunn: Who are we? Why are we?' It was produced by An Comunn Gàidhealach, a society established in 1891 and originally concerned mainly with the organisation of a national Gaelic music festival (the national Mòd) modelled on the Welsh National Eisteddfod. Since 1965, however, when An Comunn first received financial support from the Scottish Education Department and local authorities, and came to appoint its first full-time director in the Highlands, its remit has expanded into much broader Gaelic promotion activities, the production of various leaflets being one of these. An Comunn's first leaflet – *Who are the Highlanders?* – was published in 1966, and others with titles such as *Close-up on Peat, Crofting, Modern Gaelic Verse, The Story of Tartan, The Clàrsach, Scottish Gaelic Proverbs, Highland Whisky, Highland Weapons* and *Gaelic is . . .* followed soon after. The titles illustrate the Association's range of concerns with the Gaelic language, Highland culture and history; and with topics which are likely to have a wide popular interest, conforming as they do to rather stereotypical interests in the Scottish Highlands (e.g. tartan and whisky) and more esoteric and specialised ones (e.g. peat, the clàrsach).

The *An Comunn: Who are we? Why are we?* leaflet contains in very condensed form an account of why Gaelic should be valued:

> Gaelic is the pedigree of Scotland, the language of the first Scots from whom the country took its name, the language of the Scottish Highlanders whose distinctive dress and music and heroic history have given Scotland most of its colour. Scot and Gael were once synonymous terms; Gael and Scot still are. Gaelic identifies the Gael more surely than any tartan, if only through a Gaelic surname no matter how corrupt and anglicised its form may be. Gaelic distinguishes Scotland. (n.d.)

The leaflet defines Gaelic, as does Duncan, as the language of *Scotland* – as the language of those 'from whom the country took its name' and as the language which is capable of conferring a distinctive identity upon

Scotland. While this is an idea which was not altogether new in the 1960s – the Scottish nationalist Hugh MacDiarmid, for example, had made a case of Gaelic as Scotland's language in the 1920s – it is one which was far from common. Indeed, in the first leaflet published by An Comunn in 1966 the case for Gaelic as *Scottish* is not yet fully made. While this leaflet – *Who are the Highlanders?* – concludes that, as the name 'The Scots' is derived from 'the Gaels who colonised Argyll long ago', and these could therefore be said to be 'the first Scots', then 'Highlanders as their true representatives could well claim . . . to be the most Scottish of the Scots', there is no extrapolation that Gaelic should therefore be recognised as the language of *Scotland*. Language is, however, described as the key marker of a distinct identity: language 'is the surest test [of whether people really are Highlanders]. For it "identifies people". Gaelic identifies the Gael' (MacKay 1966). Realising, however, that this excludes many who live in the Highlands who would regard themselves as Highlanders but who do not speak Gaelic, the leaflet adds an afterword that: 'Residents in the Highland Counties whose parents or remoter ancestors were Gaelic speakers are Gaels by residence and by representation.' There seems to be an implication that this is not quite a proper or 'sure' Gaelic identity; but it is one which still manages to accord language a vital, if vicarious, role. The 'identity' that the Gaelic language 'identifies' according to this earlier leaflet, however, is 'Highlander' or 'Gael' rather than, as in the later leaflets, 'Scot'.

By the time of the publication of the *Gaelic is . . .* leaflet in 1969, the argument for Gaelic as the distinctive language of *Scotland* is made unequivocally:

> Gaelic is important because it identifies Scotland, just as English identifies England, French France and so on. The value of this is beginning to be realised by Scots people as more and more appreciate the need to retain identity. As it is, all that is colourful and distinctive in Scotland has been derived from the Highlanders, tartans, kilt, bagpipes and much music and a tradition of soldiers unequalled in Europe.
>
> Without the Gaelic influence we do not have a national culture which can take its place with others in the European community or strong enough to resist the onslaught of English or American institutions.
>
> In Gaelic, Scotland has a real language, its oldest institution and what is perhaps the largest body of folk song in Western Europe, and according to the Declaration of Human Rights and the recommendation of the Conference on the Multi Society held at Lljubliana this ought to be promoted and encouraged. (MacKay 1969)

Here we see very clearly the argument that Gaelic should be seen as *Scottish* and as at the heart of a strong 'national culture'. English is dismissed as a language of Scotland and is associated firmly with England and with 'the onslaught of English and American institutions'. Support for regarding Gaelic as the language of Scotland is derived from the claim that it is Scotland's 'oldest institution', from the fact that it has folklore of significance beyond the nation, and from international developments encouraging 'minority' languages and cultures (though the term is not used, presumably partly because this would be at odds with an argument for Gaelic as a *national* language).

These arguments about Gaelic as crucial to a distinctive Scottish national identity were also elaborated in various longer pamphlets and short popular histories published during the 1970s and 1980s (e.g. MacKinnon 1974, Mulholland 1980, 1984, Ellis 1985).[1] Probably the most influential of these is Kenneth MacKinnon's *The Lion's Tongue: The Story of the Original and Continuing Language of the Scottish People* (1974). Indeed, it is from this book, whose title was based on a popularly written account of the Welsh language called *The Dragon's Tongue* (Morgan 1966), that the designation of Gaelic as 'the lion's tongue' (the lion being the symbol for Scotland) has filtered into the talk of those such as Duncan. Many of the subtleties of MacKinnon's account – such as his words of caution over reading back the idea of national language into the eleventh century (1974: 17) – are, however, lost in the more polemical accounts, for example Mulholland (1980, 1984), which draw on his work.

As the title to MacKinnon's book makes clear his account casts Gaelic as 'the original and continuing language of the Scottish people'. Like the later An Comunn leaflets and many of the other pamphlets and popular histories of Gaelic, he points out that the name 'Scotland' is derived from the *Scotti* who came to settle from Ireland from about 200 AD. Furthermore, he argues, 'Gaelic was closely bound up with the formation of Scottish nationhood' (1974: 19) for it was the language of the monarchs particularly after Kenneth MacAlpin, in 844, became King of both the Scots and an earlier major group of Scotland's inhabitants, the Picts. By the eleventh century, he writes, 'Gaelic was the language of the Scottish state, its royal house, the language of learning and the church' (1974: 16). This, however, was a fairly shortly held supremacy, for since then the number of Gaelic speakers, and the areas in which Gaelic is spoken in Scotland, have been in decline. Moreover, Gaelic – which was the language of the *Scotti*, and therefore, 'Scottish' – was usurped by English as the majority language of Scotland, and it is a dialect of English that today bears the name Scots or Scottish.[2] The processes involved in this are the subject of much discussion, to which we will return, in the Gaelic renaissance accounts of Gaelic history.

The idea that Gaelic is the *Scottish* language is based, then, on the fact that Gaelic was once 'the predominant language of Scotland' (Mulholland 1984: 5) and is 'its oldest institution' (MacKay 1969; cf. MacKinnon 1974: *roimh-radh*), that it was Gaelic-speaking *Scotti* who gave the country its name, and under whom Scotland became a *nation-state*, that there is a continuing 'Scottish people', and that English somehow usurped Gaelic's proper place. The account implies a close link between language and 'peoplehood' or 'nationality'; an idea, in the words of the An Comunn leaflets, that language *identifies*, that it is 'the surest test'. Involved in this account are a number of assumptions which are typical not just of the Gaelic renaissance but of nationalist thinking more broadly. First, that 'originality' and age are sources of contemporary authenticity and legitimacy. Second, that contemporary nations, states and peoples can be projected back into the past – i.e. that these are 'continuing' entities. Third, that a distinctive language lies at the heart of a national identity. These assumptions are part of a particularly marked and consequential constellation of ideas – which entail further elaborations – that arose in Europe in the late eighteenth century; and which source contemporary ethnonationalism.

Below I explore these assumptions, and some of their elaborations, further, through a focus on ways in which the Gaelic language and its speakers have been viewed over time. This takes us on a journey of exploration of some of the categories – 'Scotland', 'Highlander, 'nationhood', 'identity' – which frame and inform the contemporary Gaelic renaissance.

Imagining 'Peoplehood' and Nation

What is a people? Deciding upon what features to look for in tracing continuities of peoples and cultures back through time is notoriously difficult. Are present day Gaelic speakers 'the same people' as the Gaelic speakers of eleventh century Scotland? Are non Gaelic-speaking Scots? And should we regard all inhabitants of the Scottish nation – Highlanders and Lowlanders – as one people? And how far back does the Scottish nation stretch? In what way can we say that it was 'the same' in Kenneth MacAlpin's day, or in the third-century kingdom of Fortriu, if its territory was not identical with today?

These are questions on which historians and others who talk about the antecedents of Scots and Gaels today inevitably – though often implicitly and sometimes unreflectively – make decisions. Sometimes it is the same name that is accorded priority, at other times it is aspects of culture or the fact of inhabiting a particular territory, or continuities of monarchy or political structures, and often it is language. My aim here is not to adjudicate but to look at the criteria that are brought to bear, at some of the alternatives that have been mobilised at different times, and to suggest reasons and contexts for some of the shifts. I do this not simply to show that Gaelic renaissance accounts of the past involve a selective and sometimes anachronistic reading of history, but to try to highlight some of the ways in which identity has been conceptualised, and to show too how the past may source some of the ambivalences about identity that I describe later in this book. I should also note that while my focus here is on Gaelic, many of the processes which I describe (e.g. the construction of continuities) are typical of modern nationalism and ethnonationalism more broadly, though at the same time the Gaelic case is specific in a number of ways as we shall see.

The Same Language/ the Same People

Those who argue that present day Gaelic speakers are the original *Scotti* focus upon the idea that both spoke the same language, i.e. Scottish Gaelic. However, not only do languages change over time, the notion of 'speaking the same language' is not as clear cut as we often assume today. In the case of Gaelic, at various times and to various ends, it has been argued to be the same as, or continuous with, languages including Irish Gaelic, Pictish, and Hebrew. Moreover, as Michael Billig has suggested, the idea that there are separate languages with distinct underlying grammars and clear-cut speech boundaries should be regarded not as a natural fact which acts as a basis upon which national social and political structures may be built, but as itself as a product of attempts to forge nations (1995). This is not to say that there is no such thing as linguistic variation. It is to argue, however, that the emphasis put upon difference or similarity is likely to belie a good deal of complexity and possible alternatives; and to highlight the non-inevitability of the implications that are drawn from linguistic difference.

In the fifteenth century, the name generally used by Lowland commentators to designate Gaelic and its speakers shifted from 'Scottish' to 'Erse' or 'Irish'. The new label was not only based on perceptions of linguistic similarity, however. It was also part of the growth of an idea that there were two distinct 'peoples' within Scotland: Highlanders and Lowlanders, and with the increasing frustration that the latter seemed to have felt with the former. Although Gaelic renaissance accounts of pre-eleventh century Scotland emphasise the extent of Gaelic spoken and the fact that the monarchy were *Scotti*, and although Scotland is commonly referred to as a *kingdom* (of either Alba or Scotland) from Kenneth MacAlpin, many historians caution against seeing this as a single *people* or a 'nation' in the modern sense. The 'kingdom' should be regarded, it is suggested, as a 'hybrid kingdom' (Grant 1988; in Lynch 1992: 53). As well as the *Scotti* there were other linguistic groups within Scotland in the eleventh century: those who had been there prior to the arrival of the *Scotti* – speakers of a Brittonic dialect in the southern and western districts, some speakers of Pictish perhaps still in the north east (Jackson 1956); and those who had moved in alongside the expansion of Gaelic – English speakers in Lothian in the south east since the sixth century and Norse into the northern and western islands and coastlands from towards the end of the eighth century (Jackson 1951). Even these we should not see as homogeneous 'peoples' or 'ethnic groups' for there was probably a good deal of linguistic and social difference within them, as well as a lack of a sense of boundaries between them. As the historian Christopher Smout has written of this period:

> It would be wrong to think of [Alba] as in any sense a state, Celtic or otherwise. There was as yet no notion of law that could be applied to all people in all places . . . Still less did anyone envisage the inhabitants of Scotland as a united or homogeneous people . . . Scotland, in fact, was much less an identifiable state than a confederacy of peoples with distinct characteristics and traditions, each prone to rebellion and to internecine war, held together only by allegiance to the person of the king. Even this was insecure. (1972: 20)

We might note here too that territorially Alba, or the Scotland of this time, was not identical with contemporary Scotland. The Hebrides, for example, did not become part of it until the end of the fifteenth century. Held under the suzerainty of the Norse, these had been under semi-independent government known as the Lordship of the Isles since 1266.

The idea that there were two main peoples or 'races' within Scotland and that these could be distinguished partly on the basis of the language which they spoke first appears in accounts by Lowland commentators in the fourteenth century. The following, by John Fordun (who was probably a priest from Aberdeenshire), is generally attributed as being the earliest clear statement of the idea of two main Scottish peoples in the late 1380s:

> The manners and customs of the Scots vary with the diversity of their speech. For two languages are spoken among them, the Scottish and the Teutonic; the

latter of which is the language of those who occupy the seaboard and the plains, while the race of Scottish speech inhabits the Highlands and out-lying islands. The people of the coast are of domestic and civilised habits, trusty, patient, and urbane, decent in their attire, affable, peaceful, devout in Divine worship . . . the Highlanders and people of the Islands, on the other hand, are a savage and untamed nation, rude and independent, given to rapine, ease-loving, of a docile and warm disposition, comely in person, but unsightly in dress, hostile to the English people and language, and owing to diversity of speech, even to their own nation, and exceedingly cruel. (1872: 38)

Fordun's 'observation', however, was not necessarily simply that; for one thing, his own Aberdeenshire and other parts of 'the seaboard and plains' were likely to have had a good many Gaelic-speaking inhabitants at this time. The clear-cut division he makes seems to have been part of an attempt to forge a sense of commonality among those who he refers to variously as 'the Teutonic' and 'the English people'. While Fordun's account may be seen as part of an attempt to forge 'a Scottish national identity', as Roger Mason argues (1992: 52), it is important to note that this was an identity among those who at the time were *not* referred to as Scots – and, moreover, it was an identity being forged in opposition to those who were. Highlanders were regarded by Fordun as a 'nation' (as he puts it) distinct from the Lowlanders.

That social identities – people's sense of being part of *a people* or other collectivity – are formed through a sense of what they are *not*, of who they are different from, is an insight which has received considerable attention and theoretical elaboration in anthropology (see Jenkins 1996 for an overview). Unlike what Fredrik Barth, one of the most important of these theorists, calls 'objective' attempts to determine whether a people (or an 'ethnic group' as he puts it) is 'the same' – tracing features which are visible to outsiders such as the same cultural practices, anthropologists have instead mostly emphasised the importance of 'subjective' features – how people are seen and see themselves. Do *they* see themselves as 'a people' and what features do they regard as important? Barth argues both that these features may not be the ones that we might assume from the outside, and that the significance of differences and the general sense of being of a particular group or people is one which will be formed through the experience of contact and trying to establish difference. Fordun's account, then, while on the one hand referring to 'the Scots' as comprised of two peoples, seems to put much greater emphasis on attempting to establish a sense of difference between 'the Teutonic' people and 'the Scottish', and through this, presumably, a sense of Lowlandness in opposition to Highlandness. The former were 'domestic . . . civilised . . . trusty, patient, . . . urbane, decent . . . affable, peaceful, devout . . .' and so on in relation to the opposed characteristics of the latter: 'savage and untamed . . ., rude and independent' and so on. It was out of such a process of self-definition by Lowlanders – involving opposition to 'an Other' – that the category 'Highlander' – a people identified with a particular part of the country and a particular set of characteristics – emerged (cf. Smout 1972, Chapman 1978, Withers 1984, 1988).

Fordun was an early example of an extremely extensive process which continued over the following centuries. The idea of two distinct 'races', characterised among other things by language, was almost invariably invoked in historical accounts of Scotland or attempts to characterise Scottish society (Smout 1972: 40). As Malcolm Chapman has argued, we need to see such attempts to draw sharp divisions and contrasts as part of a process of *self*-definition on the part of Lowlanders, and also British 'Teutons' (as in Matthew Arnold's characterisation) more generally (1978). Gaels or Highlanders were imagined as embodying characteristics which their neighbours to the South had 'grown out of' (the metaphor of child and adult being one that was explicitly used in some cases). None of this is to say, however, that these definitions were purely a matter of academic speculation. On the contrary, they were part of a whole complex of practices in which attempts were made to contain, control and improve the Highlanders. Furthermore, cultural practices – such as cattle raiding and the clan system – which were not exclusive to the Highlands, were increasingly perceived as 'Highland' ways and (especially given the fuzziness of the geographical definition of the Highlands) could provide further support for a picture of two distinct peoples. All this helped to conceptually distance Gaels and non-Gaels within Scotland. They were also, paradoxically, made more spatially distant as communications – in the form of new roads into the Highlands – opened up. 'The new land routes to the Highlands had to pass over the natural barriers of the Highlands instead of using the sea to sail round them. For the first time the Isles were placed "beyond" the mountain passes and this isolated them geographically from the Lowlands in a way that they had not been before' (Dawson 1992: 96). The idea of a 'Highland Line' – an imagined physical point of culture clash within Scotland – was established.

In referring to Gaelic as 'Scottish', Fordun was following the accepted designation of his day; and he clearly has some difficulty in finding a label for those other 'Scots', referring variably as he does to them as 'Teutonic' and 'English'. His difficulty, however, was solved by Lowland commentators later in the sixteenth century in a shift which saw the

'Teutons' labelled 'Scots' and the erstwhile Scots, 'Erse' or Irish. The linking of Gaels with the Irish was part of the process of conceptually distancing them from the centre of Scottish life – a process massively accelerated after the death of James IV (1488–1513), Scotland's last Gaelic-speaking monarch. It was an association based on a perception of both the Highlands and Ireland as being 'barbarous', especially so after the mainly Lowland Protestant Reformation of 1560, when parts of the Highlands and Ireland remained (even if often only nominally) 'Papist' if they were not still 'heathen'; and increasingly embodied in 'civilising' policies under James VI (I of England, 1603–25), the first monarch of both Scotland and England.

In Fordun's account language is seen as one of the foremost features for distinguishing between the two 'races' of Scotland. How far Gaelic speakers saw themselves as 'a people' and the place that they accorded language within this is far from clear, however. Fordun's remarks imply that there were significant linguistic and social divisions within the Highlands; and many historical accounts detail the disputes and battles between different clans, though we should not overestimate the extent of homogeneity in other parts of Britain at this time either. Gaelic poetry, which is one of the few sources to which we can turn for the historical sentiments of the Gaels, mostly concentrates upon 'clan politics' until the eighteenth century, although there are a few sixteenth- and seventeenth-century poems which employ an opposition between Gael and Saxon (*Gàidheal* and *Sasunnaich*) (Thomson 1974: 31–3; MacInnes 1989: 95). This seems to have been Highlanders' formulation of a linguistically-based difference between speakers of Gaelic and English; *Sasunnaich* referring to any English speakers rather than to the English.[3] However, as Lowland policies – e.g. James VI's attempts to establish 'colonies' in the Highlands – increasingly emphasised 'the Highland problem', an opposition between Highlanders and Lowlanders – *Gàidheal* and *Gall* (pl. *goill*, lit. 'foreigner') – becomes more prevalent in the poetry, often coupled with reference to *mi-rùin mhór nan Gall*, the 'great ill-will of the Lowlander' (ibid.). Even if Gaelic speakers had not particularly felt themselves to be a group before, and even though there was little social basis for thinking of themselves as a group, they increasingly had reason to think of themselves as one through opposition with Lowlanders.

Language, Identity and Improvement

Fordun's use of language as a central means of identifying 'races' and his depiction of each 'race' as a set of associated characteristics appears in some ways as rather like the Gaelic renaissance arguments about language *identifying* a people. However, in the intervening centuries there have been some significant shifts in the ways in which these matters are conceptualised; and by looking at these shifts we can see better what is distinctive about more recent ways of articulating identity and its relationship with language.

While Fordun distinguishes peoples or races, and while he does so on the basis of language and other observable features, he does not develop this into a demand that those 'races' should somehow remain true to their own distinctiveness. In the terms used by Charles Taylor (1989), outlined in the introduction, Fordun *individuates* Highlanders and Lowlanders – and does so in part through an implied moral distinction between good and bad peoples (to parallel Taylor's comments on personal identity) – but he does not elevate this into a 'calling' for those peoples to *express* their individuality (Taylor 1989: 375–6). The idea that *cultural distinctiveness*, just as personal distinctiveness, springs from 'some original and unrepeatable "measure"'(Taylor 1989: 376) deep within each people and that they should, therefore, 'live up to [their] originality' (ibid.) was not yet part of the way of thinking about such differences. 'Races' were different, certainly. And languages were an important part of this difference. But neither language nor other 'cultural' features of a people were yet regarded as properly inalienable from their sense of self.

On the contrary, until – and indeed ambivalently alongside thereafter – the romantic movement of the second half of the eighteenth century, Gaels were increasingly placed within a story not simply of self-evident cultural and moral *difference* but of progress and *transformation*. They came to show the state from which Lowlanders had thankfully moved away. Language difference was one of the features which was configured within this notion of transformation. For example, George Buchanan in 1582 saw the shift from Gaelic to English as 'a transmigration of languages [from] . . . Rusticity and Barbarism, to Culture and Humanity' (Withers 1984: 25). There was here no notion of groups properly expressing themselves through linguistic specificity, nor of linguistic relativism. Although languages were seen as bound in with other characteristics, these were all regarded as changeable.

One consequence of this view of language and culture was that both were regarded as proper targets for attempts at 'improvement'. Although the eighteenth century is generally known as the Age of Improvement in Scotland, both a discourse of improvement and practical attempts at it were underway well before this (cf. Lynch 1992: xvii). Where the Gaelic language was concerned, directed attempts at linguistic 'transmigration' began in the seventeenth century, under James VI (I of England). For James, Highlanders, along with the Irish, were embarrassingly uncontrollable, and they, as much as any Scottish/English divide, threatened the unity of the nation that James (before the blossoming of most European nationalisms) was trying to form. It was in this context that the association between the Gaelic or 'Irish' language and political disruptiveness and primitiveness was taken to the logical conclusion of an attempt to tame the rebels through their tongues. Thus, in the Statutes of Icolmkill (1609), which were signed by nine Highland chiefs (including MacDonald of Skye) and the Lords Commissioners for the Affairs of the Isles (Withers 1984: 28), the chiefs were obliged, among other things, to send their eldest sons (or daughters if there were no sons) to school 'in the Lowland' so that they would be able to 'speik, reid and wryte Inglische' (ibid.: 29).

Although this can be interpreted as a purely practical move – the chiefs would be bilingual and better able to understand the policies of the government – the Act of the Privy Council in 1616 illustrates clearly the nature of the identity which Gaelic or 'Irische' had acquired in government eyes. The council advised:

> that the vulgar Inglische toung be universallie plantit, and the Irische language, whilk is one of the cheif and principall causes of the continewance of barbaritie and incivilitie amongis the inhabitantis of the Ilis and Heylandis, may be abolisheit and removeit. (ibid.: 29)

The Act also decreed that any sons of Highland chiefs who could not speak, read or write English would not be recognised as the heirs to the chiefdoms. In the Highlands themselves schools were to be established for the teaching of English and instruction in religion, though this aspect of the Act was not followed until considerably later on account of the difficulties of funding the building and maintenance of these schools.

The educational policies of the seventeenth century were not put into effect, however, until towards the beginning of the eighteenth century. When education did finally come to the Highlands, it did so under the auspices of the State Church, and education itself had a centrally religious role. The Scottish Society for the Propagation of Christian Knowledge (SSPCK), approved by the General Assembly of the Church of Scotland in 1708, was the main organ of the educational programmes. The number of people affected by the SSPCK schools was, nevertheless, small throughout the eighteenth century. In Skye, for example, there was only one SSPCK school by 1719, and that had fifty-three boys on its register. By 1731, there were two schools, one with twenty-five pupils and the other with twenty-six pupils (eight of them female) – numbers which probably accounted for under 2 per cent of the population. This proportion of the population being schooled seems to have remained fairly constant throughout the century, though the rise and demise of schools around Skye meant that for particular local populations the picture often changed markedly. For example, in 1774, there was no school in the North of Skye; but in 1792 the only two schools on the island – one an SSPCK school, the other a spinning school – were both in the same Northern parish.

The SSPCK schools, born out of the aim of 'civilising' the Highlands, attempted to introduce literacy in English. An SSPCK statement in 1716 made clear the intention of the schooling:

> Nothing can be more effectual for reducing these countries to order, and making them usefull to the Commonwealth than teaching them their duty to God, their King and Countrey and rooting out their Irish language, and this has been the case of the Society as far as they could, ffor the Schollars are taught in English (quoted in Withers 1984: 122)

At the time, this intention was not contentious among the governing classes. Order and civilisation were assumed to be both right and unquestionably desirable; and the values of Gaelic, and the disordered qualities of the Highlanders, had yet to be romanticised. So too, although we see languages being associated with particular social characteristics, there is no notion of an unimpeachable link between people and language. There is no sense that 'rooting out' Gaelic might mean alienation and damage to the 'self' of the Gaels. It would change them, yes. But the transformation would be all to their own good.

However, even the introduction of English and the Bible were impeded through trying to do this solely through the English language: the pupils did not understand the stretches of text which they were instructed to memorise. Because of this, after 1723 the SSPCK adopted what was known as the 'comparative method': pupils would learn first in English and then translate into Gaelic (ibid.: 125–6). There was, however, a shortage of Gaelic books. The only Gaelic texts printed by the end of the seventeenth century were Bishop John Carswell's translation of Knox's *Liturgy* (1567), Calvin's *Catechism* (1631); the first fifty psalms (1659) and Kirk's Psalter (1684) – none of which was widely available. There had been attempts to distribute Irish Bibles but this had been largely unsuccessful owing in many cases to reluctance on the part of some authorities to sanction the use of Irish materials out of a fear that this might strengthen religious and political links between Scottish Gaels and the Irish, and in others to difficulty in comprehension on the part of Scottish Gaels.

To help ameliorate this situation, a university-educated Gaelic speaker,

Alexander MacDonald, was employed by the SSPCK to produce a Gaelic vocabulary. This appeared in 1741 as *Leubhar a Theagasc Ainminnim no a Nuadhfhoclair Gaoidheilg & Beurla* (Name Teaching Book, or a new Gaelic & English Vocabulary). Its intention was to 'introduce the English language over the Highlands and Islands of Scotland' (MacDonald 1741: vi) something 'necessary ... to make these, who can speak only Gaelic, more useful members of the Commonwealth' (ibid.: v). For MacDonald, the learning of English would not 'so speedily be got done' unless conducted at least partly in Gaelic (ibid.). MacDonald's work for the SSPCK has been seen as ironic when set against his later Jacobitism and strongly pro-Gaelic poetry (Chapman 1978: 56). However, although his apparently alternative positions on Gaelic here might be regarded as him switching camp with the emergent romanticisation of Gaelic, we should note that MacDonald himself does not appear to see his 'pro-English' work as 'anti-Gaelic'. On the contrary, he had personally felt the advantages of an English education and his motive for introducing English appears to be the benefits which it can bring. Nowhere does he talk of the 'wearing out of Gaelic' – a favourite SSPCK phrase – but instead appears to assume the development of bilingualism: the English education is for those who 'can *only* speak Gaelic' (1741: v; my emphasis). The imperialistic model of one language driving out another, while clearly sustained by some, was by no means inevitably held by those, such as Alexander MacDonald, involved in promoting English to Gaels.

Anglicisation and Suppression

Anglicisation and the decline of Gaelic are, in most revivalist accounts, depicted in terms of the active suppression of the native tongue.[4] Mulholland, for example, writes:

> The suppression of Gaelic goes back a long way, in fact to the Middle Ages. Briefly, since the invasion of Scotland by William the Conqueror and his followers in 1072 and because of Malcolm Ceann Mor's vassalage to William, Norman French became the language of the Scottish nobility. English became prominent later. Gaelic ... constantly had to fight against repression ... Thus began the sustained attack on the Gaelic language which, many would argue, continues today. (1984: 5)

The Statutes of Icolmkill and the SSPCK schools are given as evidence of this continuing process of the forceful 'suppression of native culture' (ibid.) against which 'Gaelic ... had to fight' (ibid.). However, while there certainly were attempts to 'root out' Gaelic, we should note that prior to the late eighteenth century, language specificity was not entwined with the idea of the expressive individuation of a deep-seated ethnic or national identity. Anglicising Gaels, then, was not regarded as some kind of assault upon their soul but as an 'improvement' for which they should be grateful.

We have little evidence of quite how Gaels themselves conceptualised identity in response to moves to provide English language education, though renaissance accounts generally present a picture of Gaels unwillingly being made to submit to the forceful imposition of English in schools. This has become particularly symbolised in the example of the *maide crochaidh* (lit. 'hanging stick'), 'a stick on a cord' which, according to MacKinnon 'was commonly used to stigmatise and physically punish children speaking Gaelic in schools. Its use is reported as late as the 1930s in Lewis' (1974: 55; 1991: 75; cf. Mulholland 1984: 8; Ellis 1985: 50). The ubiquity of the practice has, however, been questioned.[5] Nevertheless, the depiction of Gaelic as forcibly suppressed has an important moral place within renaissance accounts for if language is seen as the key site and symbol of a people's identity, then Gaels willingly learning English can only seem like a terrible mistake and an indication of severe alienation from their identity.

Other evidence, however, suggests that Gaels were not so resistant to learning English as the 'beating out of the Gaelic' portrayals imply. Towards the end of the eighteenth century the SSPCK changed its policy in the Highlands to advocate the teaching of Gaelic literacy (Durkacz 1983: 104). Although this change occurred at the same time as linguistic specificity began to be romanticised, the immediate motive was not a particular respect for those mother tongues but the practical ambition of saving souls as effectively and swiftly as possible, something which, it was argued, was inhibited by introducing literacy in a language other than the mother tongue (ibid.). To this end, Gaelic Bibles were produced: the Gaelic New Testament was first published in 1767 and the Old Testament in 1801, and both were reprinted many times. The promotion of Gaelic literacy, however, rather than providing a means for Gaels to resist Anglicisation, seems to have led to an expansion of English literacy. On Skye, for example, Sheriff Nicolson noted in 1867 that most of those who became literate in Gaelic also learnt to read English (ibid.: 221). Far from rejecting the unwelcome English thrust upon them, it seems that Gaelic speakers were themselves pursuing it. As Durkacz concludes from his survey of the available data on Gaelic responses to educational projects in the Highlands: 'the evidence suggests not only that Highlanders demanded English in schools, but that Gaelic monoglots demanded it more insistently than did bilinguals' (ibid.: 224). This does not necessarily mean, however, that Gaels were ready to simply divest themselves of Gaelic and to 'transmigrate' to an English-speaking identity. On the contrary, Gaelic language use has continued for long after the 'opportunity' of English became available, and for long after widespread English literacy. To regard language use purely as a matter of pragmatics, in which Gaels simply switch to whichever language offers most material benefits (a so-called rational choice model), fails – as does a model of suppression – to grasp the everyday cultural assumptions and social dynamics involved in language use and transmission. In Chapter 8, I examine the more recent history of Gaelic to try to offer a fuller account. While I do not claim that the same repertoire has necessarily been constant over time, I do suggest that language use is probably in most contexts a much more complex and socially embedded process than either the suppression or rational choice models allow.

Ambivalence, Ontology and Highlanders

Enlightenment certainties about 'improvement' – and the privileging of the rational and general over the emotional and specific – came to be challenged, though by no means overthrown, in the late eighteenth century by a constellation of ideas which provided new ways of thinking about the identity of both nations and persons, and also new ways of perceiving the Gaels and the Gaelic language. These 'romantic' ideas, which were not of course without their antecedents or complexities and variations (see Taylor 1989; Cranstone 1994), are an important source of the con-temporary popular and academic semantic repertoire for conceptualising nationhood and culture. They do not, however, supplant enlightenment conceptions; rather, the alternative ontologies that the enlightenment and romantic currents offer run alongside, generating many of the dilemmas and ambivalences of modernity. This is well evident in the Scottish case for Highlanders played a starring role in the articulation of both of the alternatives.

The 1760s saw the publication of books by two authors which are widely regarded as, respectively, central to the development of romantic and enlightenment projects: editions of Gaelic poetry describing the epic of 'Ossian' supposedly discovered by James MacPherson, the first of which was published in 1760;[6] and Adam Ferguson's *Essay on the History of Civil Society* (first published in 1767), which was one of the first attempts to analyse the formation of 'modernity' and to establish social science (Nairn 1981; Hamilton 1992). Both MacPherson and Ferguson emanated from the Highlands but lived for much of their lives in Lowland centres of learning; and for both, Highlanders – contrasted with their more 'rational' and 'progressive' neighbours – were inspirational. However, the narratives they inspired were rather different. For Ferguson, Highlanders figured in an improvement narrative of what Tom Nairn refers to as 'making it' and the 'study of the "mechanics of transition"' which lay at the heart of the new discipline of social science (Nairn: 1981: 111). For MacPherson, by contrast, what Highlanders represented was not so much a state from which to escape as a world replete with qualities which should be regained. His Ossianic poems, with their apparent naturalism and emotional content and style, represented a 'revolt of the heart over the mind [and] sentiment over reason' (Okun, quoted in Chapman 1978: 44). As such, they were widely acclaimed across Europe by those who sought a more affective apperception of the human condition than that which the 'mechanics' and 'geometrics' of enlightenment rationality seemed to offer.

MacPherson's *Ossian* provided a new, much more favourable, way of perceiving Highlanders (and many other 'primitive' peoples within Europe for whom highly regarded ancient literatures were soon discovered or forged (Morgan 1983: 99)); as well as a possible ancient and venerable ancestry with which Scotland might do nationalist battle. It did not, however, stop Highlanders from being regarded as 'primitive': it was a shift, as Stuart Piggott has put it, from 'hard primitivism' to 'soft primitivism' (1968: 77); a shift in which they remained 'Other'. Indeed, it was perhaps partly for this reason that *Ossian* did not propel a bid for Scotland to become a nation-state. Nor did *Ossian* have any immediate effects on the 'improvement' policies directed at the Highlands, though later – and in more indirect ways – it was to do so.

Romanticism, Identity and Nationhood

Romanticism, with its 'soft primitivism,' was, however, bound up with the emergence of new conceptions of both personal and national identity and the development of nation-states in Europe.[7] While enlightenment thinkers such as Ferguson contrasted themselves with 'less rational' others, and while they contrasted different types of society with one another, their concerns were not so much with *specific* societies and cultures as with a more general cosmopolitan narrative of progress. And while history was a concern, the general sense of movement in their theorising was onward and outward. This was a model in which *Being* was centrally about moving on. For Romantics, however, *Being* entailed a movement inwards and backwards – both peoples and persons being conceptualised as having 'inner depths' and specific individual experiences constituting a unique and distinctive identity which should properly be expressed. *Specific* languages and cultural traditions – including vernacular and folk languages and traditions – assumed a new importance for the Romantics, for these were regarded as the source and expression of a people's distinctiveness and inner core. This was an ontology in which persons and peoples each held some kernel of self-ness contained within identifiable boundaries. It was an ontology entailed in making nations – imagined as inherently limited and sovereign political communities (Anderson 1983: 15) – thinkable.

There is a good deal of analytical commentary on the development of the nation-state in Europe in this period, and I should note that my emphasis on the 'imaginings' involved is not intended to suggest that these were somehow primary, though nor would I regard them as mere reflections of an underlying social and economic base or attempts simply to account for what was happening anyway. Undoubtedly, there was a complex convergence and interplay of material circumstances and knowledges. The development of the identification of specific languages with specific nations is a case in point. This was an identification which was particularly powerfully articulated by the German Romantics, most notably Herder (1744–1803). Drawing analogies between individual and familial uses of language (e.g. parents 'accumulat[ing] experience not just for themselves' but also for their children (Herder, in Barnard 1969: 163)) and that of nations, Herder characterises language (in a quotation which was much adopted by later language movements) as a people's 'collective treasure, the source of its social wisdom and self-respect' (ibid.: 165). However, Herder's persuasive argument – like Fordun's account of two races of Scots – was not so much a description of the relationship between languages and nations, as an argument for the recognition and privileging of language as part of an attempt to forge national (and especially German) identity. It was a move in which language could be used as a means of identifying nation-ness. Yet, this should not be taken to imply a world of discrete homogeneous languages, each corresponding to a putative embryonic nation. On the contrary, national languages emerged – sometimes out of sentimental and political battles and social engineering but more often through more muted processes of pragmatics and compromise (Seton Watson 1977; Hobsbawm 1990: 52–4) – partly through the expansion of print capitalism (Anderson 1983). Through these processes, however, a model of identity in which language was regarded as the proper basis for nation-hood was established. This was to prove a time-bomb within those nation-states which were established in the eighteenth and nineteenth centuries.

Philology, Dictionaries and Gaelic

The new importance of linguistic specificity in the eighteenth and nineteenth centuries can also be seen in the growth of academic interest in vernacular languages. Prior to the rise of nationalism in Europe, there were virtually no dictionaries or grammars of vernacular languages (Harris 1980: 128). Philology – the study of the origins of languages – also blossomed in the age of nationalisms (Seton-Watson 1981; Anderson 1983: ch.6; Edwards 1985: ch.2). Through evolutionary models, it provided an apparently scientific means for establishing linguistic descent and origins, and was put to much use in verifying nationalist claims (McDonald 1986: 337).

In the case of Scottish Gaelic there was little formal linguistic interest in the language before the eighteenth-century appearance of *Ossian*. Edward Lhuyd had undertaken a comparative study of the Celtic languages and published the first printed Irish Gaelic dictionary together with Scottish supplement in 1707, but this was exceptional in its day (Campbell and Thomson 1963). It did, however, provide useful armoury for the Scots and Welsh later in their search for Celtic credentials on a par with those of the French (McDonald 1986: 335). The other pre-Ossianic work on the Gaelic language was Alexander MacDonald's Gaelic-English dictionary which, as we have seen, was created for the practical purpose of introducing English into the Highlands.

The first grammar of Scottish Gaelic was William Shaw's *An Analysis of the Gaelic Language* (1778), which he was partly inspired to write by the 'poems of Fingal' (i.e. 'Ossian'). Along with the first alphabetical Scottish Gaelic dictionary (1780), Shaw saw his linguistic efforts as the recording of a language in decline: 'I saw, with regret, a language once famous in the western world, ready to perish without any memorial' (1778: xvi). For Shaw, Gaelic was not only an ancient Celtic tongue, but : 'the greatest monument of antiquity, for the Gaelic language is the language of Japhet, spoken before the Deluge, and probably the speech of Paradise' (1780: 6). Nor was Shaw alone in making this particular 'philological' link. Alexander Stewart, who wrote Gaelic's next grammar (1812), saw fit to 'introduce . . . observations on the analogy between the Gaelic idiom and that of some other tongues, particularly Hebrew' (1812: x); and even later 'enthusiastic Gaelicians' (Blackie 1864: 8) made strenuous efforts to 'prove' that Gaelic was the language spoken in Paradise (e.g. MacIntyre

1865), often by engaging in fanciful etymologies – my favourite being the claim that 'Jehovah' was derived from the Gaelic *Dhe* (God) *bha* (was) *tha* (is) (in Blackie 1864: 18).

One of MacPherson's motives in producing *Ossian* was to provide Scottish Gaels with a more ancient literature than the Irish in order to 'prove' that Irish Celtic culture was an offshoot of Scottish rather than vice-versa – an argument propounded by historical exegesis accompanying the poetry (see Trevor-Roper 1983). This was also matched by various philological attempts to deny the relationship between Scottish and Irish Gaelic altogether by arguing that the former was descended from Pictish (a language ripe for speculation partly because of the paucity of information about it)[8] and therefore of wholly indigenous origin. Grammars and dictionaries also involved a prescriptive policing of the purity and boundaries of languages which were, according to the models at work, to be neatly distinguished from one another synchronically (even while their diachronic links were admitted). Alexander Stewart regarded Gaelic as 'in manifest danger of falling into [a] . . . discreditable condition, from the disuse of olde idioms and distinctions, and the admission of modern corruptions' (1812: vii–ix), and saw his grammar as a means of helping to prevent this. The makers of Gaelic dictionaries were at pains to exclude 'corrupted' forms, particularly words which have evidently English origins, even though these words may have been in regular use (see, for example, MacAlpine 1831; MacBain 1896; MacLennan 1925). Languages, like nations and cultural identities, were to be kept distinct. The use of English in Gaelic speech was, therefore, a sign of decadence: 'your modern Highlander cannot ask for his breakfast or dinner without using the Saxon tongue, not because he is forced to do it, but because he has got into a bad habit' (Blackie 1864: 25). It was only with the publication of Thomson's *New English-Gaelic Dictionary* in 1981 that words which would previously have been rejected as English and therefore corrupt are included; though, the use of English in Gaelic speech is still often regarded as a sign of the decay of Gaelic, not least by Gaelic speakers.

Effects of Romanticisation

Despite the growth of interest in Gaelic in the eighteenth and nineteenth centuries, there was little concerted attempt to do anything to maintain Gaelic speaking within Scotland. Many Gaelic societies were set up on the Scottish mainland and in England, but these were often more concerned with 'the external vestiges of Gaeldom – the kilt, the music, and whisky' (Withers 1984: 206) than with language; and none had policies designed to promote Gaelic within the *Gàidhealtachd*.[9] Indeed, English-language education continued apace; and it seems to have been largely assumed that Gaelic would eventually succumb to progress. Dictionaries and grammars were a means of recording that which was sadly, but inevitably, giving way to the language of civil and rational thought.

Romantic ideas did, however, affect Gaelic speaking within the Highlands in more indirect ways. Within the prevailing milieu of soft primitivism, Gaelic was caught within the net of two contrary claims about 'primitive languages': that they 'were incapable of anything beyond minimal generalisation and abstraction . . . [and] conversely, . . . incapable of precision and specification' (Henson 1974: 10). Gaelic was widely assumed to be ideally formed for the earthy or airy emotionality of poetry but unsuitable for science and mathematics – ideas which found their way into schools and other spheres of life (Chapman 1978: 131; Chapter 8). MacPherson's 'search' for ancient Gaelic poetry also opened the floodgates of vast folkloric enterprise in the Highlands (Dorson 1968: especially chs. IV and XI; Chapman 1978: ch.5); and this too reinforced the idea that some aspects of Gaelic culture – the old and traditional – were valued highly by the outside world. As with the Gaelic grammars, however, this folkloric activity was undertaken very much in the spirit of capturing traditional culture before it disappeared, and thus simultaneously reinforced a perception of Gaelic as dying. At the same time that the idea of a coherent, estimable Gaelic culture was born, then, it was also seen as near to its end; and Highlanders often found themselves charged with having neglected to properly maintain it. Also, as I discuss in the following chapter, the romanticisation of the Highlands was involved in the developments and legislation arising out of the Land Wars in the nineteenth century. This established the *Gàidhealtachd* as an area with distinct land-holding patterns (i.e. crofting) and to some extent helped to maintain a Gaelic-speaking population in the area. Romanticisation, then, was far from being simply a distant academic movement: in numerous ways it entered the world of those living within the Highlands.

Scotland, Gaelic and Nationhood

Ironically, given Highlanders' place in the formation of the romantic nationalist model of identity, neither the Highlands nor Scotland established themselves as nation-states. Scotland in particular might have been expected to do so given that pre-Union (i.e. pre-1707) independence was relatively recent and that it had some politico-economic autonomy on which to build in the form of its own Law, Church, Education and Mint;

but there was little nationalist activity in Scotland in the nineteenth century (Webb 1978: 46; Nairn 1981: 10). In part this seems to be, as Nairn suggests, on account of the strength of the alternative cosmopolitan enlightenment model within Scotland (Nairn 1981), and the fact that for the most part intellectuals tended to regard themselves as neither specifically Highland nor Scottish but as part of either a British or broader European intelligentsia (ibid.: 123–5; Hanham 1969: 67). Moreover, Scottish Highlanders – in whichever way they were primitivised – also made it difficult for Lowland Scots to imagine Scotland as a single 'community;' and the Jacobite rebellions of the first half of the eighteenth century, which were increasingly, though to some extent mistakenly, seen as a mainly Highland affair, had 'tainted opposition to the Union of 1707 with Jacobitism,' and in effect, therefore, also with Catholicism (Hanham 1969: 67).[10]

Concerted attempts to establish Scotland as a nation-state had to wait until the 1960s. As Webb notes: 'Explicitly nationalist organisations have existed since 1853, but only in 1961 did the movement begin to suggest that it might disrupt the political system' (Webb 1978: 102).[11] 1960s Scottish nationalism was to some extent part of a broader emergence of ethnonationalism in Europe at this time, an emergence which was a surprise to many observers and theorists and which has been the subject of a good deal of debate. One area of controversy has been over the extent to which European ethnonationalism was a 'reawakening' or an 'invention' of ethnic ties.[12] The positions, however, have often been over polarised, for while 1960s ethnonationalism frequently drew (as in the Scottish case) on earlier definitions of peoplehood and traditions, it also involved asserting a new primacy – and a new set of accompanying political and cultural expectations – to the 'revived' ethnic identities. Moreover, both positions need to explain the reasons for the new visibility and new demands of sub-national ethnic allegiances in the established nation-states at this time. Explanations here have focused variously on economic and political dissatisfaction with established nation-states;[13] and increased tolerance of minorities in reaction against the experience of Nazism in Germany, and as part of a more general critique of imperialism and modernity.[14] However, no single explanation can deal with all cases, and it seems that a variable set of factors – together with the 'pirating' of the notion of 'ethnic identity' (itself informed by earlier romantic-nationalist ideas) – needs to be invoked.

Language issues were never so central to Scottish nationalist concern as they were in many of the other emergent European nationalisms of the 1960s, such as Welsh and Breton nationalism.[15] In part this is because

Gaelic remains very much a minority language within Scotland, where less than 2 per cent of the population are Gaelic speakers;[16] and, according to a survey in 1981, less than half of Scots agree that 'the Gaelic language is important for the Scottish people as a whole' (MacKinnon 1981).[17] Nevertheless, it was within this growth of Scottish nationalism – a nationalism that gained new impetus in the 1980s with the discovery of North Sea oil (referred to as 'Scotland's oil' by the Scottish National Party) and with a glimmering possibility of greater autonomy within the European Community – that a new interest in Gaelic language and culture, and policies directed at promoting and maintaining the Gaelic language, were generated.

The Gaelic Renaissance

The 1960s saw the first significant state support for Gaelic and the beginnings of what was to become a massive increase in pro-Gaelic policy-making and developments throughout Scotland (Table 2.1). It also saw a concerted attempt to define Gaelic as *Scottish*, as we saw in the An Comunn leaflets. Those such as MacKinnon were quite explicit about the importance of this as a way of maintaining Gaelic: 'The immediate task of the promoters of Gaelic in national life is to get over the view that Gaelic is above all the Scottish language' (1974: 117). It would only be by enlisting the support of Scots as a whole that Gaelic would be able to survive. Even those accounts which argued for a resurrection of 'Celtica' – the Celtic nation – made their case not in terms of the Highlands alone but with reference to Scotland as a whole (Ellis 1969; Ellis and Mac a'Ghobhainn 1971; *Celtic League* 1969–72; also, MacDiarmid 1968).

While the Gaelic renaissance can be seen as part of a broader 'ethnic revival' (Smith 1981), it has taken place more under the wing of the state than has much ethnonationalist activity elsewhere.[18] There has been relatively little belligerent activism, and most of this has been relatively low-key compared with that of, say, the Basque country or even Wales and Brittany. Nor has Gaelic activism been part of demands for political autonomy within the Highlands and, despite its associations with Scottish nationalism, nor has it been part of such claims for Scotland.

In 1968 the SNP took its first steps towards embracing Gaelic by passing a conference resolution to establish a 'Gaelic Secretariat', though it was not until 1974 that a resolution was made to formulate a detailed policy on Gaelic. Demands for the support of Gaelic have not, however, been at the centre of the SNP political agenda and most nationalist activism (for example, bombings by the Scottish National Liberation Army in

Table 2.1. Some Developments in the Promotion of Gaelic 1950–90

1951	*Gairm*, a Gaelic quarterly produced at Glasgow University is published for the first time.
1961	The Celtic League is founded.
1965	*An Comunn Gàidhealach*, The Gaelic Association, receives financial support from the Scottish Education Department, local authorities and private sources, and appoints its first full-time director and establishes offices in the Highlands.
1968	*Crann*, a Gaelic and English magazine, is started by students at Aberdeen University.
1968	*Club Leabhar*, a Gaelic publishing house, is set up.
1969	The National Mòd Bill, establishing an annual Gaelic festival along the lines of the Eisteddfod is passed by parliament.
1970	*Comann na Canain Albannaich*, an association promoting all of the Scottish languages, is founded (it is disbanded in 1975).
1971	*Tocher*, a Gaelic, Scots and English magazine is started by the School of Scottish Studies, Edinburgh.
1972	*The West Highland Free Press* is established in Skye. Although it is not a Gaelic paper it is supportive of the language, carries some Gaelic columns, and for several years has a monthly Gaelic supplement.
1973	*Fearann Eilean Iarmain*, a company directing various enterprises is set up by Iain Noble in Sleat, Skye. The employees are to conduct their business in Gaelic.
1974	The Scottish National Party confirm their policy on the promotion of Gaelic (first devised in 1968) at their party conference.
1974	The Western Isles becomes a single administrative unit with their own islands council, *Comhairle nan Eilean*, which is responsible among other things for the Gaelic education policy in the schools.
1975	The Bilingual Education Project (concerning mainly primary education) begins in the Western Isles.
1975	*Comhairle Oileanaich Gàidhealach Alba*, the Association of Gaelic Students, is founded. There are signs of Gaelic 'activism': demonstrations, mainly by students, outside the BBC offices in Glasgow to protest at the low output of Gaelic on radio and television.

Table 2.1. Some Developments in the Promotion of Gaelic 1950–90 (*continued*)

1976	*Radio air a' Ghàidhealtachd*, a Gaelic radio station based in Inverness, begins broadcasting.
1977	*Cinema Sgìre*, a community film and video unit, is established (until 1981).
1977	Highland Regional Council sets up a Gaelic sub-committee.
1977	*Proiseact Muinntir nan Eilean*, a community education project based in the Western Isles is established.
1977	*ACAIR*, a Gaelic publisher based in Stornoway, Lewis, is founded. *Cliath*, a primary school book project, to be published by ACAIR receives funding.
1978	A bilingual-medium education project begins in Skye primary schools.
1987	*Fir Chlìs*, a travelling Gaelic repertory company is founded.
1978/9	Various radical Gaelic pressure-groups appear, notably *Ceartas* (Justice) and *Strì* (Struggle).
1979	*Radio nan Eilean*, a Gaelic radio station, is set up in Stornoway.
1980	The first International Celtic Film Festival is held in the Uists.
1981	A Bill for Gaelic is defeated in Westminster. This is followed by activism.
1981	The first Gaelic folk festival, *Fèis Bharraidh*, is held on Barra.
1981	*An Litreachadh Ur*, the revised Gaelic orthography, is instituted.
1982	Gaelic is given recognition in the Nationality Act.
1982	A report on Gaelic, *Cor na Gàidhlig*, commissioned by the HIDB is published. This provides policy recommendations for many of the Gaelic developments to emerge in the following years.
1982	*Comhairle nan Sgoiltean Araich* (CNSA), the Gaelic pre-school playgroups association, is established. Its aim is to promote Gaelic-medium playgroups. In 1983 it is awarded funding by the HIDB to provide a full-time National development officer.
1983	The first students begin the Gaelic-medium business course at *Sabhal Mór Ostaig* (Skye's Gaelic College).

Table 2.1. Some Developments in the Promotion of Gaelic 1950–90 (*continued*)

1983	The first national *Airigh Shamhraidh*, Gaelic Summer School, is held in Skye.
1984	European Parliament establishes Lesser-Used Languages Bureau.
1984	*Comunn na Gàidhlig* (CnaG), an association designed to coordinate Gaelic organisations and promotion, is established.
1984	*Comunn Luchd Ionnsachaidh*, a Gaelic learners association, is established.
1985	*Parantan airson Foghlam Gàidhlig*, Parents for Gaelic-medium Education, is set up in Inverness.
1985	Gaelic-medium playgroups and primary classes open in Inverness and Glasgow.
1986	*CnaG* produced *Towards a National Policy for Gaelic*.
1986	Secretary of State for Scotland announces a Specific Grants Scheme for activities in connection with education in and about Gaelic (£250,000 for 1987–8).
1986	More Gaelic-medium primary units open, including in Skye and the Western Isles. There are six such schools in total.
1987	National Gaelic Arts Council, funded mainly via the Scottish Arts Council, is established. This in turn helps establish and fund a number of theatre companies and drama projects, notably: *Ordag is Sgealbag* (a children's educational theatre company), *Dràma na h-Alba* (a national drama organisation), the National Gaelic Youth Theatre for over-16s, and *Smathsin* (a Gaelic comic).
1988	Gaelic-medium stream opens in Carnan and a number of other places.
1989	A conference is held leading to the formation of an organisation to coordinate Gaelic folklife festivals: *Fèisean nan Gàidheal* (the National Association of Gaelic Arts Festivals).
1989	Government White Paper on broadcasting acknowledges the importance of Gaelic language programmes.
1990	Announcements made about major new funding for Gaelic television. Gaelic Television Committee established to oversee the developments. Programmes to begin in 1993.

the 1970s) has not been on behalf of Gaelic or the *Gàidhealtachd*. The year 1975 saw the first Gaelic activism and this, as in many areas of Europe, was university-based, which in Scotland meant that it was based in the Lowlands. An Association of Gaelic Students in Scotland (COGA – Comhairle Oileanaich Gàidhealach Alba) was established in Glasgow, Edinburgh and Aberdeen Universities and claimed more than three hundred members. In 1975 they held demonstrations outside the BBC in Glasgow in protest against the paltry number of hours of Gaelic broadcasting. This seemed to follow closely on a Welsh example. Later in the 1970s organisations such as Ceartas ('Justice') and Strì ('Struggle') appeared. Strì was instrumental in establishing a Gaelic playgroups network and seems to have drawn its members mainly from universities, though there were some members from the Isles too.[19] The main activity of Ceartas, following the Welsh example, was the daubing of English-language road signs. Membership again seems to have been fairly small and young and probably drawn from the same stock as the other organisations. By the early 1980s these organisations had disappeared. Another which appeared in their wake was Faire ('Watch' or 'Guard') which was set up in Skye and said to be 'a grass-roots stirring of a different kind from that emanating from the universities' (*Cor na Gàidhlig* 1982: §45.04). However, by the mid-1980s this had also disappeared. The only major Gaelic militantism during the 1980s followed the defeat of a Gaelic Bill in Parliament which had been put forward by Donald Stewart, SNP MP from the Western Isles, though even this was short-lived.

The Gaelic renaissance, then, has been characterised by an absence of the high degree of politicisation and activism characteristic of some other ethnic resurgences. There has been no widespread withholding of tele-vision licence fees (as in Wales), though some members of Strì did refuse to pay; no organised violence against outsiders (as in Corsica); very few demonstrations; and even the damage to road signs has not been extensive. The majority of Gaelic pressure-groups have been established within pre-existing frameworks (e.g. as sub-committees on local councils) and most have state support, as do most Gaelic publishing and arts. Indeed, many of those which were established outside the state framework have come under its wing (e.g. An Comunn Gàidhealach). The National Mòd (a Gaelic festival modelled on the Welsh Eisteddfod) was established by a parliamentary bill in 1969 and is run by An Comunn Gàidhealach. Research commissioned by the Highlands and Islands Development Board (the Scottish office agency dealing with the Highlands) in 1981 led to many of the new renaissance developments during the 1980s. These included the establishment of Comhairle na Gàidhlig (CNAG –

the Committee on Gaelic) to provide 'information, liaison, research and development facilities' (ibid.: §87.05) and generally oversee the renaissance; as well as the funding and often organisation of more specific projects such as the Gaelic playgroups network, a youth activity project (Airigh Shamhraidh), and an annual Gaelic festival. These Gaelic developments could be seen as essential to maintaining a Gaelic-speaking population within Scotland, though it might also be argued that state support effectively contained any possibilities of more militant activism.

Some of the impetus for Gaelic revival has also come from the supranational institutions of the European Community; which in turn have been influenced by lobbying from some of Europe's more vocal minorities. Primarily under the auspices of the European Bureau for Lesser-Used Languages, established by the European Parliament in 1984 (and based in Dublin), there have been a number of initiatives aimed at protecting and promoting 'Lesser-Used Languages' (see Williams 1991a). While these did not provide significant direct funding for Gaelic-language projects during the 1980s, they undertook research which made comparisons with other minorities possible (and showed Gaelic as relatively 'neglected'), provided further legitimation for Gaelic revival projects and a promise of future funding. Moreover, within the European Community emphasis on greater regional autonomy – a 'Europe of the Peoples' or 'Europe of the Regions' – Gaelic could act as a marker of the distinctiveness of Scotland (language being a very contentious issue within the European Commission and Parliament more generally).[20] This was something which seems to have become increasingly recognised by the Scottish National Party (which has become more actively supportive of Gaelic during the 1980s as well as more pro-Europe) and by Labour. However, it has been a Conservative government which has directed funding towards Gaelic, something which may have been intended partly to counter their image in Scotland as 'the English party', though might also be intended to indicate that cultural difference can be effectively pursued within a United Kingdom context.

Throughout Scotland in the 1970s and since, there was an increase in numbers of Gaelic evening classes and a spread of Gaelic teaching in schools and universities; and an unprecedented number of courses appeared for learners.[21] Between 1961 and 1971 there was also a surprise 9.8 per cent increase (i.e. 8000) in the number of people reporting as Gaelic-speaking in the Census returns. This was the first increase since 1891 and the publication of the figures was delayed while they were checked (MacKinnon 1978: 3). The breakdown of the figures suggested, however, that the upturn was not just a statistical irregularity but a change in people's assessment of whether they spoke Gaelic or not. The increase was one of bilinguals and was concentrated in the Lowlands, particularly Lowland cities. Indeed, nearly all *Gàidhealtachd* regions recorded a decline. MacKinnon suggests that young men from the Highlands working in Lowland towns make up a good deal of the number, although this is not simply an increased presence of exile Gaels but: 'changes in education policy and public opinion now prompt larger numbers of these to "remember" their ability to speak Gaelic and have it recorded on the Census' (ibid.: 7).[22] From the Census we have no way of knowing whether people are claiming to speak Gaelic on the basis of half-a-dozen evening classes, whether it is individuals like Duncan who are swelling the numbers, or, conversely, whether people claiming not to speak it in fact do so fluently – as Duncan's father might perhaps do. Nevertheless, the increase is significant even if what it represents is a change in sentiment towards Gaelic.

Although much Gaelic promotion has been supported by officially-constituted state-funded institutions concerned with development and administration, this is not to say that Gaelic promotion has simply been imposed from outside the *Gàidhealtachd*. As we shall see in Chapter 8 below, there are mediating institutions, such as community, district and regional councils, and particular individuals who act as local activists. Yet, as we shall also see, the models of identity and culture invoked by those devising the promotion policies are not always entirely the same as those held by local people.

In this chapter we have seen how the idea of a 'Gaelic people' with particular cultural and linguistic characteristics first arose in opposition to the definition of Lowland Scots. From the perspective of those living outside the Highlands, it was only with the romanticism of the eighteenth century that this culture came to be seen as in any way valuable and that the notion of an inalienable cultural identity, in which language was central, arose. This idea found itself in competition with another, very different, modernist idea: that of improvement. These alternatives set up divergent ontological models both for what it was to be a person and to be a people or a nation.

The transnational ethnic revival beginning in the 1960s or thereabouts involved a widespread 'pirating' of the earlier nation-state model. Linguistic specificity, now firmly cast as at the heart of a coherent cultural identity, became increasingly politicised. Within Scotland this lead to a flourishing of Gaelic policies and developments throughout Scotland, and Gaelic coming increasingly to be cast as a, or even 'the real' (original), Scottish language. To an unprecedented extent, Gaels found themselves regarded as a valuable repository of culture, tradition and community within Scotland. Outsiders like Duncan arrived, armed with a discourse (and perhaps leaflets and books) of identity and culture. How those living within the Highlands experienced this and how it met up with other ways in which they conceptualised themselves is the subject of later chapters.

In the next chapter we turn to another dimension of history which has also been important in formulating ideas of Highland peoplehood and culture: the history of the clearances, evangelical revivals and land wars. This is a history which intertwines with that discussed in the present chapter; and like that discussed here has been a significant focus of the post-1960s Gaelic renaissance.

Notes

1. There are earlier examples of this argument. The Scottish nationalist poet Hugh MacDiarmid, for example, attempted in the 1920s to argue for a resurrection of a version of Scots as a step towards making Scotland a Gaelic-speaking nation (McClure 1979: 28; Grieve and Scott 1972; Brand 1978: Ch.6; Bold 1990).
2. Whether Scots should be regarded as a dialect of English or a distinct language, and whether it is Scots (of which there are various versions, e.g. Doric and Lallans) rather than Gaelic that should promoted as Scotland's language, are matters of some contention within Scotland, see McClure 1979; 1988; and Fenton and MacDonald 1994.
3. Whether the term *Sasunnaich* is being used to refer to those speaking English (which would include Lowlanders) or more specifically to those South of the Scottish border is not always easy to determine from historical records. John MacInnes' careful sifting of evidence on Gaelic perceptions of the Lowlands suggests that it could be one or the other depending on the context and that a less linguistic usage may have become more prevalent by the nineteenth century (1989; cf. Mac Gilleain 1985a: 255–6). The *exclusive* use of the term *Sasunnaich* to refer to people from England (rather than speakers of English) may, however, have first been a Lowland use of a Gaelic term rather than Highlanders' own understanding of it.
4. MacKinnon 1974 is, however, more sophisticated and offers a multi-factorial model through which to understand the processes of language shift. Accounts which draw on his work are rarely so nuanced, however.

5. Chapman (1992: 102–3) argues that all of the references to the practice derive from one citation in Campbell 1950. During my own fieldwork, despite my questions on the subject, I was not told of any instances of children being beaten for using Gaelic and nobody had heard of the *maide crochaidh* being used on Skye, though some had heard of its use on Lewis from the radio. I was, however, told that children would be rapped over the knuckles for speaking in class without the teacher's permission – whatever the language.

6. See Stafford 1988; Kidd 1993, ch.10.

7. Rousseau was a key figure in this. For relevant commentary see Cohler 1970; Solomon 1988; Taylor 1989; Llobera 1994.

8. The antiquarian William Skene popularised this idea with some zeal (1836) – making clear that he regarded links with Ireland to be nationally unpalatable, as have others since (e.g. Robertson 1865: 120; Coghill 1928: 15). There has been extensive debate among linguists, particularly in the 1940s and 1950s, over whether Pictish is a P-Celtic dialect (i.e. a version of Brttonic); a Q-Celtic dialect (i.e. related to Gaelic); or a non-Indo-European language (O'Rahilly 1946, Appendix II; Jackson 1956; Wainwright 1956); with the weight of opinion being in favour of it being P-Celtic, though possibly also including a non-Indo-European language (Jackson 1956: 152). Pictish links are still popular, and sometimes partly so on account of the possibility that they offer for an indigenously Scottish ancestry (see, for example, Lynch 1992: ch. 2).

9. The main Gaelic societies established in the wake of *Ossian* were The Highland Society of London founded in 1778; the Gaelic Club of Gentlemen in Glasgow, 1780; the Highland Society of Scotland, 1783; the Gaelic Society of Inverness, 1871; the Gaelic Society of Glasgow, 1877, and An Comunn Gàidhealach, 1891. See Withers 1984: 203–8 for further details.

10. Murray Pittock (1991) describes the idea that the Jacobites were Highlanders as a 'myth' (they made up less than half of the Jacobite army), and shows well how the myth was promoted and fostered particularly by Sir Walter Scott as a way of marginalising Jacobitism and thus uncoupling it from Scottish nationalism. For further discussion see McLynn 1996.

11. See Kellas 1989 for the share of the vote that the SNP has taken in elections pre-1989. For discussions of the growth of Scottish nationalism see Webb 1978; Bogdanor 1979: 93–9; Nairn 1981: ch.3; Kellas 1984: chs.7–8; McCrone 1991; Finlay 1994; Harvie 1994.

12. Those who have emphasised the constructed nature of ethnicity in

ethnic revival include Anderson 1983, McDonald 1989, Roosens 1989 and those who have argued that this was more a matter of a new way of representing pre-existing ethnic groupings include Edwards 1985, and most especially Smith, of which his 1986 book makes the argument most forcefully. See Eriksen 1993 for an overview and discussion.

13. This includes theories of uneven development, e.g. Hechter 1975, and of globalisation, e.g. King 1991. See also Melucci 1989. Evans 1991 is a useful discussion of the internal colonisation thesis.

14. See, for example, McNeill 1986; Hobsbawm 1990.

15. For discussions of Welsh nationalism see Davies 1989; Borland, Fevre and Denny 1992; Bowie 1993; Jenkins 1995; and for Breton, McDonald 1989.

16. In Wales in 1971 Welsh speakers constituted 20 per cent of the population. For analysis of the Welsh situation see Khlief 1980; Jones 1981; Bellin 1984; Davies 1989: ch.3; and for the Irish see Hindley 1990. For more general discussion of minority languages and ethnic identities see Stephens 1976; Haugen, McClure and Thomson 1981; Edwards 1985; Fishman 1989; Grillo 1989 (especially chs.3 and 5 which include comparative discussions of Welsh, Irish, and Scottish Gaelic); and Williams 1991 (especially Williams 1991a). Fishman 1991 is a discussion of different policies aimed at reversing language shift.

17. 40.1 per cent of respondents agreed with the statement and 42.4 per cent disagreed. 5 per cent of Lowlanders thought that Gaelic should be given official recognition in Scotland; 48.4 per cent that Gaelic should be encouraged throughout Scotland as a whole; and 23.6 per cent that they would welcome more opportunity to learn Gaelic themselves (MacKinnon 1981: 6–9). SNP supporters were considerably more in favour of Gaelic than individuals who supported other parties (ibid.: 17).

18. In addition to references in footnote 15 see also Heiberg 1989 for the comparative Basque case; and for various comparisons and overviews, Foster 1980; Mitchison 1980; Smith 1981; Rokkan and Urwin 1982; Tiryakian and Rogowski 1985, Connor 1994.

19. My information on these organisations is drawn partly from published sources (especially *Còr na Gàidhlig* 1982) and also from interviews and conversations with former members of the groups and Gaelic officials.

20. For anthropological discussion of the European Community see Wilson and Estellie Smith 1993 and McDonald 1996 which includes

anthropological discussion of language questions within the European institutions. Hunter 1991 and Parman 1993 discuss the implications of European integration for Scottish crofters; and McCrone 1991 and Harvie 1994 (ch.7) and 1994a discuss the implications for Scotland.

21. For overviews of the situation see Thomson 1976, 1979; MacAulay 1979; MacKinnon 1991: part 3. New Gaelic courses appearing included J.A. MacDonald 1968; R. MacKinnon 1971; I.A. MacDhomhnaill 1976; *Can Seo* 1978/9; Blacklaw 1978; Owen 1979, 1982.

22. The Census returns give a greater proportion of men than women speaking Gaelic in the Lowland areas (MacKinnon 1978: 7). Mac-Kinnon feels that these are not likely to be learners because 'We could . . . expect larger numbers of learners to profess reading and writing abilities than native speakers' (ibid.) – the figures show the reverse. However, we might note that many of the new Gaelic classes put their emphasis on *conversation*. Furthermore, literacy, particularly in Gaelic, may be viewed as a more sophisticated activity than speech, requiring a higher degree of competence to 'count'.

3

'The Crofting Community': Land, Religion and the Formation of the Highland People

I found it hard to remember that Big Donald had not actually lived through the Land Wars, that he had not taken to the hills to avoid the sheriff-officers when they came looking for the ring-leaders of the rent strikes, or any of those events described in the novels in which he was widely said to have been the model for the local crofting hero. Even now in his sixties he certainly looked the part: ruggedly handsome, tall and broad-shouldered, and with a full-head of only slightly greying hair. When I sat in his kitchen while he filled in forms for the Department of Agriculture and heard him grumbling about 'They'll be wanting to know how many mice we have in the byre next', I heard the voice of a man who surely would defy any forces threatening 'the people' and 'the community', a man scathing of 'the powers-that-be'. Big Donald had, however, been born in the 1920s and though he went up to the hill to get his sheep often enough, he was too young to have hidden out there and been a great Land Wars hero. Sometimes too, he would surprise me by talking not of the tragedy of the Clearances, when people were evicted from land to make way for sheep, nor of the defiance of the people against the lairds (land-lords), but of petty arguing between neighbours at the time. On one occasion, for example, he told me about how a president of the Land League in the area had tried to get extra land for himself; and on another, when I tried to draw him out about the period, he remarked gruffly: 'There's landlords and landlords. And there's crofters among the worst of them. They were all after their own, same as today'. No doubt he was keen to halt the questions from the eager anthropologist; but his remarks point too, to an alternative picture of social relations than that of a single people acting for the collective or community good. This is not to say that Big Donald did not believe that there had been popular defiance in the 1880s, nor that many landlords had acted badly. He was willing enough on some occasions to castigate particular landlords, to chortle that 'the people' had 'told the government where to go', and to tell of, say, the way that local women had made a mockery of the governmental show of force by linking arms with the marines that had been sent to the area in 1884 to try to put down the rebellion against rent rises. But the past offered, he implied, complexities too; and at the local level it could not necessarily be safely mined for a vision of how things ought to be now. There were different histories that could be told.

This chapter looks at some of the different accounts that are told of late eighteenth- and nineteenth-century Highland history – a history which has become the subject of a considerably expanded popular literature during the Gaelic renaissance. Eighteenth- and nineteenth-century Highland history is rich in images of dislocation and oppression (the Clearances), and of resilience and peoplehood (the Land Wars and evangelical revivals); and it is in this period that some of the most distinctive institutions of the contemporary Highlands – crofting and the Highland Presbyterian churches – were formed. It is also to this period, rather than some ancient Celtic or Viking past, that those living in the Highlands today usually refer when talking of 'our past'; it is to this that those eschewing the romanticised history of clans and tartans often turn; and it is a period which is the subject of a good deal of contention among historians. This history is, then, an important source of contemporary, sometimes conflicting, imaginings of the Scottish Highlands.

The aim of this chapter is twofold. First, to describe some of the alternative emphases of historical accounts of the eighteenth- and nineteenth-century Scottish Highlands; and the implications that such accounts have for the present. Second, related to the former, I explore the formation of the notion of 'the people' – and the 'bringing home' to the Highlands of expressive individualist ideas about culture – during this period and at some of the alternatives which events and memories also offer. I look particularly at the formation of crofting and Highland Presbyterianism, both of which – although sometimes assumed and often projected as much older – were largely shaped into the forms which we would recognise today in the nineteenth century; and both of which provide, as I discuss in the following part of this book, important contemporary idioms of collectivity, though also of social division.

While both crofting and Highland Presbyterianism can be regarded as part of what is distinctive, and even 'traditional', about the Scottish Highlands (albeit with parallels elsewhere) this should not be taken to imply that they are somehow totally indigenous creations. On the contrary, both can also be seen as formed at least partially in relation to, and by means of, modern developments: including, the philosophy and economics of 'improvement', capitalism, the spread of print and literacy, and roman-ticism. As in the previous chapter, I do not attempt here to provide a detailed or comprehensive historical account. Rather, my aim is to highlight certain themes and debates relevant to consideration of contemporary notions about identity.

This chapter begins by discussing some of the accounts of crofting history that have been published during the Gaelic renaissance, and in particular the substantiation of the idea of a 'Gaelic culture' and 'Highland way of life' that these involve; and some of the differences amongst historians over interpretations of the Clearances. Such accounts are made familiar to those living in the Highlands today through popularisation in the local and national media, and to some extent in schooling (see Chapter 8), and as such they are a very audible source for imagining culture and peoplehood today. The chapter goes on to look at accounts of the evan-gelical revivals and Land Wars in relation to notions of 'peoplehood' as well as social differences, focusing particularly on the relationship between the locality and the broader social and political world; and returns at the end of the chapter to consider the implications of these histories for contemporary social relations and local ambivalence over the past, such as that expressed by Big Donald.

Highland History and the Gaelic Renaissance

Since the 1960s there has been a growing literature on eighteenth- and nineteenth-century Scottish Highland history, and especially a proliferation of popular and social historical accounts. This proliferation of historical accounts which focus upon 'the common people' and minority groups is part of a wider development throughout Europe and many other parts of the world,[1] and is itself often closely associated, as it is in Scotland, with socialist and ethnonationalist politics. Themes which recur in such accounts, especially those directed more explicitly at contemporary pol-itical concerns, are the projection back of the notion of a 'people' and the materialisation of this through descriptions of the people's 'way of life'; oppression of 'the people' by those in power – a conflict which may also be mapped onto an ethnic divide (e.g. Scotland versus England); and the resilience or rebellion of 'the people'. This is not to say that these themes are not to be found in earlier accounts. On the contrary, in the case of the Scottish Highlands we find many of them in nineteenth-century books and articles about the Clearances, as I shall discuss below.[2] However, since the nineteenth century there has been no similar clustering of publications on crofting history until the post-1960 literature associated with the Gaelic renaissance and the allied upsurge of Scottish nationalism.

This 'people's history', as I shall call it,[3] although varied in its scholarship, has focused particularly upon the Highland Clearances, events mainly of the nineteenth century when landlords encouraged or forced many of those living on their estates to leave, generally in order to turn the land into sheep farms or sporting estates; and the Land Wars or Crofters' War, when 'the people' rebelled against their treatment in the 1880s and which led to new crofting legislation – the Crofting Acts of 1886. This effectively established crofting in the form in which we know it today. The Battle of Culloden (1746), at which the Jacobite Charles Edward Stuart's attempt to take the throne was quashed, has also been a focus as a key moment in the 'destruction of the Highland people and their way of life' (Prebble 1966: 9); a representation which casts the transformation of the Highlands in terms of a single causal moment; and which also implies that the same forces – namely 'the government' or even 'the English' – were responsible for the changing nature of Highland society as were responsible for the defeat of the Jacobites, a construction which simultaneously casts the Jacobites as synonymous with Highlanders, or even as synonymous with Scots.[4]

The popular interest in Culloden notwithstanding, the main emphasis of the people's histories has been on the effects on, and responses of, the common people; and they have often sought to avoid and dismiss romanticised images of the Highlands. John Prebble is the first and most famous of these authors to write in the post-1960 period, with his tremendously popular semi-fictionalised historical accounts which include *Culloden* (1961) and *The Highland Clearances* (1963),[5] all of which have remained continuously on sale in paperback. Like other writers of popular Highland history, Prebble is concerned to link history with the present and to point out the lessons of the past. For example, in the Foreword to *The Highland Clearances* he writes:

> This book . . . is the story of how the Highlanders were deserted and betrayed . . . It has been said that the Clearances are now far enough away from us to be decently forgotten. But the hills are still empty . . . The chiefs remain, in Edinburgh and London, but the people are gone.

Finally, we have not become so civilised in our behaviour, or more concerned with men than profit, that this story holds no lesson for us (1963: 8).

Other popular accounts which make a polemical case against the Clearances include Ian Grimble's *The Trial of Patrick Sellar* (1962) and Ian Fraser Grigor's *Mightier than a Lord* (1979). There is also James Hunter's important scholarly history of the clearances and Land Wars: *The Making of the Crofting Community* (1976); and his *Highlanders* (1992). The Clearances and crofting history have also been the subject of chapters in books on particular parts of the Highlands, such as Francis Thompson's *Harris and Lewis: Outer Hebrides* (1968), some of which, like Hunter and MacLean's *Skye: the Island* (1987), are intended as both attractive coffee table books and serious accounts of crofting history. The post-1960 period, and especially the centenary of the Crofting Act, has also seen a widespread republication of classic accounts of the Clearances from the nineteenth century such as Alexander MacKenzie's *History of the Highland Clearances* (republished in 1986 with an introduction by John Prebble), and the writings of John Murdoch (also republished in 1986, with an introduction by James Hunter).

The popularisation of history, and attempts to encourage local people to record their own histories, has also been a feature of the people's history movement and, in Scotland, of the Gaelic renaissance. In the Highlands, as elsewhere, it has seen the development of folk museums and local history societies; and Gaelic radio and television regularly discuss the Clearances and Land Wars – particularly during 1986, which was the centenary of the Crofting Acts. In addition to popular historical books there have been significant attempts to 'bring' history to local people in other media; and these have often sought to make linkages between the past and the present. John McGrath's play, *The Cheviot, the Stag and the Black, Black Oil* (1974), which toured the Highlands in 1973 and was later adapted for television, makes connections between eighteenth- and nineteenth-century clearances – the replacement of people on the land by cheviot sheep and deer – and the oil boom of the 1970s, to argue that Highlanders have continuously been subject to exploitation by those out to make a quick profit. In the play, which was performed as Scottish nationalism and the question of 'Scotland's oil' came strongly onto the political agenda, Highlanders are presented as *Scottish*, and there is an attempt to present not only a message of exploitation but of resistance to, and victory over, it. As McGrath writes in the preface to the play: 'I resolved that in the play, for every defeat, we would also celebrate a victory . . . At the end, the audience left knowing they must choose . . .

they must have confidence in their ability to unite and win' (1974: xxvii). Also shown on television in the 1980s was *The Blood is Strong* (written by Tom Steel), the first of a number of programmes to deal with the Clearances and crofting history. This too, if less directly than McGrath's play, was concerned with associations between oppression of the nineteenth century and the contemporary Highlands, a linkage made metaphorically in the title through the idea of blood and kinship. Another important representation of crofting history, which was also the source of much discussion within Highland localities, was an exhibition, *As an Fhearann: From the Land: Clearance, Conflict and Crofting*, created to mark the centenary of the 1886 Crofting Acts. This toured the Highlands during 1986 and 1987; and was also concerned to contrast 'the "traditional" [romanticised] picture of the Highlands and Islands of Scotland . . . with a rich range of alternative images of a harsher Highland history' (exhibition book cover). The introductory essay by Malcolm McLean in the book published alongside the exhibition makes clear that the exhibition was also seen as having contemporary significance:

> The Crofting Act legislation continues to shape the pattern of life in the Highlands to this day . . . but it did not restore the lost lands or resolve the Highland land question. That is an issue which continues to fester on quietly into the late twentieth century, erupting at irregular intervals into the public consciousness. Politically and economically the Highlands, and especially the Islands, are remote from the centres of power and continue to occupy a marginal and somewhat neglected position, similar to other peripheral regions and minority cultures worldwide. The crofting system which stemmed from the Act has provided the social fabric and hard-wrought material stability, for the Gael, but the gradual erosion of the Gaelic language and culture continues (1986: 6).

Questions of the contemporary state of 'Gaelic language and culture' are here tied in with questions of the nineteenth-century Land Wars.

James Hunter has been still more explicit about the lessons of Highland history and their relevance for the Highlands today. *The Making of the Crofting Community* (1976) ends with a 'Postscript: The Crofting Community Today' in which he argues that 'the crofting problem is still with us' (1976: 207) and makes a number of suggestions of ways of overcoming it. He has also been involved in putting this into practice, having been employed to assess prospects for crofting and a revitalised crofting union in Scotland, and then influential in the establishment of the Scottish Crofters Union in 1985 and its first director; and he has sought to make Highland history known to a wide audience within the Highlands today by giving talks and writing articles in the *Press and Journal, The West Highland Free Press* and *The Crofter* (the publication of the Crofters Union) – articles in which he frequently brings together discussions of politics from recent days with those from the nineteenth century. In his more recent book *The Claim of Crofting* (1991) Hunter discusses crofting history since the 1930s, including the establishment of the Scottish Crofters Union; and argues that crofting is both an effective and ecologically sound form of agriculture, and that it has not been as demanding on the public purse as is often claimed. His accounts of the 'insidious threats' to the crofting 'way of life', and of crofters' battles and campaigns to maintain crofting, constitute a historically-grounded moral argument for contemporary crofters in making them custodians of this continued tradition. Hunter is concerned to distance himself from 'propagandists' of both the nineteenth century and recent years who, he suggests, have not helped the Highland cause by their impassioned arguments against landlords. While his own account is thoroughly researched and scholarly, however, he too is concerned to draw on the past to articulate an argument about the future: to stake a contemporary claim.

Disputing History

The people's histories are not, however, without their critics; and indeed there is fierce debate among historians of the eighteenth- and nineteenth-century Highlands about the interpretations of events, and particularly the attribution of cause and responsibility. Historians such as Gray, Gaskell, Devine, and Richards,[6] who can broadly be classed as economic historians, have seen the events of the eighteenth and nineteenth century less in terms of exploitation and oppression, and more as a matter of broader, inescapable, agricultural and economic developments.[7]

There are many specific points of different emphasis between these two types of history, some of which will be discussed below. In general, however, the economic historians are criticised by those such as Hunter for tending to ignore questions of the people affected by the improvement policies (1976: 4). By basing their documentary research primarily on estate papers, and paying less attention to alternative sources such as poetry and pamphlets produced at the time, the argument is that they have been more sympathetic to Highland landlords than they might otherwise have been (1976: 4–5), and have perhaps substituted landlords' own modes of legitimising their actions for analysis and thus absolved landlords of blame.

For their part, the economic historians – of whom Richards has perhaps made the case most cogently (1982, 1985) – argue that Hunter, and to an even greater extent popular historians such as Prebble and Grimble (who he categorises as the 'passionate' school), romanticise the pre-Clearances period and therefore regard the events of the nineteenth century as a sinister and cynical betrayal and destruction of Highland culture, and that they exaggerate the extent of the brutality involved. The class-conflict model, which depicts 'the people' as exploited by the landlords, is, according to Richards, too crude to explain what was going on in the Highlands and the extent to which land-owners were themselves the victims of forces beyond their control. The people's historians, suggests Richards, may have been relying too much upon nineteenth-century radical newspaper accounts and pamphlets, and have substituted the frameworks employed there for *their* own analyses (Richards 1985: ch.5).

The contemporary significance of this dispute is not lost on the historians, though Richards is more reluctant to draw out contemporary messages than is Hunter. In an article in the *West Highland Free Press*, a weekly newspaper widely read throughout the Highlands and especially on Skye where it is produced, Hunter writes:

> The general point about all this is – why do so many historians feel impelled to make excuses for what happened in the Highlands in the nineteenth century? I think it is because it is difficult to look at these events as something that is of no consequence to the present day . . . But we are still living in the Highlands with issues that relate directly to that period – control of the land and the viability of communities. When people like Richards write about these things as if what the landowners did was perfectly justifiable, what they are saying is that what we have today is equally justified (1.11.1985).

Richards for his part disagrees that his form of analysis indicates that he is somehow 'against the people':

> Dr Hunter . . . [is not] on safe ground assuming that other writers are any less well disposed to the Highland poor than himself. The assumption of moral superiority in historical debate is not easily conceded (1985: 147).

Below, my aim is not to try to adjudicate between the different histories – which agree on many points of fact – but to show how particular constructions of events may inform contemporary social imaginings. My emphasis is particularly upon the people's histories for these have been most influential within Highland localities themselves and closely associated with the Gaelic renaissance. This is not to deny, however, that economic histories may also affect contemporary Highland life. Indeed, I suggest that they are part of a continuing rhetoric of 'improvement' which forms an alternative strand in imaginings of the Highlands. The people's histories – of recent years and the late nineteenth century – are, however, particularly important for the extent to which they articulate a notion of 'the people' through both a class-like model and through linkages with concepts such as 'way of life', 'tradition', 'community' and 'distinctive culture'. It is to this semantic constellation that I now turn.

'A Distinctive Crofting Culture'

One characteristic feature of the people's histories of the Highlands is that they describe a process of threat not simply to a particular pattern of agriculture or even a group of people, but to a distinctive and ancient 'way of life' (this is a phrase which resounds through many of these accounts)[8] or 'culture' ('the Gaelic culture'), 'tradition' or 'community'. As we have seen in the previous chapter, the claim to age and to cultural distinctiveness has become a predominant means through which group rights have been articulated, particularly since the 1960s, though drawing on earlier romantic-nationalist ideas and in particular the eighteenth-century idea of cultures as expressively individuated.

In his book *The Claim of Crofting*, James Hunter sets out the 'claim' in a number of statements, including the following: 'a claim that crofting is . . . intimately linked with the survival of Scotland's ancient and distinctive Gaelic culture' (1991: 22). In some ways this is an odd claim for, as Hunter's own work argues, crofting itself is not particularly 'ancient', and its origins lie not so much in a distinctive Gaelic culture as in capitalist enterprise. Crofting involves fairly small, individually held pieces of land; and was originally introduced in the eighteenth century to replace an earlier system of landholding known as runrig. In the runrig system a middleman, a 'tacksman', rented land from the laird and then sub-let the land to a group of three to eight joint tenants. They divided the infield land into strips which they worked individually and periodically reallocated; and they shared common grazing land.

For some people's historians, the runrig system has been seen as part of kinship-based (or 'tribal' as Prebble also puts it) communal way of life – a Highland 'community'. Many people's historians of both the twentieth and the nineteenth century argue that 'the land had been the communal possession of the clan, and that each person had possessed inherited rights which were not subject to the arbitrary power of the chief' (Richards 1982: 53–4); a view which, as Richards argues, makes the actions of landlords in reorganising land appear to be a betrayal of a tacit agreement and even a direct attack upon Highland morality. However, he maintains that although the joint tenants lived in a settlement together, the extent of their shared social life is unclear, the land was worked individually, and the settlements themselves were not nucleated (cf. Millman 1975: 96). Nor can it be said, argues Richards, *contra* some popular assumptions about the pre-Clearances period, that life in 'the old Highlands' was egalitarian at the level of 'the people'. On the contrary, he claims, 'Even below the level of the tacksmen the organisation was intensely stratified' (1982: 77; cf. Gray 1957: 49). Moreover, Richards and others (e.g. Condry (1980)), claim that Highland society was probably not nearly so kinship-based as is commonly assumed. Although the word 'clan' comes from the Gaelic word *clann*, meaning children, it seems that while lairdship was hereditary, tacksmen and tenants of farms were not necessarily related to the laird, though they might take his name (Condry 1980: 183). Nevertheless, tenantry may have been partly conceptualised in terms of kinship and patronage – rather than being simply an economic transaction; and the language of kinship may have been significant for the connotations of moral responsibility that would seem to be implied. Certainly, the long tradition of elegiac poetry dedicated to clan chiefs (from at least the fifteenth century but continued even into the nineteenth century),[9] the concept of *duthchas* – a notion of inheritance which may also mean native land,[10] sentimental poetry about Highland geography (particularly nineteenth century), and oral testimonies in the later nineteenth century, suggest a set of relationships which are not primarily economic, such as an expectation that lairds would surely take care of the common people if only they were properly aware of their plight (MacGilleain 1985; for an example from Carnmore: Napier Commission 2638).

Whatever was the case, however, runrig was replaced throughout the Highlands from the late 1700s, and on Skye 'By the year 1811 runrig had come to an end' (Nicolson 1930: 393). Its demise was part of a reorganisation of landholding that also saw what Richards refers to as the 'eradication' of tacksmen (1982: 65). This, he argues (and Hunter agrees), 'was associated with a larger flow of rent income to the landlord' (ibid.); and also the establishment or extension of farms ('tacks') held under single tenants without the subletting of former times. This was part of a move towards the consolidation and enclosure of land that was seen in other parts of Western Europe too, being regarded as a particularly profitable mode of agriculture according to the agronomics of the day (Richards 1982: ch.1). During the early years of the 1800s, as this reorganisation was underway, landlords in most areas were also reluctant to see the population on their land fall. In the feudal scheme of things, the population of an estate was regarded as a source of fighting manpower and prestige

(Richards 1982: 58). Moreover, in many parts of the Highlands labour-intensive agricultural schemes were introduced by landlords during the late 1700s as part of their attempts at agricultural 'improvement'. One of the most significant of these – though one which affected the area in which Carnan lies to only a small extent – was the production of kelp, alkaline substances produced from the burning of seaweed.

The establishment of crofts, then, was part of a reorganisation which aimed to maintain a large population while decreasing the amount of land available. Crofts were to provide their tenants with basic subsistence to supplement their wage income from working the kelp – a system which, Hunter has argued, enabled the lairds who controlled both wages and rents, to bind people inescapably into working for them in generally harsh conditions (1976: 18). Crofts were also, as a survey for the improvement of Lord MacDonald's estates (of which Carnan was part) in Skye put it, to be located in 'the least profitable parts of the estate [where they would] not interfere with, or mar, the laying out of better farms' (Blackadder 1799: 7–8). Far from being an ancient 'way of life', then, crofting was a mainly nineteenth-century introduction whose format was principally dictated by what those in charge of the reforms saw as the most economically viable solution.

Nevertheless, crofting has since come to be regarded as a valuable 'way of life' in itself and one bound together with the Gaelic language (even though not all crofting areas, e.g. Shetland, are Gaelic-speaking). This perception is one that developed during the nineteenth century, and involved a coming together of local ideas about land, socialist politics and analogies with events in Ireland, and the growing romanticisation of 'Gaelic culture'. This was a period in which the idea of Highlanders as a 'distinctive people' with a particular 'way of life' or 'culture' worth preserving was brought thoroughly home to those living in island and upland areas of Scotland. It was put into place finally by the 1886 Crofting Act. However, this articulation of Highlanders as 'a people' was by no means merely an imposition from outside. On the contrary, it also involved Highland dwellers in mobilising analogies (as with Ireland) and in themselves staking claims, particularly during events which came to be known as the Land Wars or Crofters' War.

The Clearances

During the nineteenth century the removal of people from land of which they had formerly been tenants became much more widespread, and increasingly lairds attempted not simply to move tenants to other parts of the estate but to 'clear' them from the estate altogether by inducing them to emigrate. The main reasons given for this are that lairds no longer had a military interest in maintaining large populations on their estate; that between 1810 and 1825 kelping became increasingly financially redundant;[11] that the populations on most estates had expanded markedly during the eighteenth century;[12] and that lairds saw the development of single-tenant tacks as sheep farms or the establishment of sporting estates as the most economically promising utilisation of the land. That this is a period which saw the common people in extreme destitution is agreed by historians; as is the view that lairds were engaged in what they believed to be an economically rational form of land reorganisation. However, while the economic historians generally regard lairds as acting in a reasonable, if perhaps unfortunate, manner by this course of action, the people's historians castigate the emphasis on economics itself, regarding it as a breaking of relationships which they believe should have been, and were previously, based in an ethic of patronage. John Prebble's *The Highland Clearances*, for example, has the word 'Betrayal!' in bold type on its back cover and the words: 'In the terrible aftermath of Culloden, the Highlanders suffered at the hands of their own clan chiefs . . .While their chiefs grew rich on meat and wool, the people died of cholera and starvation or, evicted from the glens to make way for sheep, were forced to emigrate to foreign lands' (1963). That the lairds were profiting from the people's hardship is made unequivocal.

The economic historians, however, emphasise the extent to which the transformation of the Highlands was part of a broader set of developments afflicting rural areas of a modernising Europe. Almost every part of Europe had seen a significant population increase since the middle of the eighteenth century, something attributed variously to vaccination against smallpox, new crops and increased transportation of foodstuffs. The population increase in the north and west Highlands of Scotland was particularly marked – between 1755 and 1801 it grew by 34 per cent, and between 1801 and 1840 by 53 per cent (Richards 1982: 98–99) – a consequence of the above, the potato being the crop producing fairly high returns from a poor soil. This population increase and the reliance on the potato were a main cause of destitution, according to the economic historians who also stress the extent to which material hardship and periodic famine were longstanding within the Highlands. They also argue that the land reforms were for the most part carried out without resort to violence. As Richards sums up: 'The episodes of brutality during the clearances were, in proportion to the dimensions of the events, relatively few, and, in any case, scarcely unprecedented. Nor, in the final analysis, is it at all clear that the levels of welfare – economic, social, even psychic – were lower after the clearances than before' (1982: 7).

For the people's historians, however, the clearances were the result of lairds' defection to a metropolitan way of life. The 'congestion' of the people on estates was a consequence of lairds' own earlier desires for a sizeable labour force and the expansion of farms. Most people's histories emphasise the opulent lifestyle, often lived away in Edinburgh and London, that many lairds had adopted; and episodes of undoubted cruelty, such as the evictions in Sutherland.

It is generally agreed that the land reforms were influenced by fashionable agronomic ideas of the day, and more generally by enlightenment philosophies of 'improvement'[13] – philosophies which often made landlords reluctant to give aid to the people during the time of destitution for fear of making them 'feckless' (cf. Withers 1988: ch.2). They may also, however, have been influenced by the growing romanticisation of the Highlands as an empty landscape. Murray Pittock suggests:

> Some of the Clearances were . . . idealistic rather than primarily economic. What could be more picturesque and appropriate for a primitive land with a primitive history than to 'conserve' its primitivism, by turning populated and cultivated land back into wilderness? . . . Scotland could once again be the deer-hunting paradise of would-be ancient hunters, eager to follow in the remote steps of Fingal/Fionn, or the more recent ones of the Prince Consort (1991: 108; cf. McGrath 1986: 39).

There was, of course, some variation between different areas, depending upon the policies which their landlords adopted and their suitability for particular reforms; and much of the variation in matters such as population size in the Highlands today is a result of the fate of particular areas in the nineteenth century. The estate of which Carnan is part, which I call 'Carnmore', had been held by the MacDonalds of Sleat since the fifteenth century (Nicolson 1930: 36). In the eighteenth and early nineteenth century they owned about half of the Island's acreage, as well as estates in the Outer Isles; and with mounting financial difficulties, instituted many reforms. Carnmore, which was unsuitable for substantial alkali manufacture but which was successful in grain production, had a population increase of a third between 1755 and 1790 (Nicolson 1930: 332). Five single tenant tacks on the estate were established in the early 1900s, initially for cattle farming, and later expanded for sheep, and those who had occupied this land were relocated to increasingly congested and marginal areas.[14] While some of these were allocated the newly established crofts, others cultivated part of the land of the tenant and contributed to the rent (cottars) or lived on the common grazing with no access to arable land (squatters).

The potato blight of the 1840s resulted in particularly severe destitution at a time when Lord MacDonald was in extreme financial difficulties, owing over £200,000, despite his new sheep farming ventures. In 1855 he sold the estate to a landlord from the Lowlands, Captain Fraser. The new landlord increased the size of farms still further and greatly increased the rents on crofts; and the emigration which had begun under MacDonald accelerated dramatically. Between 1840 and 1880 it was estimated that 1,500 people left the estate (Napier Commission, Appendix A: V). Overall, the island lost about 83,000 people during this period – an enormous number, especially considering that its current population stands at around 8,000. Fraser also built a shooting lodge as part of a programme to encourage 'Highland Sport' but apart from the boys employed as beaters during the beating season the 'new tourism' did not seem to have brought economic benefits to local people (Napier Commission: 2519).

It was under Fraser's lairdship that the inhabitants of the estate began to actively resist – primarily through rent-strikes and the occupation of land which had been taken over by farms – the way in which they were being treated. The lack of any sense of personal moral ties with the new landlord was one factor involved in the increase in resistance; and there seems to have been a tendency for inhabitants of the estate to look back to the time when MacDonald was laird – when there had been severe, if not perhaps quite such extreme, hardship – with nostalgia. For example, one crofter from the area reported that local people under Fraser: 'can only live now by practising the utmost economy. I remember in my township none of the families would need to go to borrow anything from another family. They were not in the necessity of borrowing anything when they were tenants of Lord Macdonald' (Napier Commission: 2795). Moreover, in the second half of the nineteenth century, disputes which had formerly been regarded as primarily specific to particular estates (itself a perception perhaps associated with the vertical models of social relations that clanship suggested) became increasingly articulated through a class-like model of 'the people' versus 'the lairds'. In other words, the horizontal oppositional model of social relations, as employed by people's historians in the nineteenth and twentieth centuries, became a model through which grievances were expressed. However, as I describe further below, it was by no means the only model in operation.

'Peoplehood'

The extent to which those living on Highland estates thought of themselves as a part of a broader 'people' during the Clearances period is difficult to assess, though for the most part it seems that prior to around the 1880s they probably did not. Certainly, one question that is often asked is why there was not more concerted resistance by 'the people' to the reforms which were causing them such hardship. In fact, there seems to have been more resistance than used to be assumed, but it was sporadic and localised, and not part of any wider coordinated movement (Hunter 1976; Richards 1982). In the 1880s, however, this was to change and 'crofters', as they were increasingly referred to, were to come to articulate themselves increasingly as 'a people'.

Also involved in this developing conception of peoplehood was the increase of literacy and evangelical protestantism, which in the Highlands were often bound together, as we saw in the previous chapter. The role of religion in the formation of what James Hunter calls 'the crofting community' is, however, deeply ambivalent, for while on the one hand the evangelical protestantism offered models of 'peoplehood' and was often critical of landlords, on the other it has been widely argued to be one reason why the Highlanders were not more resistant to the events of the Clearances (e.g. Richards 1982: 40; S.MacLean 1986). In popular accounts, evangelical religion tends to be ignored, or else portrayed as a reactionary force (e.g. MacColla 1945; I.C.Smith 1968). It is problematic too, in that while on the one hand a popular movement, it can also be seen as responsible for the demise of much of the musical tradition of the Highlands; and more generally, as Malcolm Chapman has put it, as 'a subversion of most of the imagery that has been used to express the nature of Gaelic society' (1978: 25). However, nineteenth-century evangelism was simultaneously a popular movement and moreover offered a model for self-expression which shared much – while not being identical – with that offered by the radical land politics of the Crofters' War. Moreover, when those living in Carnan today evoke historical images of 'community', they are as likely to refer to the evangelical revivals as to the Land Wars.

Evangelical Protestantism

Although the Highlands have often been associated, to some extent exaggeratedly, with Jacobitism, and the latter with Episcopalianism, most areas of the Highlands lacked access to religious instruction or any place of religious worship until the late eighteenth century and many for long after that. The Reformation of 1560, therefore, had little effect in the Highlands prior to the nineteenth century despite James VI's attempts to introduce the Established (national and Presbyterian) Church in the Highlands as a means of bringing the Highlanders into the fold of national control and mores (MacInnes 1951). From the late eighteenth century, however, the Highlands of Scotland,[15] in common with 'most parts of Europe' (McLeod 1981: 36), experienced a form of protestant evangelism which:

> reasserted the doctrines of the Reformation: the Bible as the unique word of God, the utter sinfulness of the natural man, the possibility of redemption through God's grace, justification by faith alone. [Evangelical movements] emphasised that becoming Christian required an experience of conversion, in which the sinner knew God's forgiveness and was born again (McLeod 1981: 37)

In the northern Highlands, where evangelising became widespread in the early nineteenth century (MacInnes 1951), the preachers were from a group within the Church of Scotland known at the time as Evangelicals. In the disruption of 1843, after years of disputes with those they pejoratively labelled 'the Moderates', the evangelicals broke away from the Church of Scotland to form the Free Church. Both churches officially follow the *Westminster Confession* of 1643 (see Sher 1986), a document drawn up consequent to the efforts of the Covenanters in order to provide a clear and comprehensive Calvinist interpretation of the Scriptures to act as a guide for church organisation and doctrine,[16] and which defines their form of organisation, which is designed to avoid undue hierarchy, as presbyterian — a system referred to by Lenin as the most democratic form of government in the world (Highet 1950: 5)! Evangelicals and moderates disagreed, however, over the interpretation of the *Westminster Confession*; with evangelicals increasingly impatient with moderates' interest in liberal enlightenment ideas and their failure, as evangelicals saw it, to properly follow the rules involved in 'calling' a minister to a parish. Under the moderates, the right of a congregation and/or the presbytery, to appoint a minister, or at least to have the right of veto on a minister selected by the patron — who was in the majority of cases the landlord — had been lost or at any rate not put into effect.[17] Moderates, according to evangelicals, were compromised by their deference to landlords.

The evangelicals who preached on Skye were not all ordained ministers: indeed, an important feature of the religious revivals that began in the nineteenth century was the extent to which lay preachers were involved. The first of these was a man known as Blind Donald Munro (*an Dall*

Munro), who was converted by an evangelical preacher who visited Skye in 1805 (MacCowan 1902: xiv–v), and who is remembered (as are other evangelicals) as a kind of spiritual folk hero on Skye even today. MacCowan (an evangelical historian) refers to him as 'the father of evangelical religion in the Isle of Skye' (1902: 1); and he epitomises important themes in Highland presbyterian evangelism. Although Donald Munro was already an SSPCK catechist, he is usually described as an uneducated layman; and sometimes even equated with a 'Holy Fool' – a popular character in evangelical and popular accounts who appears lacking in wits but who nevertheless is able to grasp important religious truths that elude more educated folk. Central to the message preached by the evangelicals was that salvation was open to all regardless of social and educational background. Donald Munro is also described as undergoing a dramatic religious conversion. As a moderate, he had not in fact received God's grace and was spiritually barren – so the evangelical account goes. The fact that he played a fiddle demonstrates this; and on 'seeing the light' he realises the sinfulness of his musical accomplishment and destroys his instrument. The denial of this-worldly gratification was a marked theme of the Calvinist revivals; and Donald Munro called upon the people of his locality to bring their musical instruments too to be burnt to show 'renunciation of worldly pleasures' (Nicolson 1930: 367).

The laymen such as Donald Munro who became spiritual leaders were known as *na Daoine*, 'the Men' – an idiom which at once implied their equality with one another and their difference from those who were not of their group. Some ministers, often of what Sorley MacLean refers to as 'the tacksman class' (1986: 14), also had significant roles in the revivals, however. On Skye, the Reverend Roderick MacLeod, known as *Maighstir Ruairidh* ('Mister Roderick'), was particularly influential. His ministerial title of '*Maighstir*' ('Mister' or 'Master'), and even more his nickname – 'the incongruously Episcopalian title' of 'The Bishop of Skye' (MacLeod 1985: 174), indicate that he was regarded as of socially higher status than the mass of the population. Through *Maighstir Ruairidh*, however, local events and national ones were linked, for in a nationally publicised case he refused to administer the Sacraments to any who he considered not to have received God's grace. This included a number of well-to-do families. Later he also lodged appeals complaining about the issue of patronage and the fact that congregations of communicants were not being allowed to exercise their right of veto (a right to which the Church of Scotland responded in 1840 by removing it).

At the Disruption, MacLeod and one other minister on Skye joined the Free Church and large congregations followed them (MacLeod 1985:

187). Landlords, including Lord MacDonald, generally refused the evangelicals permission to build places of worship; and so services were held outside, often, according to the evangelical historians, with thousands in attendance and hundreds fainting and falling into fits of religious ecstasy (ibid.; Hunter 1976: 101). This millenarian picture is one which some Carnan people readily recount today – telling of great crowds standing listening attentively to *Maighstir Ruairidh*'s sermons while hail stones beat down upon them; a 'memory' which has clearly been sustained at least in part by ministers who, as I have myself witnessed on a number of occasions, portray such visions in their sermons, so reminding local people of the religiosity of their forefathers.

One reason for the success of evangelical protestantism in recruiting converts from the common people, it has been suggested, is that it drew on earlier folk beliefs (McLeod 1981: 39; Hunter 1976: 101). Of equal or greater importance, however, was the fact that evangelical protestantism offered people with little formal learning or institutionalised power 'the chance of interpreting the Bible for themselves, unhindered by an educated clergy or by persons of higher status' (McLeod 1981: 37). 'The Word' (*Facal Dhé*) or 'the Truth' (*an Fhirinn*), as the Bible was also known, was theoretically available to all. This in itself was a kind of challenge to 'persons of higher status'. The message of opposition to established powers was made explicit by some of the preachers. A commentator of the time noted:

> Some of these reformers of religion, as they wish to be considered, intermix their spiritual instructions with reflections on the incapacity and negligence of the clergymen of the Established Church and on the conduct of landlords whom they compare to the taskmasters of Egypt (Stewart 1825: 130–1; quoted in Hunter 1976: 96).

Despite this, however, evangelical sermons have not in any case been accredited with inciting any form of direct action against lairds. More generally, the message of Calvinism was one of accepting this world as 'a vale of tears' (S.MacLean 1986); and indeed Jane Nadel, in her study of Ferryden near Montrose, has argued that religious dissension provided the common people with the means of 'transform[ing] their self-image without being forced into threatening confrontations that they could see no hope of winning' (1986: 51). The inequalities of this world were made irrelevant by the possibility of rewards in the next.

Moreover, while on the one hand evangelical presbyterianism offered a collective and egalitarian model of social relations – one in which 'the Truth' was not restricted to those with wealth or education – it simultaneously forged new social distinctions. Those who received God's grace, especially 'the Men' (women were not as likely to be converted in the early days), were fundamentally set apart from those who had not; something which was usually marked by a physical sign – on Skye they wore multi-coloured nightcaps (Hunter 1976: 101). Thousands may have flocked to hear the evangelical message and even joined the Free Church but the number who actually became communicants was very small, partly on account of the rigorous expectations of a non-worldly lifestyle to be adopted by the communicant, but also because anybody deigning to 'put himself forward' would be examined for his knowledge of 'the Truth', a procedure which, in this age of low literacy levels, necessarily excluded many people.

As popular agitation over land grew during the course of the nineteenth century, the Free Church played little part in articulating crofters' grievances. One reason for this, according to Smout, was that 'Dependence on voluntary sources of funds made it increasingly dependent on rich middle-class benefactors who alone could meet call after call to enable it to compete with its rival at home and abroad' (1986: 189). In the Land Wars, perhaps ironically, it was the Church of Scotland rather than the Free Church which often took a radical role (cf. Hunter 1976: 155).

Not only did the churches disrupt a sense of collective peoplehood through the horizontal divisions between Members (those who had been saved) and Adherents (those who had not); they also effected vertical splits within localities between the different churches. After the Land Wars there were further secessions: the Free Presbyterian Church, which regarded even the Free Church as 'a plain apostasy from Scripture truth and the Disruption testimony' (Burleigh 1960: 361), was founded in 1892; and a number of other churches, such as the United Free Church, came and went in the first three decades of the twentieth century. This left even relatively small localities, such as Carnan, with three different churches; something which has considerable importance for the nature of contemporary social relations as we see in Chapter 6. No doubt one reason for the secessions was the disavowal of ecclesiastical hierarchy within Calvinist doctrine. Ministers and others who might set themselves up as authorities were open to challenge, making 'the Truth' potentially highly contestable, even though it was defined as inherently incontestable and absolute.

Also involved in the splits and unions within particular localities – and the allegiances which individuals adopted – were issues of land-holding. The precise nature of this is difficult to determine from the historical records available, and churches did not formally play a role in the reallocation of land. Nevertheless, ministers and elders were sometimes represented in the Land Court which, after the Land Wars, was established to oversee issues of tenancy and land boundaries; and from accounts that local people give today it seems that some individuals changed their church allegiance partly in order to try to maximise the likelihood of a favourable outcome of Court decisions. For example, I was told how the tenant of one large farm, which was due to be subdivided in part into crofts, changed church three or four times during the 1920s as the Court was making its decision.

The place of the churches in the nineteenth-century formation of the idea of 'the crofting people' was, then, ambivalent. On the one hand, evangelical religion seemed itself to suggest egalitarian and anti-authoritarian models of peoplehood; a model in which evangelism could be seen as a means through which 'the crofting population stood up to their landlords' (Hunter 1976: 106). However, while it clearly did contain this oppositional potential, it simultaneously set up divisions within what Hunter calls 'the crofting community' – divisions between churches, and divisions among congregations. Moreover, its role in effecting any this-worldly opposition to landlords was, as we have seen, often tenuous. The ambivalent potential of religion in models of peoplehood and 'community' is, as we shall see in Chapter 6, one which is also characteristic of the churches in contemporary life within Highland localities. On the one hand, the northern Highlands today are characterised by a strict Calvinistic type of Presbyterianism that is often referred to as 'Highland Presbyterianism' or 'the Highland ethos'; and this provides a means through which the distinctiveness of the area can be articulated in opposition to the 'morally depraved' world beyond. At the same time, however, the churches also articulate differences within the locality through a discourse of moral differences and hypocrisy. And while the churches may be characterised through the notion of 'Highlandness' or even 'Gaelicness', their place in relation to 'traditional Gaelic culture' (as we have seen with regard to music) and the Gaelic language is also ambivalent.

The Crofters' War

The Crofters' War (or Land Wars) is generally defined as an event of the 1880s. However, as more detailed scholarship of Highland history has shown (Richards 1973, 1982, 1985), the kinds of acts which were later to be labelled as the Crofters' War – creating an impression that Highlanders had been wholly passive previously – had many earlier precedents. More-over, they also continued in many places after the war was supposedly won in 1886. In the 1880s, however, 'disturbances' (as they were often called) came to be perceived differently both within and outside the Highlands – a shift in perception in which the expansion of print media, and particularly the use of pamphlets by activists, played an important part.

Parallels drawn with Ireland, which had long been taken as a comparative case with the Scottish Highlands, were particularly influential in affecting perceptions of Highland events. In 1879 the Irish Land League had been established and had gathered an enormous following in rural Ireland, linking together anti-landlordism with Irish nationalism, particularly through its president and parliamentary spokesman, Charles Stewart Parnell. This had resulted in 1881 in the Irish Land Act which established rights to security of tenure and judicially determined rents (Hunter 1976: 132). Disturbances in the Scottish Highlands soon became characterised as an analogous Land War, something aggravated in part by the sometimes heavy-handed approach that the authorities, nervous of events taking too Irish a turn, took in the Highlands. The governmental decision to send marines – 250 of them – to Carnmore in 1884 (as Big Donald had recounted to me) was one such example. The Irish parallel was also mobilised locally. Information on the Irish case was widely available in newspapers, pamphlets produced by the Irish Land League, and contacts between fishermen from the two countries; and it was clearly taken as inspirational. As one crofter from Carnmore said in 1886, describing the actions of himself and others on the estate: 'We were hearing of good news from Ireland. We were much inclined to turn rebels ourselves in order to obtain the same benefits' (Napier Commission: 2804). In Carnmore the parallel with Ireland was particularly marked, for substantial rent increases – known as rack-renting – were experienced by both (though not by most other Highland estates). The idea of a rent-strike, which began in 1881 was derived directly from the Irish example. So too was the nickname of one of Carnmore's local activists who, sharing part of his name with the famous Irishman, was dubbed 'the Skye Parnell'.

Influential concern over the state of the Highlands also came from those, generally living in Lowland Scotland or England, with either a romantic interest in Gaelic culture or a motivation to understand the dispute in terms of socialist politics – or possibly both. A 'pro-crofter coalition', established in 1882 to put the crofters' case (in the absence at that time of any popular association or Highland equivalent of the Irish Land League), was just such a mixed bag of luminaries, many of whom had 'no organisational links with crofters themselves' (Hunter 1976: 137). Hunter lists them as follows:

John Stuart Blackie, professor of Greek and passionate Celticist; Dr. Roderick MacDonald, president of the Gaelic Society of London; John MacKay, a member of that society and a prominent Gael; Angus Sutherland, president of the Glasgow Sutherland Association; Alexander MacKenzie, a founder member of the Inverness Gaelic Society and editor of the influential *Celtic Magazine*; and G.B.Clark, a Scottish doctor residing in London where he had had a long career in radical and socialist politics. This increasingly effective pressure group had as its parliamentary spokesman, Dr Charles Cameron, a Glasgow Liberal M.P. and chairman of the Federation of Celtic Societies; Charles Fraser-MacIntosh, Liberal M.P. for Inverness and a leading Gaelic scholar and antiquarian; and Donald H. MacFarlane, Irish nationalist member for County Carlow but a Highlander by birth (ibid.: 136–7).

Even John Murdoch, a Gaelic-speaking socialist who felt that the pro-crofter coalition did not go far enough in that it did not advocate the abolition of lairdship entirely, infused his talk of 'class', 'alienation' and 'system of oppression' with a romantic-nationalist language of 'race, lore and language'. Murdoch was probably more responsible than any other single individual in the nineteenth century for formulating and attempting to activate a vision of 'the Highland people' (cf. Hunter 1986: 11); and in articulating his account and bringing it 'home' to Highlanders he drew on his experience in Ireland, and on both socialist and romantic-nationalist ideas. He travelled widely in the Highlands, giving talks to crofters; and founded in 1873 a highly influential newspaper, *The Highlander*. At times Murdoch's conceptualisation of 'the people' is primarily a socialist one which crosses the boundaries within Britain to imagine a working 'people' of Scotland, Ireland and England together oppressed by 'the landlord class'; and at others he refers to Highlanders as 'Scottish', and talks of 'the Scottish people', while noting that 'an important section of the people of Scotland . . . have shown their sympathies to be much more with the English in power than with their own countrymen north of the Forth' (1986: 100). Most often, however, Murdoch talks of Highlanders as a 'people' whose case stands on the ground of tradition as much as contemporary iniquity. 'The LAND QUESTION,' as he put it (e.g. 1986: 147), was in the Highlands not simply a matter of landlords exploiting the people, but it went against 'the old doctrine of the Land for the People [which] comes down to us from antiquity' (1986: 195). According to Murdoch, this doctrine was encoded in the Gaelic language and entailed a view of 'landlordism [as] . . . a violent encroachment upon the divine rights of the people' (quoted in Hunter 1976: 158). In formulating his arguments, Murdoch also often expressed himself in the language of romantic-nationalism. The following, for example, where he explains why *The Highlander* contains articles in Gaelic, has clear echoes of Herder: 'We go in for the preservation and cultivation of the language [ie. Gaelic] for the sake of the people whose mental treasury and repository of culture it is' (Murdoch 1986: 154). A main aim of the journal, he observed in its first issue, was to

> encourag[e] . . . them to assert their nationality and maintain their position in the country to which their numbers, their traditions and their character entitle them. It is a good and righteous thing for our people to cherish a measure of pride in the stock from which they have sprung . . . The particular type of humanity to which we belong is itself worthy of being preserved and developed. Instead of affecting to surrender the type of humanity which we have received, we are bound to hand it down with all the fullness of development of which it is capable. That is what intelligent men in other lands demand of us. They deprecate a tame uniformity, the result of one race giving in to another (1986: 146).

Such expressive individuation was for Murdoch a kind of moral calling in itself, and one which could not be achieved if Highlanders did not strive to maintain their 'own distinctive character' (ibid.).

Murdoch and the pro-crofter coalition articulated their arguments on behalf of Highland society, then, not simply in terms of the hardship and inequities which local people were being made to suffer, but in terms of 'Gaelic culture', 'tradition' and 'a Highland people'. An ancient, and supposedly superior, way of life was summoned up to legitimate the case for land law reform – reform which was sometimes conceptualised in terms of the 'restoration' of rights which it was assumed 'the people' had once had in clan society. Those living on Highland estates were expressively individuated as 'the Highland people', with a distinctive mindset, and a 'race' with their own 'lore and language' (Murdoch 1986: 146). This was the first real attempt to press for policies intended to 'preserve Gaelic culture'.

This pressure was acted upon officially in 1883 when the government established a commission to look into and report on 'the crofting problem'. The pro-crofter coalition assumed that the Commission, headed by Lord Napier, who was himself a Highland landlord with cleared land, would not be sympathetic to crofters; and they continued to press for reforms and established an organisation called the Highland Land Law Reform Association, which although founded in London, modelled itself partly on the Irish Land League and encouraged the formation of groups within the Highlands which would be affiliated to the main organisation. In fact, as was widely agreed at the time, the Commission did a thorough job of touring the Highlands and taking testimonies from thousands of crofters as well as ministers, farmers and others; and its recommendations, which were the basis for the 1886 Crofting Act, were in crofters' favour. The Act established the rights of crofters to security of tenure and compensation for improvements. The Crofters Commission, which was set up under the Act, fixed 'fair and reasonable rents' and average croft sizes and cancelled most arrears. In providing a basis for the continuation of crofting within the Highlands, the Crofting Act effectively enshrined in law the idea that the inhabitants of what it called 'the crofting counties' were culturally distinctive.

What the Act did not do, however, was to restore any land which had been lost in the expansion of farms. For this reason there were continued protests – especially the occupation of farm land – often organised under the auspices of the Highland Land League, an organisation which had evolved from the Highland Land Law Reform Association but with a much more popular base. In 1897 the Highland Congested Districts Board was set up to try to deal with the problem of land shortage by buying land in order to create and expand crofts. However, the Board had no compulsory powers of purchase and it was not until after 1911, when the Land Court and Board of Agriculture were given some such powers, that landholding changed significantly, with more land becoming available for crofting. This was still far from universal, however, and many areas – particularly estates which had been cleared in their entirety and so had no clamour for land from 'congested districts' – were not redistributed. So while some districts, such as Carnmore (which had been bought by the Board in 1904), were substantially reallocated and in the first decades of the twentieth century saw the amount of land available for crofting increased significantly, others remained as sheep farms or deer parks, practically or entirely devoid of agriculture or human inhabitation. Clearances, crofting legislation and the redistribution of land were, then, crucial in shaping the patterns of Highland landholding today, and the marked variations within the Highlands.

Local Complexities

The events of the nineteenth century could be said to have established a class-like model of 'the people' in opposition to 'the landlords' or, as local people today more ambiguously and expansively put it, 'the powers-that-be' (discussed further below). Certainly this was a model articulated in accounts of the time, as well as in more recent histories of the period.

It is also an idiom in which social relations today may be expressed by those living in Highland localities, as we will see further in Part II. However, as we have seen in the case of religion, the past – and its contemporary consequences – also offers alternatives to the notion of an egalitarian 'people' or 'community', as was made clear by Big Donald.

During the Crofters' War it was not the case that all crofters supported the protests. Carnmore was acknowledged as one of the more active centres of local protest, with Land League meetings held in several townships and a variety of actions taken – including rent-strikes, the driving of cattle onto farmland, and sometimes the 'deforcement' of sheriff officers and policemen by throwing mud, stones or tipping the contents of chamber pots onto them. However, even here the participation, even in rent-strikes, was not universal, though it is difficult to assess the numbers involved. This was clearly a source of dissension in the locality, as evidenced by police reports of incidences of damage to the property of those who paid their rents (Scottish Record Office: AD 56 5). The example that Big Donald had mentioned, of a former Land League president who had tried to get more land for himself, also illustrates some of the local complexities. According to police, court and newspaper reports of the time, in 1893 cattle were driven onto an area of land whose tenant, Archibald Macdonald, was a former president of the Skye Land League. Macdonald, as became clear at the trial, had recently acquired the tenancy to the island on the death of the previous tenant by drawing upon his kinship links with the factor. Other applications for the tenancy had not even been considered – a procedure quite out of keeping with the spirit and rules of the Crofting Commission. The apparent hypocrisy of Macdonald's position was remarked upon by the Sheriff during the trial: 'you are a wealthy man and they are poor. You took the land from the people. The whole thing shows that your acting professedly in their interests in the past was a sham' (*Scotsman* 26.10.1893). However, although the Sheriff clearly articulated the event in terms of a conflict between rich and poor and an exploitation of 'the people' by the wealthy Macdonald, the matter was still more complex, for those who had occupied the land, as was evident from the names involved and as was observed by the policeman in his original report, were a group of the wealthier crofters (SRO: AF 67 50). Far from being a class-like conflict between rich and poor, then, this was a dispute between relatively powerful individuals. That even the Sheriff was predisposed to configure events through a model of the poor people versus the wealthy, however, illustrates the salience of this form of representation at the time.

After the Crofters' War, as before it, those who were not lairds were not all of the same social level, despite the impression given by the oppositions used between 'the people'/'crofters' and 'landlords'. Even apart from the tacksmen who held farms, the families who owned the mill and the Inn, and schoolteachers, are remembered as having been 'a bit above other folks'. Mill owners, for example, were able to wield a good deal of local power through setting the prices for the grinding of meal – prices which, as disgruntled crofters reported to the Napier Commission, local people had to either accept or else buy their meal from dealers instead of make their own (NC: 2496–502). The machinations surrounding the school board seem likewise to have involved a good deal of petty tyranny (e.g. NC: 2625–43). In addition to these social distinctions, there were individuals with relatively large or small crofts, with good or poor land, with half crofts or with no land at all.

None of this is to say that invocations of 'the people' or the oppositional model are somehow false. On the contrary, they were and still are an important reality in the construction of both the past and the present in the Highlands. It is to say, however, that there are also other histories which can be invoked; and that the past is not necessarily so unequivocal a model for contemporary identity as those who urge 'the people' to recover and recall their history seem to assume. Although 'the past' and 'heritage' have become key features of the romantic-nationalist model of what it means to be 'a people' and to 'have an identity', oral history and the detailed histories of particular localities will not necessarily support all contemporary visions of identity. As I discuss further in Chapters 4 and 5, maintaining social relations today may entail a *forgetting* of the past – or at least of some pasts.

This chapter has explored the formation of notions of peoplehood and their alternatives in the nineteenth century. It has been concerned to show how certain imaginings of social relations were mobilised both at the time and in subsequent accounts. In particular it has sought to highlight the mapping of an oppositional 'people's history' and a new definition of Highlanders as 'crofters' onto emergent ideas about 'Gaelic culture' and the expressive individuation of national identities more broadly. While the past is today used particularly to substantiate – to add a historical depth and a sense of shared experience to – contemporary constructions of a 'crofting community', I have suggested that it is in this case a much more ambivalent source, containing other stories too. In the following part of this book I turn to constructions of identity – stories of who we are and who we are not – mobilised during the mid-1980s in one Highland locality. Here I show how accounts of the past – and categories sourced by past events – are mobilised or ignored in daily life.

Notes

1. For a broad discussion of this see Samuel 1994. For discussion in relation to Scottish heritage see McCrone, Morris and Kiely 1995.
2. E.g. MacKenzie 1883/1986; MacLeod 1856, 1892; Ross 1852, 1854.
3. This name is one which has been applied to a much broader context: see Samuel 1981. Although it has not been used explicitly in the case of Scottish Highland history the division between historians which I discuss here is one which they recognise themselves.
4. See Pittock 1991 for an extensive discussion of representations of Culloden and more generally of what he calls 'the Stuart myth'. There is a good deal of debate among historians about Culloden, largely over the extent of support for the Jacobite cause within Scotland and how close it came to success. For some recent discussion see McLynn 1996.
5. John Prebble has also published *Glencoe* (1963), *The Darien Disaster* (1968), *The Lion in the North* (1971), all of which share the common theme of the destruction and betrayal of Highland society.
6. For references see the bibliography.
7. Although I divide the historians broadly along lines which they themselves would recognise and which they at times mobilise, I should note that the picture is sometimes more complicated. James Hunter's scholarly study, for example, pays a good deal more attention in its detail to contextual matters than it does in its more programmatic statements. Likewise, Thomas Devine, whose emphasis is usually upon broad currents of history, has also argued that Highland landlords had unusually strong powers and that emigration in the nineteenth century was 'a consequence of estate strategy . . . [and] emigrations were the ultimate manifestations of the power of Highland landlordism' (1992: 100). See also Devine 1994.
8. As it does in discussions of crofting today: see Chapter 5, and other anthropologists of the Highlands such as Condry 1980 and Parman 1990.
9. For relevant examples and discussion see Thomson 1974; MacGilleain 1985; as a nineteenth-century example I am thinking of Màiri Mhòr

nan Oran, Mary MacPherson, who although a great heroine of the Land Wars also composed poetry in honour of Lord MacDonald.

10. See Withers 1988 for a discussion. The term refers to an idea of the hereditary right to land. It is probably related to the term *dualchas* which is used, among other things, to refer to 'heritage'. See Macdonald 1997 for a discussion of its connotations and contemporary use.

11. Prices for kelp began to fall from around 1810, a decrease accelerated after the import taxes on another form of alkali, Mediterranean barilla, fell after the Napoleonic wars. The industrial production of alkali from salt was perfected towards the beginning of the 1820s, and in 1825 salt tax was abolished, making kelp production redundant.

12. From the middle of the eighteenth century almost every part of Europe had seen a significant population increase, though that in the North and West Highlands of Scotland was particularly marked (Richards 1982: 13, 98). The latter increased in population by 34 per cent between 1755 and 1801, and 53 per cent between 1801 and 1840 (ibid.: 98–9).

13. See, for example, Campbell and Skinner 1982; Hont and Ignatieff 1983, Allan 1993.

14. My account here is based on papers lodged in the Scottish Record Office (SRO), including GD 221, Lord Macdonald's papers; HD Highland Destitution files, and papers at references AF and AD. NC refers to the Napier Commission report.

15. This was the case in many parts of the Highlands, though some, such as the Southern Highlands are today mostly Catholic, following a reintroduction of Catholicism after the Reformation by Jesuits (Smout 1969). There were also popular Catholic revivals in some rural areas: see Taylor 1985, 1992 for discussion of examples from rural Ireland; and Badone 1990 for a broader range of cases.

16. At the time, the *Westminster Confession* was intended 'to provide the basis for a complete British uniformity' (Smout 1969: 63) and it even looked likely that the Church of England might become Presbyterian (Burleigh 1960: part III, ch. IV; Smout 1969: 62–3), but in the end it was only adopted by the Scottish parliament and General Assembly. There was a great irony in this as Smout observes:

> Thus by a strange accident it was not at the Reformation or in Edinburgh but eighty years later at a conference in London where eight Scots participated among more than one hundred Englishmen that the worship, doctrine and model of government which was to guide the Church of Scotland over hundreds of years was formally drawn up. (ibid.)

The paradox is even greater for the Highlands, for although they were not asked to sign the Covenant, and felt the effects of the Reformation late, the *Westminster Confession* became the scriptural standpoint from which the Disruption, and the stricter Presbyterian churches associated particularly with the Highlands, followed.

17. The legal position here is rather complex; see Burleigh 1960: 338–48.

Part II
Identities

'Nationality is... not just a matter of institutions, or of "high" culture, but of all the elements that make up the texture of life' (Janet Adam Smith on the Scottish poet Robert Ferguson, 1970: 118)

In the Gaelic renaissance the Scottish Highlands are cast – not for the first time – as a repository of 'real' Scottish identity. Highlanders are regarded as having the right ingredients of 'a people': that is, a history, a culture, a community and a language. At the same time, however, 'real life' Highlanders are often thought to be somehow alienated from their true identity and out of touch with what ought to be their authentic way of life. Moreover, they may also find themselves assumed to be ill-educated rural rustics, bogged down in their own primitive culture.

In this part of the book I am concerned with ways in which people in one particular Highland locality defined what it was to be one of them. In my fieldwork I tried not to presuppose any particular identity categories (e.g. national) but to investigate what emerged during routine conversations and events. What kinds of classifications were invoked? How did those living in Carnan see themselves? In what forms were ideas of collectivity and division expressed? Whether there would be a strong sense of a singular homogeneous identity or not was a question to be investigated. So too was the issue of whether there would be importance attached to such matters as having a culture and a heritage, and to being a community. As we shall see, the picture is not straightforward.

One point which I am concerned to emphasise about this part of the book is that I am not trying to uncover *really real* Highland identity. I see identity not as an inherent fixed matter but as *produced* and fluid (albeit within limits). In this part of the book I try to give a sense of some of the identity alternatives which those in Carnan produce. Because my focus is on a relatively short period of time, mainly between 1984 and 1987, the description here is largely synchronic. This is not meant to imply, however, that the classifications and evaluations mobilised will always be as described here. On the contrary, I would assume that there will be flux. Nevertheless changes are likely to occur in relation to the repertoire of possibilities – itself changeable though more slowly than particular performances – and I try to give a sense of some of the shifts underway through description of generational differences.

4

'A Way of Life': Crofting, Tradition and People

One Summer, as a back-packing tourist in Skye – before I had embarked on 'fieldwork proper' – I got off the bus which had met the ferry, along with all the other tourists. It was late afternoon and still bright and clear. In one of the fields near the bus-stop a crofter was walking a cow back towards the road. In his navy-blue dungarees, sturdy boots and cap, and with his collie at his side, he looked thoroughly the part. We dug in our rucksacks for our cameras and, like a bedraggled paparazzi, angled them towards him. He glanced up, smacked the cow hard on the rump, and turned to walk back towards the shore.

This is a memory I find myself reflecting on later as I look out of my window in Skye and see Murdo Alasdair bringing home the cows with his dog Suzy. 'Suzy the Floozy' he would call her when she went sniffing at people and other dogs. Dogs almost always have English names – Laura, Suzy, Dan, Misty, Pat – a residue, people say, of the fact that the first shepherds in the Hebrides came from the mainland with the sheep in the nineteenth century. Murdo looks the perfect crofter and I would rather like to take his picture. But my memory holds me back.

Much of Murdo's croft, like so many of them, is overgrown, thick with rushes and marram grass. He keeps four cows and some fifty breeding ewes but often tells me that it is hardly worth the effort. Although it would not be profitable at all without the subsidies, it only takes a bad year with hay fetching a hundred pounds per ton to make it 'a dead loss' he says. He keeps at it himself – 'it's my way of life' – but would not encourage young people to go into it, for 'there's no future in it'. Other times, though, he is scathing of these young people who are 'too fond of their own home comforts' to ensure that the crofting 'way of life' continues. The disappearance of this way of life 'would make me sad, aye. It's not just about sheep, you know'. One Gaelic word for 'land', Murdo tells me, is *tuath*; 'and you know what else *tuath* means? It means people. *Tuath*

Carnan – that would be the people of Carnan. *Tuath* – land and people – they're tied together you see'.

Crofting is for many people synonymous with the Scottish Highlands. It represents not just a particular mode of agriculture but, in a set of ideas crystallised in the nineteenth century, a whole way of life. Often assumed to be a relic of the ancient past, crofting summons up a world of closeness to nature, self-sufficiency, unhurriedness, tradition and neighbourliness. Crofters are part of a 'crofting *community*'. As we have seen, however, crofting agriculture was introduced as part of a thoroughly capitalist venture, and as such driven by motives of profit, maximum exploitation of the land, and a kind of time-discipline; and in many respects it is not an especially communal means of working the land. Moreover, the notion of crofting as traditional – as a distinctive part of Highland culture – can prompt a vision of the Hebrides as either a superior haven, or as an old-fashioned backwater; and of contemporary crofting as either a continuation of a valued past or as evidence of its demise. A similar ambivalence is also evident in the interventions of organisations concerned with crofting, such as the Highlands and Islands Development Board (as it was called in the 1980s), whose aim is on the one hand to 'preserve' a Highland 'way of life' and on the other to 'develop' – and thus change – the area (Carter 1974; Condry 1980).

Carnan crofters are well aware of the romanticised and the derogatory visions of the crofting way of life as both Murdo and the crofter who turned his back on the tourists illustrate in different ways. Nevertheless, this means neither that they accept that imagery nor that they necessarily reject the ideas of crofting, place and people as important in their sense of themselves. As we have seen in the previous chapter, the development of crofting in the nineteenth century was part of the making explicit of ideas about a distinctive Highland culture in which people have a special connection to the land. Certainly, the etymology of *tuath*[1] which Murdo gives suggests that this idea is one which has resonance for him. At the same time, however, the neglected state of so much croft land and the fact that 'youngsters' seem increasingly to be turning their backs on it might suggest that crofting is of dwindling significance. So what does crofting mean to crofters? And how does this relate to romanticised ideas about the crofting way of life and having an identity?

Legislating the Crofting Community

Crofting very directly bears the imprint of history for much of the legislation which governs it even today arises directly out of the 1886 Crofting

Act. As we have seen in Chapter 2, this Act was concerned to provide rights for crofters but it has also had the effect of creating a particular type of 'crofting community' which, although bearing similarities, is in many respects unlike that which preceded it. This is a community defined centrally by kinship continuity of landholding over the generations, equal rights for all 'the people' (crofters), and activity in crofting agriculture. These definitions have a very direct impact on local people's lives, though they do not always do so in quite the ways or spirit intended by the Act.

As the Crofters Commission itself points out: 'It is not . . . easy to give a simple and concise definition of a croft' (1976: §20). Nevertheless the official definition of a croft operational in the 1980s is that it is a small-holding within the 'crofting counties' with an annual rent not exceeding £100 or an area of inbye land not greater than 30 hectares (Crofters Commission 1976: §§ 21–5; DAFS 1986: §§ 11.1–2). Most of Carnan's crofts are owned by the Department of Agriculture and Fisheries (Scotland) (DAFS) and their occupants are tenants. Tenancies, however, are inherited, and since 1886 have passed down through families. It is very difficult for outsiders or incomers to acquire crofting tenancies in an area with a minority of incomers such as Carnan because the township has the right to object to applications for tenancy and the Crofters Commission, which deals with croft assignation, is supposed only to accept *bona fide* crofters. This means that even the most well-intentioned and enthusiastic incomers are unlikely to be successful in their applications because of an inability to demonstrate experience of crofting. In Carnan during the period of my fieldwork only one incomer family ran a croft and they did so as tenants of a man who had bought his own croft. In tangible ways, then, crofting is exclusive of incomers and outsiders, and creates a 'community' with the idea of stability through kinship and landholding.

Not only does this legislation control access to agricultural land, it also effectively controls access to housing for the majority of houses in Carnan are built on crofts. Indeed Carnan is in one of the areas with a particularly high proportion of the population, over a third, registered as crofters (as usually only one person per household would be registered as such the overall number of people in 'crofting households' would probably be about three times this number as the mean size of household in the area is just over three). The only housing exceptions are the council estate and a dozen or so properties on a feu (perpetual lease at a fixed rent). This means that not only is it difficult for incomers or outsiders to croft in Carnan, it is also difficult for them to live there at all, and they have had to rely upon sub-letting. Although legislation enacted in 1976 has given all crofters the right to buy their crofts from their landlords, something which potentially has considerable consequences for who comes to hold crofts (for purchasers are later able to sell to whoever they wish, something which tends to mean to the highest bidder),[2] in Carnan, as yet, most people remain tenants and the proportion of those who have come to the area with no kinship connections to it is fairly low: 16 per cent.[3] The reluctance to buy stems partly from the fact that many crofters tend to regard themselves as owners already (they often told of their fathers or grandfathers 'buying' a croft when what they meant was buying the tenancy to a croft); and from concern over losing rights to grants and subsidies, which might mean a very significant diminution in income.[4]

Working the Croft

Though often thought of as small-scale farmers, it is misleading to regard crofters as such. Crofting agriculture was not set up to provide crofters with the whole of their income and it is mostly oriented towards subsistence rather than market (Collier 1953). Moreover, they do not generally think of themselves as farmers; and crofting is not primarily classified as 'work' in the sense of a centrally economically-oriented activity (cf. Cohen 1987). To be a 'crofter' is not to have a particular job. As one said, and others echoed, 'Even if we do not work the croft exactly we're still crofters – crofters in spirit if you like'.

In Carnan very few households derive their income from crofting alone. The one which comes closest to it in the central three townships has two large crofts. They keep some twenty head of cattle, several hundred sheep and a number of goats and are the only ones to make silage as Winter feedstuff for their livestock. Like many other crofters they grow their own potatoes and various other vegetables such as swedes and cabbages; they cut their own peat; keep some chickens for eggs; and do some fishing for home consumption. In addition, they supplement their income by letting the house on one croft, by doing bed-and-breakfast in the Summer, and by managing a small light-house on a nearby island.

Non-croft work has always been important for crofters, both that available locally (from kelping in the eighteenth and nineteenth centuries to tourism today) and that available 'away' (from herring fishing to the oil-rigs). However, by all accounts the amount of work put into the croft has decreased over the last century and the emphasis has changed from cattle to sheep husbandry (Mewett 1977; Ennew 1980; Parman 1990) which involves less labour and less financial investment. Many households in Carnan keep some sheep – perhaps twenty or so – but do so they often say more for the subsidies available than for what they can make from selling wool or lambs. It is difficult to calculate the economic viability of crofting for individual households, for there are so many fluctuating factors such as the prices of feedstuff and livestock and the changing subsidies available, and as Parman notes crofters themselves may have a tendency to underestimate their gains (1990: 54). However, even if the profits are relatively small, given the high levels of unemployment labour is not a scarce resource and crofting also provides 'an occupational baseline, a continuity within a shifting employment pattern' (Ennew 1980: 57). It provides some additional income and is something to 'fall back on' if there is no other work available and can be fitted around other work with short-term migratory patterns (such as work on the rigs).

Crofting and Tradition

Crofting has more than an economic role, however. It is also of symbolic importance in articulating the present to the past (cf. Cohen 1987). This articulation, however, offers very different possibilities. On the one hand, it creates a sense of continuity between past and present – and on the other a sense of demise. As an activity consciously marked as 'traditional' – even though tractors pull the ploughs and the sheep-dip is factory-produced chemicals – it is also a locus of complex and often ambivalent reflexivity, in which local people may bring together images of the past, contrasts with the present, awareness of outsiders' valuations of the traditional, and awareness of some of the images involved in 'tradition invention'.

Crofting was sometimes described to me using an idiom of continuity through kinship: 'my father and his father before him worked the croft'. It can provide a tangible connection with the past, inscribed in the often mundane details of crofting life such as fetching the cattle home and scything the hay – something which might be verbalised in people's accounts of participating in, or watching, these activities in their youth. Crofting – done properly – was often talked about as a sign of independence, of a proper connection to the land, and of unwillingness to rely upon imports; in other words, in moral as much as practical terms. Nevertheless, the symbolic significance of crofting does not drive most people to actually work their land. This contrasts with the situation in Shetland where crofting is enthusiastically pursued to an extent which belies any economic advantage and which can even pose difficulties for individuals (Cohen 1987).

In Carnan, even those who do croft do not see themselves as simply continuing a tradition, for their own crofting is almost universally perceived by them as but a pale reflection of the past. Nostalgic contrasts of earlier times with the present were a continuing refrain:

It's not like it used to be . . . When we started out [1930s] you wouldn't have seen anybody buying in hay. The crofts were worked right down to the shore. They can't be bothered with the croft today.

Well, just look – it's all that thick grass – and sheep. There's few that keep cattle to speak of. And few that really work the croft to its full extent. It's becoming a thing of the past.

The thing is today that there's plenty of subsidies, and plenty that are happy to have them. But there's not so many happy to put the work in. I mean real work like they used to . . . In the past it was more, you know, thinking about your neighbour and not just yourself. More Christian [laughs]. Everybody would muck in, you know, at the peats, or if there was somebody getting on a bit who needed a helping hand . . . It's not like that today

These accounts of the state of the land are far more than that, of course. They also evoke a community superior to that of today – a world in which people could 'be bothered', where people would help their neighbours and work together. Crofters of the past are described as *cruaidh* or 'hardy' – an adjective which seems to bring together the notions of being tough in withstanding the elements (I was often described as *cruaidh* if I had walked somewhere in bad weather) and adversity generally, and in working hard. By contrast, people today are described as having been made 'soft' (*bog*) by relying upon modern conveniences. There is more than a hint at a kind of moral equation here; that it is because people have become less willing to put the work in – because they have become reliant upon imports rather than their own hard work – that the local community has declined. This is an equation which may draw in part upon Puritan ideas (see Chapter 6) and a more widespread 'Protestant ethic', though it is also an equation suggested by the discursive linking of land, community and work. The decline in the tending of the land, then, is cast as a metaphorical decline in community relations and vibrancy, and in personal toughness and resilience. Such ideas were particularly clear in discussions of communal activities such as summer transhumance, peat cutting, and waulking tweeds.

Summer transhumance to the 'shielings' (*àirighean*) with the cattle – a practice which stopped in the late 1800s in Carnan – is especially romanticised. So potent is its imagery that one woman talked to me of it almost as though she had been there:

And it would be the young ones going up [to the shielings] you know . . . and, oh well, such a good time was had by all. It was like a holiday, you see. Everyone was mucking in and having a good time

In a Gaelic television programme on shielings an old man from Lewis, where shielings continued into the 1940s in some parts, said that it was strange but the weather always seemed to have been warm and sunny in those days. This is in part a vision of past youth, but it also is an impression fostered in Gaelic song and poetry (see, for example, in Fergusson, MacDhomhnuill and Gillespies London 1978). Although this transhumance no longer continues, a new Gaelic renaissance project to bring teenagers to Carnan during the Summer holidays to experience local crofting life has been given the same name: *airigh shamhraidh* (summer shielings). This naming draws on the connotations of youth, Gaelic and a vibrant community which are so readily evoked by the shielings.

This romanticised view of the past conjures up a world of stability and integrity and people may certainly find pleasure in summoning up such imagery. However, by contrast with this, contemporary life is seen as disjointed, declining and individualistic. As much a projection of an idealised crofting identity, this vision of traditional life is also a counter to the present, and a moral repertoire by which the conduct of individuals may be judged. To be 'not a good crofter' is according to this perspective not just an agricultural failure.

However, this is not the only way in which the decline of crofting is spoken of in Carnan. In explaining the decline to me many said that it was due to the need for wages, money, with which to buy material goods such as cars, freezers and washing machines and while on the one hand this reliance on money and conveniences was sometimes disparaged, it was also seen as inevitable, and the goods themselves were generally seen as desirable. As in other parts of the United Kingdom, goods and services such as electricity, the telephone and the car have become regarded as necessities which few people would contemplate giving up. On the one hand this was expressed through a kind of robust pragmatism that should also be seen as part of the local repertoire: for example, 'You've got to make a living', 'You need a car to get from A to B these days'. It was also, however, part of a more negative evaluation of the traditional: as one woman put it – 'We do not want to be left in the byre'.

Traditional communal activities which continue today, such as peat cutting, are marked by the same ambivalences in their evaluation that we see with crofting agriculture generally. On the one hand, they are valued for continuing a former striving to work the land and make the most of local natural resources. Yet, as I helped at the peat cutting, I was also constantly told that, enjoyable a time as we were having, it would have been more fun in the past with people working not so much as families but more communally, and with 'everybody' participating. And, of course, today it sometimes rains. Moreover, while most people said that they liked the smell of peat and would choose it over coal 'any day', there were also those like Peggy Morag who said 'If it wasn't that it's free I'd surely not be out here breaking my back lifting peats'.

Perhaps it is in part a consequence of the idealised view of the communal crofting past – a view constantly reinforced in the media – that the present is perceived as decadent. Against the backdrop of such a past, the present population is cast as in indubitable decline. Given this, what is surprising in a place like Carnan is not so much the negative comments about contemporary crofting and community as the fact that they can act as idioms of collective identity at all, and that that collective identity seems in many ways to be very actively maintained.

Performing Tradition

Carnan crofters are thoroughly aware that certain activities are regarded as 'Gaelic' and 'traditional' by outsiders, and as such highly valued. This was constantly marked in their discussion and performance of traditional activities in my presence. While we were cutting the peat, gathering in the hay or branding the sheep, for example, they often made remarks such as 'You'll not be getting this down in England', 'Well, you're getting some tradition now Sharon' and 'I hope you're taking notes on this!' They sometimes volunteered to have their photographs taken (something which in other contexts of daily life they seemed generally unwilling to do) and typically posed in the act of working. They also gave running commentaries on their activities, giving details of the Gaelic terms for the implements used and traditional ways of, say, stacking peats or binding stooks of hay.

Such is the semantic force of the association of former communal crofting activities with an idealised community, that there have even been attempts to revive activities which have no current practical use at all. An example of this was a group of women in a neighbouring area who in the early 1980s began a 'waulking group'. Waulking is a stage in the traditional production of tweeds when the length of cloth (the tweed), having been soaked in stale urine, was pounded and kneaded by women sitting at a table. As they worked, they sang, and these songs – which tend to have a particular form and often to be about subjects such as courting and love – are known as waulking songs. The 1980s waulking women had no tweeds to pound but gathered in order to sing the songs; though for being filmed for Frank Delaney's series *The Celts* they bought a tweed – but chose to soak it in soap suds rather than stale urine (such are the aesthetic limits to authenticity!). At one level, these women, in their performance for a series such as *The Celts*, might be regarded as fulfilling somebody else's vision of the traditional Hebrides. However, the 'tradition' also provided the women with a legitimate reason for getting together and singing (something which can sometimes be difficult in the Presbyterian Hebrides) – 'it was very much a social thing' one of them explained to me. It also gave them an externally validated status that they seemed proud to have achieved. Not only have they been televised, they have also come to be regarded as experts in waulking, and have since found themselves consulted on the proper way to waulk tweeds and recorded by the School of Scottish Studies. In a sense they have reappropriated custodianship of traditional Highland knowledge and have found a legitimate source of pride (one which, importantly, is not equated with personal advancement or 'pushiness'). They have done so, however, through a circuitous route which has involved outsiders (many of the songs had been collected by the daughter of a Lowland incomer teacher for participation in the 'collection' competition at the National Mòd), and the knowledge itself has been transformed from the practical, semantically inconspicuous, knowledge of everyday life to a more self-conscious and specialised type. What had previously been custom has been turned into tradition; and this tradition has been reappropriated.

The congruence of local actors' and outsiders' interests that we see in the waulking example, is not, however, a feature of all such 'performances'. Indeed, a marked discongruence can arise where either local people refuse to perform as expected or where they perform a domain of life which does not fully fit outsiders' visions. Examples of the former, like that described at the beginning of this chapter, are widespread. To turn your back upon the tourists is a relatively 'muted' strategy – at any rate it was silent and possible to appropriate into an alternative, less confrontational mode ('Perhaps it's time for his tea break' suggested one of the puzzled onlookers) – but it was, nevertheless, a refusal to be part of the 'tourist gaze' (Urry 1990). After every Summer there are a few letters in the local press from aggrieved visitors to the Highlands to complain about the brusque treatment that they sometimes received from one or two residents – perhaps waitresses or petrol-pump attendants; treatment which they clearly feel is not in keeping with the Highland hospitality which they had expected to find.

One particular arena of cultural disjuncture which can give rise to a discongruent touristic performance centres around attitudes towards animals. On one occasion I was invited, along with another woman and her two young children who were holidaying nearby, to witness the skinning of a dead lamb. This was part of a long-used practice in which the skin of a dead lamb is placed on an orphaned lamb to encourage the mother of the dead lamb to accept it. We all stood in the dingy byre, solemnly watching 'Camby' wield his knife, and listened to his cheerful explanations of ewes' behaviour, the difficulty of skinning if the knife was not sharp enough, and his jokes to one of the children that he'd be the next one 'for the chop' if he wasn't careful. It was hard to know how to react. At one level I felt privileged to be witnessing an 'authentic' part of crofting life – blood and death themselves helping convey that sense of the really real. Yet I also felt disturbed by Camby's 'performance' of it: his banter on the one hand presenting the skinning of the lamb as a matter of fact, and on the other as a tourist show. As he continued, our squeamishness became more evident – a possibility released by one child's tearful response – something clearly of surprise to Camby. We all became rather subdued, Camby muttering 'well, now' and talking of other matters until the job was finished. This was a cultural performance which had fallen flat, for instead of evaluating on the terms which he had expected – as a glimpse into real crofting life – we had brought to bear our own sentimental ideas about lambs and distaste in witnessing butchery. The problem here seemed to be the event selected by Camby for 'staging' as an 'authentic', and thus touristically appropriate, spectacle. Despite the rhetoric of authenticity surrounding the tourist quest – and the idea of reality being 'backstage', 'behind the scenes' or wherever tourists may not be privileged to go – what counts as appropriate is, in fact, highly selective (cf. MacCannell 1989: 96; Gewertz and Errington 1991: chs2 and 3). It is only that which fits into the semantic field already mapped out.

In Carnan there is frequent talk of tourists and their expectations – the shocked look on the face of the tourist who finds that there is only one bus to the ferry per day and it has already left, or that there is no cinema on the island, or that there will be no shops open on Sunday, or that there are no ceilidhs this month. Stories are told of having laid on a haggis hunt for the gullible visitors, or persuaded them that local people believed there to be a monster in the loch, or other ways in which tourists might be persuaded to part with their money. There is also a large repertoire of 'stupid tourist' jokes which highlight derogatory tourist perceptions and turn the images on their heads. These jokes often figure a crofter working in his field. Tourists come by and begin to ask him questions which suppose him to be uneducated, untravelled or irrational. For example, 'Can you count? . . . How many of us are there here then?'; 'Have you ever left the village? . . . Did you find Portree a big city then?'; 'Do you think you can see great distances? . . . How far then?' The crofter speaks slowly as though dim of wits and with a poor grasp of English but then topples the images by revealing his or her wit, education, cosmopolitanism and rational sense: 'There are one hundred of us here . . .. Because I am one and you are two nothings'; 'Well I did not find Portree as big as I found Paris, Sydney or New York'; 'Look up there. I can see the moon, can't you?' In these jokes we are told that crofters are well aware of touristic images of them; and that it is possible to be a crofter *and* educated, to be local *and* cosmopolitan, to speak Gaelic *and* to be rational.

Contested Crofting Histories

Crofting also has more specific historical associations than the rather nebulous romantic ideas about traditionality. This is the Land Wars history discussed in Chapter 3. The idea of the Highland people, or crofters, as a 'class' formed during the Land Wars provides a source for contemporary representations of 'locals' as egalitarian, and at least one framework for their conceptualisation of bureaucracy and 'the powers-that-be' (cf. Parman 1990: 64–5). This is not to say, however, that Carnan crofters talk often, directly and fully of the Land Wars – indeed, I suggest that it is significant that they do not – but that they sometimes speak within a set of concepts that were spun out and woven together at this time. However, their acceptance of the class-like model of social relations that this semantic field implies is far from absolute, but is brought into play in particular contexts. As we have seen in Chapter 3, the Land Wars period offers up alternative historical imaginings of social relations – Highlanders as 'a people' or a more fragmentary picture. Which are invoked is related to the technologies of remembering and to the social politics of the detail.

Remembering Crofting History

Many of the stories that I was told about the Land Wars period were ones which had been published in popular, accessible sources (cf. Condry 1980: 143); and indeed many people told me that much of what they knew about the period had been derived from their own reading, and the accounts they told were often not about the local area (even when I had asked about local cases) but about other parts of the Highlands. This was not entirely the case, however. The fact that 'the Skye Parnell' had been from the area was widely mentioned, together with his descendants today. But I was surprised to find that some of the colourful events which had occurred locally about which I had read in the Scottish Record Office – including instances of local women emptying the contents of chamber pots over policemen – were known by very few people.

Part of the reason for the absence of such events in many contemporary local accounts is that they are not encoded in locally accessible texts and that patterns for transmitting knowledge orally have been disrupted. Some older men described ceilidhs (i.e. informal social gatherings – not necessarily involving any singing or musical performances) which they had attended in their youth where they would hear the older men talking of political events and reminiscing about the Crofters' War. This clearly could make an impression on the younger men, for as one told me of his elders: 'They had a heroic aura about them.' Big Donald, with whom I began Chapter 3, had learned much of the Land Wars from time that he spent at the Church of Scotland manse as a child, the Church of Scotland in Carnan generally having been much more pro-crofter than the Free Church. The house in which I lived for part of my fieldwork was another place in which some of these gatherings had taken place. It was the house to which newspapers and letters were delivered (until about the 1950s) and served as an obvious locus of information. Even at this time, however, only a minority of youngsters would have witnessed this talk of the past, and they were not *told* the history, rather they witnessed it simply because they were there. Today, although there are informal networks for the dissemination of news – people phone around, the postman stops for a chat, they bump into others in the local shop, or stop their cars to lean out and talk to each other in the street – it is relatively fragmented and sequential by comparison with the collective venues of the past. This means both that there is less opportunity for children to overhear political and historical discussion and that the nature of that discussion is likely to be more episodic. Given that there are no yet established frameworks to transmit unwritten information from one generation to another (though this is an aim of a recently established local history society) it is not surprising that the most impressive accounts of the past come through text and the media.

'Non-remembering' of the past may also have another dimension in some instances, however. Those older local people whose accounts were not so restricted to what was available in popular sources were much more likely to recount events which told of 'the people' collectively or otherwise avoided highlighting differences between families. For example, one octogenarian, Calum, would – when it suited him – tell me about how 'the people' had stood up to the landlords and would tell me stories about, for example, the coffin of a man evicted by Carnan's landlord in the 1870s having been washed out of its grave by a flood and thrown up into the landlord's living room;[5] or would recount the rhyme that had reputedly been said at the graveside of the detested factor of Lord MacDonald.[6] And he would sometimes intermix his accounts with examples from more recent history which often expressed ways in which 'the people' got the better of the landlord. One song, for example, called *Reithe air Tìr* ('The Grounded Ram')[7] conveyed very vividly and humorously popular opposition to the 'Department' (DAFS, which became the 'landlord' of the estate in 1904). The song describes a dead DAFS ram somehow being washed up on the shore at a local township. The people all go down to the shore to take bits of the ram − one to make *maragan* (a type of sausage) and another the head for soup (a Highland delicacy). Such is the resourcefulness of the people that even the hooves get used for something. Then, when the Department official comes round − as he always does in such narratives − the locals have to make their excuses and hide their produce. I was told a number of other such songs and tales too by Calum and others about such matters as hiding the whisky from an illicit still when the taxmen came to investigate and setting up a pretence of proper schooling when the Inspector calls. All these celebrate local people outwitting the 'powers-that-be', making the best of their situation, and manipulating the images they project to those who interfere.

Calum's stories and songs were almost always couched under the general rubric of 'the people' and he never mentioned specific families, except his own. I noticed, however, that he rarely told me of the 'witty old men' if his wife, Peggy, was present, and on the few occasions on which he did begin to tell such stories she would interrupt the conversation and change the subject (generally to the weather). She would herself tell me stories about the past sometimes but these were mostly of a more personal nature: her school days, her father's farm, the Sabbath School they ran, her days 'away'. In her biography we can see reasons why she had reason to feel ill at ease with the stories of radical popular protest. Her father was known locally as the 'King' (*Rìgh*) of one of the townships and his farm was broken up by the Land Court and made into crofts. Because the individuals in accounts of the past are perceived to have a connection through kinship with those today, talking in individual terms about that past cannot be seen as innocent of contemporary connotations. The few older people who did affirm some of the more individualised accounts at the prompting of information I had already gained through my archival research made this clear by their statements that what they had told me should only be seen to concern a past that had gone and that retained no relevance today: 'But all that's long gone', 'That was yesterday and today's today' *'Bha sin an dè agus se an diugh an diugh'*. For example, when I asked about the example of the man who had been the Land League President who had tried to acquire land for himself – a man whose descendants occupy the croft which he held – I was told 'that was long back. It's of no relevance today'. Because these descendants and Peggy are well liked and respected, historical accounts which implicate their particular genealogies are avoided and 'forgotten'.

The experience of Calum and Peggy is no doubt more widespread within today's 'crofting community'. Older people in particular are aware that beneath the ideological construct of 'the people' lies a good deal of messy complexity. For the most part this is allowed to lie dormant through a rather general presentation of history in terms of class or occasionally ethnic (Scots versus English) conflict or, particularly among those in a position to know something more of the historical details, by simply avoiding speaking about this history altogether. However, this history, like ideas of belonging through kinship, can also be used – though rarely – as an expression of present difference within the community. On one occasion, for example, when a woman was telling me of what she regarded as a 'snobbish' attempt of another local woman to teach her children English (see Chapter 8), she added in a conspiratorial tone: 'Her family held one of the farms before the Land Courts saw to it'. Big Donald's grumpy references to differences among crofters, although it rarely touched on particular individuals (and he avoided making any reference to the name of the Land League President or those to whom he might have been related), seemed also to be bound up, though in a generalised way (I think), with irritation at the behaviour of some crofters today.

If different social relations produce different histories (Davis 1989), it is the playing down of intra-community fissions that produces a 'forgetting' of the details of the past. This itself has consequences. Younger people are unlikely to learn the historical alternatives to the egalitarian model of the people and this leaves the way open for a more politicised conception of crofting history among them. One of the ironies of the current movement to establish local history societies – something intended to strengthen contemporary communities through providing them with a sense of their identity and roots – is that some of the details of local pasts are divisive. Perhaps this is part of the reason why many of the older people in Carnan would not participate in it. As one said: 'It's something for the incomers really'; and another: 'I don't think that we need all that today. There's things that's best forgotten'.

Crofting, People and Class

The set of ideas about the 'crofting community' born in the rhetoric of the Land Wars also fosters symbolic oppositions between crofters and 'away', and within Carnan between locals and incomers. In this history, rights to the land become something which was fought for (whether individual families did so or not), and the language of the fight is that of class opposition. In Carnan, the position of landlord is now occupied by the state (DAFS), personified by the secretary of state for Scotland, and this shapes the relationship with the state, and with various state organisations such as the HIDB. Such organisations tend to be regarded as outside forces – as centres of power deriving from 'away' and its codes – and they often find it difficult to avoid paternalistic roles (see Chapter 7). The confrontational class-like model – crofters versus the landlords/government/the secretary of state/the Highland board – is frequently found in the local media, and as we have noted it often draws explicitly on the rhetoric of the Crofters' War.

Because the idea of 'crofters' refers to local people in general – 'We are all crofters to some extent' writes Kay MacLean (n.d.), a young woman from Carnan – it provides an apt idiom for the expression of attachment to the land and for the presentation of islanders as a 'class'. The idea of the land, crucial in this constellation of ideas, establishes the sense of connection over time; it anchors people to place. This connection is not, however, typically made in detailed specific forms – i.e. not through genealogies associating particular families with particular crofts or townships. Rather, it is done through more general claims – e.g. 'We're all from this place and our fathers before us' – and through the idea of being crofters. This is not to say that local people are unable to recount past holders of croft tenancies – they can often do this very well as I found when I took old valuation rolls round to people's houses to discuss these with them. However, it is not through family or kin holding of specific pieces of land that belonging and land rights are expressed. Carnan, like many other parts of the Hebrides, has seen significant mobility within the area over time and most families cannot lay claim to more than two or three generations having held the same croft, though in most cases they can claim to be from the same area of Skye over several generations. The general claim, then, as well as providing a collective idiom, also has better reach into the historical terrain.

By presenting themselves through a single 'occupational' idiom, crofters convey the notion of egalitarianism. This is most strongly expressed in the idea that the Highlands are classless: 'We don't have class and that here', 'We don't bother about class'. To make social distinctions on class lines is perceived as characteristic of 'away' and particularly of English life. However, although rejecting the terminology, they do seem to see themselves as something akin to a class in opposition to 'class-society' away. Through their claim to 'classlessness' crofters articulate their difference and opposition to others, especially to those in political and economic power. Through the semantic blurring of 'crofters' and 'people', and of a specific type of landholding and a more general 'way of life', 'crofting' has both a concrete reference in everyday life and a much broader semantic reach.

In everyday life crofting acts as a particular source of difference, and sometimes resentment, between locals and incomers. That croft tenancies in Carnan are almost completely exclusive of incomers, though not of individuals who have lived 'away', is in part a consequence of local crofters' working of crofting legislation. When a croft falls vacant it is up to the township committee to make representations to the Crofters Commission on the suitability of applicants, and it is generally said that the township will get its way (and all cases which I know of in Carnan suggest as much). Even incomers who are well liked locally will be excluded in this way. Indeed, I was often surprised in conversations with crofters who were friendly with incomers that they would sometimes express anger at the idea of *coigrich* ('strangers') or 'white settlers' coming into the area. These were people who might even at other times encourage me to stay. The issue which sparked the anger was often housing. Incomers are said to have pushed up the price of housing, thus preventing local young people from staying in the area. There is a resentment against the idea of being 'taken over' and a constant perception that this is happening (cf. Ardener 1989: 218). The land is seen to 'belong' to the 'descendants of Carnan folk', to the descendants of those who lived through the Land Wars. The fact that most crofters are not legally owners of their land or that many crofts lie unworked makes no difference to this sentiment.

Crofting acts as a source of difference between locals and incomers in other ways too. Incomers, beginning with romanticised views of crofting, often turn swiftly to more jaundiced perceptions, complaining about such matters as the untended state of much croft land, the 'rubbish' which accumulates on crofts and local people's attitudes towards livestock. Locals, likewise, share stories about the incomer couple who try to grow tomatoes or who create a beautifully artistic peat stack but leave no gaps for the water to drain away. These classifications are in many ways more flexible than the allocation of crofts, for as incomers become more conversant in Highland ways they too can begin to tell stories of the naivety of the newly arrived and may even begin to contemplate using the old dormobile as a shed. This is a gradual business, however, and some areas of difference are more resilient than others

The treatment of livestock, or of animals generally, involves a particularly sharp mismatch of perceptions. Incomers almost always feel that local people do not treat animals well, and some that they are actually cruel: stories were told of locals not feeding their sheep, dogs and cats, and of not using the vet when they should. Local people are often aware of these views and they may respond to them with the subtle humour which often serves as a means of commenting on outsiders' views. For example, one day when I was sitting in the kitchen of a croft house, Alex, a local crofter, came in and took one slice of *Mother's Pride*. As he left, he said to me, 'the dog's dinner', winked and grinned.

Very few local people have pet dogs though most have working dogs, usually collies. The dogs generally live outside the house, in the byre, shed or unused car, though sometimes they are allowed into the kitchen. The generous treatment which incomers lavish on their pets is treated with amusement: 'It's like a baby', 'I wouldn't mind being that dog myself'. When one incomer's dog was bought a set of special doggie wellingtons this was the source of much comment. So too is the fact that incomers may ask after each others' dogs as though they are relatives. Locals, however, have started asking after incomers' dogs too in the absence of human relatives to inquire about. Although these matters may seem trivial, they are part of the lived experience of difference between incomers and local people and they indicate different responses to the crofting way of life. For incomers, the 'hard' attitude towards animals jars with their preconceptions of crofting as a harmonious relationship with nature, while for locals incomers' sentimental attitudes are a peculiar luxury of those who do not have to make their living from animals.

Egalitarianism and Natural Ability

The rhetoric of an egalitarian community of crofters is, then, defined partly through contrast with 'away' and with incomers.[8] However, while in contrast with 'away'[9] crofters claim themselves to be 'classless', they do identify differences of social status and power, often related to material differences, within the locality. For example, I was told of one family whose members were said to 'run things round here' during the Land Wars and through to the 1930s, and to consider themselves 'a step above other folk'. This was explained by a list of their different qualifications and positions of social influence – they ran the post office and the threshing mill, one was a doctor, another a teacher, and others had posts in the civil service away. The list was concluded with the statement: 'So you can see that money-wise they were much better off than their neighbours'. At stake, however, was clearly more than a matter of money. Money was a kind of translation for me of their local social distinction and local power. Likewise social differences today are often expressed in indirect ways, such as through the use of titles. Doctors and schoolteachers, for example, were nearly always referred to in this way, e.g. Mr MacLeod, rather than the more usually used first names, patronymics or nicknames.

Scholarship and professional status were usually spoken of very highly, however, and individuals and families were often described to me in terms such as 'He's a very good scholar', 'They're all good scholars'.[10] (By contrast, to describe somebody as having 'plenty of education' was not necessarily so favourable.) Mostly, this was expanded upon through accounts of the qualifications of the individual concerned or those of their relatives, though in some cases it would be said that although a good scholar a person had not 'taken it up' – i.e. translated their natural skills into formally recognised qualifications. As the following obituary suggests, scholarship is seen to be evidence of 'natural ability', though natural ability does not necessarily evidence itself in professional qualifications:

> Among many families in [Carnan] and Skye who valued education and were
> determined to pursue it at considerable sacrifice, the M..s were pre-eminent.
> B..'s brother and two uncles became doctors, and numerous relatives achieved
> distinction in other professions . . . B.. himself had a very keen natural ability,
> though he didn't pursue a scholastic career. (*West Highland Free Press*)

The idea is not that professional status should be admired in itself, but for the 'natural ability' which it reflects: a good scholar is naturally able. There is here an idea of natural ability running in families, for the formal achievements of relatives can be given as evidence of someone's unformalised ability. These natural differences between people contravene any simple idea that all are equal. Because they often lead to professional and material differences too, the latter are by implication given a natural basis.

Of course, there are those – especially from 'away' – whose professional status and qualifications are suspected to have been achieved without a proper basis in natural ability. This confusion which the education system, and 'pushing' children more generally, can have is commented upon through stories of individuals who have not had their potential fulfilled or who have been pushed into lives which did not suit them. The ideas here seem to be sourced too by Calvinist notions of a 'calling' – a life course laid down for each individual – which should be followed.

For example, I was told of two brothers, the eldest of whom was 'pushed by his mother' into the ministry, and the youngest of whom was left the croft. It was the eldest, however, who was interested in crofting and 'in the place' (i.e. the locality) rather than his brother. The outcome of this 'going against the grain' was that the elder brother finally 'took to drink' and was dismissed from the ministry; and the younger left for the mainland to use the croft only as a holiday home. Many similar accounts are told locally, some of them undoubtedly apocryphal.

Local renditions of the more generally Scottish 'Lad o' Pairts' figure also reflect upon the education dilemma. The Lad o' Pairts is a boy (typically), 'often the son of a crofter or a peasant who had the ability but not the means to benefit from education' (McCrone 1992: 95), who somehow manages to get an education for himself. The difficulty which a local boy has in attaining what would readily come his way if he had been born into a different social milieu is clearly articulated in these stories, so highlighting the perceived opportunity deficit of a place like the Highlands – and perhaps suggesting that its inhabitants must in general have more natural ability than their counterparts elsewhere to succeed as well as they do.

When I was told of individuals said to be 'good scholars' I was often given very specific details such as their class of degree, where it had been taken and the names of their professors. The detail is an extension into a more distant context of the detail which local people typically hold about one another; and it serves to 'empiricise' achievements won 'away'. Education is acknowledged as a passport to a life away from the Island, and success in the educational and professional sphere almost always means success achieved through the English language, and regulations and classifications which emanate from 'away'. Even 'natural ability', then, tends to be translated into recognisable forms through non-local registers; even while at the same time 'away' is appropriated into local idioms.

Crofting and Masculine Identity

Even though success by the codes of away is seen to reflect natural ability, there is often ambivalence surrounding it. This is especially the case for men, and is related to the central place of crofting in articulating masculine identity. For while crofting articulates with the idea of 'the people', it also articulates more specifically with men.

Take Robert. He had not followed his father to work on the croft. Instead, as his parents proudly told me, he had 'done well for himself', got himself a career as a solicitor and left home to work on the mainland. At weekends he would often return in his smart new Ford Escort, with his bag of washing, to visit his parents and enjoy what they laughingly described as 'home comforts'. One winter evening when Robert was home I went round, as I sometimes did, to have a 'blether' with his parents, Angus and Tina. Robert and Angus were sitting in the ample armchairs, pulled close to the fire, half watching a football match on television. After we had chatted for a while, Angus stretched himself and rose from the armchair, winked at me and said: 'It's all right for those that work behind desks but I've got cows and hens to feed'. This was obviously part of a well-rehearsed repartee, and Robert replied 'You should save yourself the trouble. What's the point of slaving away at the croft? Going out in all hours? It's a thing of the past, Dad. You should join the twentieth century'. To which Angus retorted: 'Well, what sort of job is it for a man sitting behind a desk all day? Look at the weight you're putting on'.

While Angus was proud of his son, he also expressed some regret that Robert had not decided to follow him onto the croft even to a limited extent. While there is great respect for scholars and the idea of 'doing well' in professional and financial terms, there is also a sense that working behind a desk is not a fully masculine occupation, and there can sometimes be a strong feeling among those who have chosen such a course that they are thereby alienated to some extent from the place and values of their birth. This is well illustrated by the character of Alasdair, caught between the world of the schoolmaster (to which his pious mother wishes him to aspire) and that of the men of the township fighting (in the 1880s) for their land, in Allan Campbell McLean's *Ribbon of Fire* (1962) – a novel popular in Carnan, and based in part upon local people. An ellipsis between crofting, people and men, sets up this tension, and presents following a career into a rejection of the ideals of egalitarianism and the crofting way of life.

Croft work, much of which is carried out individually, is gendered, though not strictly so. Women are more likely to carry out the tasks close to home – feeding the hens, collecting the eggs, tending the vegetable patch – and men the fetching of livestock from the moor, and the dipping and shearing of sheep. The main crofting unit beyond the croft itself is the township which is responsible for communal crofting activities: arranging fanks and the hire of a bull together.[11] Although not debarred to women, fanks are an important site for the affirmation of male crofting identity.

Physically, a fank is a set of folds for sheep which lies on common ground outside the township. It is also an event: the communal activities of sheep husbandry such as dipping, dosing, branding and shearing flocks. The sheep are owned individually, and some tasks such as shearing and branding are conducted individually at the fank, with some reciprocity and sharing among friends, though in the communal environment. Other tasks, such as dipping and dosing, are more fully communal. All of these tasks could be carried out individually on the croft (indeed, one man who finds the walk to the fank difficult does so), though the division of labour at the fank is probably advantageous, particularly for those with large numbers of sheep. As important as the pragmatics of the fank, however, is its social dimensions. Indeed, there are men who have no sheep of their own who attend nevertheless.

Unlike peat cutting, and planting and gathering potatoes, which are organised on a family basis, fanks are attended mostly by men. The only time in the year where women regularly take part in the fank is at the shearing when they may help pick over the fleeces and roll and bag them. A few women occasionally help shear, which is done by hand. During the colder winter months, however, women are rarely seen at fanks and the atmosphere is very much of male camaraderie. I attended many fanks – Summer and Winter – during my fieldwork.[12] Despite my gender, I generally had the sense that I was regarded rather like a child, and as such mostly invisible. This was probably encouraged by the fact that I was not fully fluent in the Gaelic that was generally spoken there or in the agricultural practices themselves; and perhaps by the naivety of some of my questions (e.g. 'What are *magairlean* (testicles)?'). Even if there are individuals present 'without the Gaelic', conversation mostly continues in it, with perhaps occasional instructions or the punch-lines of jokes being translated into English. That this male crofting world and male crofting identity in Carnan are so strongly Gaelic has prompted a few young men who did not learn Gaelic as children, but who strongly desired to participate in this crofting world, to learn it. The same pattern of identification is evident in those families where boys whose mothers do not speak Gaelic have learned fluent Gaelic from their fathers through participation in crofting activities.

Another aspect of the male world of the fank is the drinking that goes on there. When the men take a break they get out their flasks of tea and Tupperwares of sandwiches, and a half bottle of whisky is either passed or else little glasses are filled for each individual. I never heard any discussions of who should provide the bottle but the principle seemed to be that of a round in a bar (i.e. turn taking). Whisky is the only drink that is ever passed, and it is itself a drink associated with masculinity (Macdonald 1994). The sharing of drink at the fank is also a symbolic

Figure 4.1. At the fank: shearing (by Julie White)

affirmation of the ideal of egalitarianism and male solidarity. At the fank there is no sense of any individual being of higher standing than others: the comparatively wealthy oil worker works alongside the unemployed, the traffic warden alongside the lorry driver. There is a respect for those men who are particularly skilled at certain tasks such as shearing, but this does not confer any status other than respect for their 'natural ability' and 'handiness'.

Through crofting men gain access not only to one of the most significant male reference groups, but also to the political institution of the township, and to the ideal of egalitarianism and its connotations of 'the people' and radical history. This is something which is partly shaped through an opposition with women. One story which I heard at a fank illustrates this well. It concerned a woman, not from the local area, who had inherited a croft and decided that she wished to work it and keep sheep. She became, as was her right, part of the township and attended fanks. Soon, however, 'she was trying to get the upper hand' – trying to boss people about and lay down rules about how things should be done. She 'just couldn't keep her hand out'. Worst of all, she disapproved of the drinking that went on at the fank and tried to get it stopped. The story illustrated well what seems to be a more general theme in local social relations: the suggestion that egalitarianism and the ideals of the crofting community are especially threatened by women.

For men under the age of thirty at the time of my fieldwork there seemed to be something of a shift away from the close association between crofting and male identity. While some of these men do take a great interest in crofting and do participate in it, they seemed to be a minority. Of course, those who do not show an interest now might do so if they come to inherit a croft themselves – something which tends not to happen until a man is into his forties – although statements by many of these young men that they are not interested in crofting, that they 'can't be bothered' with it, suggest that this may not happen. These young men seem to derive their masculine identity not from crofting but from their peer group and its activities, especially the cars and motorbikes which they drive around in (at great speed), and from the football club. Certain jobs, such as those in the construction industry and on the rigs, also confer their own masculine identity. Gaelic is not so much part of these men's world as it is for their elders, though a substantial minority do prefer to speak it. The spatial and linguistic divisions in the local bar, however, suggest an age division between men over thirty who tend to speak Gaelic and those younger who use English.

The values of these younger men are not, however, simply those of 'away'. Indeed, in conversation these men often fiercely contrasted the locality with 'away', and said how much they desired to remain on the Island. In some ways their reasons are not so different from those of their elders, for they have their 'mates' and family there whereas in the city 'you can just be lost'. In the 1980s period of high unemployment, cities such as Glasgow had become much less financially promising. 'I'd rather be unemployed here than on the mainland', said one young man, 'Here you've got people around you . . . you could die in some of these places and nobody'd notice . . . there's not so much crime [here] and the air's cleaner'. Despite the strength of the idea of community evoked by such statements, the Gaelic language, crofting and other aspects of the 'traditional way of life' play little part in it. These men select some elements of the repertoire of possibilities available to them – but they do not take on board the full complement of characteristics which the media and others suggest are properly part of 'having an identity'. A television documentary made about young Highland men which represented them as delinquents who had abandoned their culture, language and crofting way of life, and which depicted drinking and playing pool together in the Hotel Bar as symptoms of a modern pathology, was the source of much annoyance among young men in Carnan. 'It's like they see us as good for nothing', said one, 'but it's not like that. We're not all sitting around in gloom feeling sorry for ourselves or trying to drink ourselves to death to get away from it all. These things always focus on the negative side. It's like, if it's not about some old *bodach* [old man] sailing out to sea on a wee boatie or singing Gaelic songs all day long there's some problem there'.

We should note too, however, that while these men express a lack of interest in *crofting* – in working the croft – they may nevertheless still identify with the broader definition of *being a crofter*. As one said when I asked whether he thought he would become a crofter: 'Well, I don't think I'll make my living by working the croft if that's what you mean . . . But, you know, I don't know what else I will think of myself as. So I'm a crofter *in a way*. Even now [laughs]'.

In this chapter I have suggested that 'being a crofter' is an important identity for many of those living in Carnan. This does not, however, mean that they necessarily feel that they must work the land, nor that crofting and other aspects of 'the traditional way of life' are regarded in the same way as they are by outsiders (for whom they tend to be part of an attractive 'alternative', 'non-materialistic', 'pre-modern' lifestyle). There is, however, a particular constellation of associations made between 'crofters', 'the people', land, being of the place, way of life, opposition to 'away' and the powers-that-be, and at least some renditions of masculine identity. This is part of a repertoire through which social classifications and evaluations can be made. On the one hand the category 'crofters' can also map onto broader, still more inclusive, categories, especially 'the people' and 'Highlanders'. On the other, however, it can be a source of differentiation within the locality, where some are conceptualised as more fully crofters than others. Divisions of localness, gender and age, in particular, but also of social standing and religious status may be articulated through the idiom of crofting. It is because of this conceptual intermeshing of social categories — and its very everyday and 'close-to-home' realisations — that crofting has considerably more semantic significance than might be implied by the often neglected state of croft land today.

The metaphors and everyday practices through which identities are articulated are not, however, fixed. Nor are they completely fluid and changeable. Rather, they are created in relation to the repertoire of possibilities available, a repertoire which itself changes as new variations are tried and fed back into the set of possibilities. The women who become experts in tradition and the young men who fiercely articulate a vision of the locality as a community while rejecting stereotypical romanticised visions of a crofting way of life, are appropriating ideas about Highland culture, and changing both those ideas and their own experience of their lives at the same time.

In the following chapter we see further how ideas of 'being of the place' are conceptualised and 'belonging' ascribed. We look here too at those who while clearly living *in* Carnan — and as such thoroughly part of our study here — may be classified, and classify themselves, as not fully part of the place.

Notes

1. According to MacBain's *Etymological Dictionary of the Gaelic Language* (1911) the words share a common Indo-European root.
2. In some areas of Skye and other parts of the Highlands crofters made a collective decision to buy their crofts in 1886. Because crofts have

then often been sold on the open market in these areas they generally have a much higher proportion of incomers than does an area such as Carnan. The character of areas and the proportion of incomers is also shaped by the landlord, many Highland estates being held by private landlords who can exercise a good deal of control on tenancies. See Hunter 1991 for relevant discussion.

3. Calculated on the basis of my data from the central three townships of the Carnan area.

4. In those cases where local people *have* bought their crofts, they told me that they had done so because of fears about such official interventions as compulsory purchase orders during road building schemes.

5. This is a story which was published in *The Highlander* in the 1870s. It sounds too apocryphal to be true but the grounds on which the landlord sued the paper were that it would injure the sale of the estate (Murdoch 1986: 157)!

6. This is a rhyme which some others knew too and was probably widely known in Skye earlier in the century. It is published in Hunter 1976: 122, though he does not specify that it was Lord MacDonald's factor.

7. The song was probably composed around 1910. Sadly, Calum refused adamantly to be recorded singing though he did sometimes recount the words to me slowly, though he would tend to run out of patience with this in his enthusiasm to make sure I understood the funny parts of the story in English.

8. Egalitarianism has been identified as a significant feature of Highland life by several writers (e.g. Caird and Moisley 1961); and is also commented on in various other British rural communities, e.g. Cohen 1982, 1987; Phillips 1986. However, as John Davis has observed in the Mediterranean, communities that present themselves as egalitarian to the outside world may well have often rather fixed and strict lines of division within (1977: ch.3), so it is important to recognise – as some observers fail to do – that a rhetoric of egalitarianism does not necessarily mean that a community operates in a fully egalitarian manner.

9. This concept is discussed in the following chapter. Very roughly it applies to the mainland, though as we shall see it is more a symbolic than a cartographical concept.

10. I can not resist noting here that a word that is very widely used in Carnan – *tapaidh* – which is usually translated as 'clever' but which is applied to cleverness with the hands and not just intellectual abilities, also forms part of the word that is usually translated as 'thank you' (*tapadh leat* – literally, cleverness be with you).

11. Townships vary greatly in size, Carnan's generally being fairly small (twenty-seven crofts is the largest). Small townships group together for the purpose of fanks. Increasingly today, crofters rely on artificial insemination with semen bought mail-order, rather than a communally hired bull.

12. These were mostly the fanks of one particular township. The patterns I describe may be widespread but are unlikely to be universally the case particularly in townships with small populations or large numbers of incomers.

5

'Being Part of
the Place':
On Belonging

W hy did we come? Well, Roy was made redundant and although he'd started doing all right driving a cab it wasn't what he really wanted. It was, well, you know, we'd had enough really. We lived in Oldham, you know? There's nothing wrong with Oldham, it's a nice place and we had a nice house – a palace compared with this! But like everywhere it had got more and more built up, noisier, break-ins and that. And Roy used to help on a farm when he was a lad and I think that deep down that was what he'd always wanted to do really. He'd go on about it you know. And then we started coming up here – I mean not just to this place but you know touring around Scotland – and we started to think maybe we could buy up somewhere and do it up and do a bit of farming. So we were looking for a croft. It would have suited us down to the ground that – a croft – you know, growing your own stuff and keeping a few chickens and that. But we didn't get anything we went after. It's right difficult you know because it's not just like buying any where. The Crofters Commission wants to know that you're going to be a proper crofter so they always go for the local. It's such a joke. I mean, look around – how many of the crofts round here are looked after proper? We'd have worked hard, we would, right hard. We'd have grown things, made a real go of it. And it wasn't as though we didn't have any experience, you know, what with Roy's farm work. Anyhow, to cut a long story short, we got a chance of this house – it's been feued off – and although there's no land, hardly enough even to let the dog out, we thought it was worth it. We thought if we could live here for a bit then we'd have more chance of a croft. I'm not so sure now though, you know. It's funny round here. People are that friendly. I couldn't ask for better neighbours. And everybody says 'Hello' and stops to have a chat. But then, just when you'd thought you were really, you know, accepted, something brings you up short. We went after a croft round here and we'd thought we were really in with a chance but it went to, well I shouldn't say, but I can't see

him working on it like we would have. Yes, a local. And I'm thinking to
myself, some of these that's being ever so friendly like must have given
us the thumbs down. They're clannish when it comes down to it. So, I
don't know. We'll see I suppose. It's all right at the moment with Roy
doing the school run but it's not what we really wanted. Do I regret it?
No, no, I don't think so. It's really beautiful up here and when I think
back to what life was like. And I think we'll get to be more part of the
place as time goes by. It's funny though, you know, you just think you're
really getting there when you put your foot in it. Like saying something
about somebody's uncle or third cousin. Or like this woman did and going
down to the cemetery at a funeral. Have you seen the funerals here? Well,
everybody turns out and there's a line of cars like nobody's business. I
mean it's a really nice thing, you know, people care, want to show their
respects. And this woman, you know, an incomer, she'd wanted to show
her respects too so she got herself rigged up in black, you know, and a hat
– you have to wear a hat – and went off to the church. It's right different
from in England the churches here, you know. And then, she'd gone off
down to the cemetery with everybody else – or so she thought. But then
somebody taps her on the arm and says 'There's no need to come down'.
You know, polite, but it was only then she saw that it was only men going
down – all the women had stayed behind. Yes, they just sit in the cars
waiting at the top or go off home. So you see, you think you're getting
the hang of it all and then you put your foot in it!

In this chapter I look at ideas about 'belonging' and 'being part of the
place'. What sort of barriers did those like Sheila feel were against them
in being 'accepted'? How was 'localness' defined? Who was 'us' and
who was 'them'? And what were some of the effects of such classifications? Answers to such questions, I argue, are not fixed and absolute;
and nor do they necessarily take the form which the romantic-nationalist
model of identity would suggest, i.e. a package of 'culture' in which
language is especially significant, in which an ancient shared past
is assumed, and in which ethnic or national identity is the preeminent
collective identity. On the contrary, in everyday life the predominant
categories of collective identity that are invoked tend to be at once more
geographically and culturally fuzzy – 'here', 'away' – and more apparently
concrete and immediate – 'crofters', 'incomers'. This means both that
there is considerable flexibility – and room for ambivalence and dissent
– in identifying practices; but also that they are experienced as part of
everyday encounters and social relations. Such identifying practices are
embedded in the everyday exchanges and practices of local life and are

manifest in such matters as knowing who is related to whom, knowing how to behave at funerals, jokes, ways of decorating the home, and attitudes towards animals. These are not the kinds of features which, according to the romantic-nationalist model, are typically regarded as part of the way in which having an identity and having a culture is expressed. Even where there is resonance between romantic notions and those produced locally – for example, the importance attributed by both to notions of place and of kinship as ways of identifying – there may be subtle yet significant differences between the two. Not only do apparently 'banal' expressions of identity (Billig 1995) provide a means of expressing, affirming or challenging local social classifications, however, they are also idioms through which 'wider' identities, such as those of the nation, may be expressed, and thus 'localised'.

Localness

Discourses of belonging – of who is and who is not 'part of the place', who is and who is not authentically 'local' – have been described for many British localities; and indeed 'belonging' or 'localism' has become possibly the dominant theme of the anthropology of Britain.[1] However, as many studies have pointed out, we need to take this preoccupation with localness not simply as evidence that there are more locals, or more kinship (or however localness is imagined), in the kinds of places where the preoccupation has been reported, but as expressive of certain meanings, social relations and moral evaluations. While those studied may readily reel off definitions of what it means to be 'local', and while there may in some circumstances be very clear-cut divisions made between, say, locals and incomers, in practice ascriptions may shift, defining features be recast, and other cross-cutting definitions be assigned greater significance. This means that we need to look at 'localness' and 'home' as both socially produced, and potentially contested and shifting.

'Localness' and 'home' are not, however, only produced locally or by 'locals'. They are also produced by incomers such as Sheila. More generally, the idea of certain places as 'local' – and the conceptualisation of them as inherently different from, and somehow out of kilter with, the rest of modern society – is one which has certainly been fed back to areas such as the Scottish Highlands, through development policies, media images, and visitors (cf. Nadel-Klein 1991). However, this does not mean that it is only in these terms that localness is defined by those living in the Highlands.[2] I should note, however, that although I talk of 'Carnan', this is not intended to reify locality, and as we shall see this particular definition is one which has a very mixed resonance locally. Moreover, I do not intend to imply that those features which I describe are necessarily exclusive to this locality: indeed many of the features which are described locally as characteristic of 'here' are ones which many other areas might equally claim; and what is important is not so much their 'real' geographical extent as the place they have in local definitions of self.

In Carnan the use of the term 'local' is widespread, particularly as a noun, to refer to certain persons – a term used in both English and Gaelic speech, and, less often, as an adjective. 'Locals' are also sometimes referred to (by themselves and others), in part of widely used colonial discourse, as 'natives'. The main distinction made is between 'locals' and 'strangers' (*coigrich*) or 'incomers' or 'white settlers' – a distinction which both locals and strangers/incomers attribute primarily to the fact that 'locals' are 'from the place', that they are related to many of the other inhabitants, that they 'are crofters', and to a wide range of knowledge and behaviour which might include speaking Gaelic or knowing whether to go down to the cemetery, but which might equally concern ways of treating animals or how potatoes are cooked and eaten. All of the latter could, however, be variably applied and invoked, for there were locals who did not speak Gaelic and incomers who boiled their potatoes in their skins and peeled them at the table. As such it seemed possible to learn how to belong; and I was certainly not the only incomer to be told 'You're becoming a native now' when I mastered certain local knowledge or behaved in particular ways. However, at the same time 'incomer' status could always be suddenly remembered, and of course in effect was by the very fact that it was remarked upon. Moreover, while at one level 'being of the place' and having kinship connections with it might seem empirical and uncontroversial, and was often presented as such, in practice there was a great deal of flexibility over how these were construed.

'Home' and 'Away'

Probably the most pervasive way of talking about 'us' and making con-trasts with 'them' was a distinction between 'home' or 'here' (*a bhos* – over here) to 'away' (*air falbh*).[3] These terms are vague with regard to geographical reference though if pressed Carnan folk say that the division lies between the islands (*na h-Eileanan*) and the mainland (*Tir Mór*). However, it is less the spatial dimension which concerns them than the social and ethical difference which the terms symbolise. 'Away', *air falbh*, is used most frequently in conversation and makes explicit or implicit contrasts with island life, which serve, relationally, to strengthen images of 'home'.

Facts and ideas about the nature of 'away' and the contrast with 'home' are gathered from the press, from incomers, from experience of 'away' and from 'exiles' – those who used to live in the Highlands but now live 'away'. On the one hand, this tends to support positive images of 'home'. The very idea of 'exile' (*fuadach*),[4] which derives part of its resonance from the nineteenth century experience of emigration and clearance, summons up the impression of forced separation and a wish to return. The poetry of exiles, particularly during the early phase of settlement in places like Canada in the nineteenth century, often expresses the sentiment of 'home-sickness' (*cianalas*) for the places which they have left and hope to return to. As Derick Thomson notes: 'The commonest theme of Gaelic verse in the nineteenth century is that of 'homeland' . . . . The homeland is seen primarily in a nostalgic light; a place of youthful associations, family and community warmth, a Paradise Lost' (Thomson 1974: 223).

Such nostalgia is constantly fed back into local conceptions by exiles today; so reinforcing both the idea of connection to place and the idea that local places – 'the homeland' – are special and different from else-where (cf. Parman 1990). Like exiles, I am always asked on my return to Skye whether I have missed the place (*'an robh thu ag ionndrainn an àite?'*); and through my affirmative answers I too support an image of Skye as the sort of place with which one builds up an emotional attachment. Many holiday-makers return to the same holiday cottages year after year and they are talked about approvingly in contrast with the tourists who only come once and 'race about here, there and everywhere' rather than establish a more enduring relationship to a locality. The idea of nostalgia for the homeland is also continued through the Gaelic media where a typical radio programme format is to interview an exile who talks nostal-gically of his or her 'own country/area/land' (*mo dhùthaich fhèin*) or 'the country/area/land of my people/relatives' (*dùthaich mo chuideachd*). These programmes are talked about with admiration for the way that exiles may have maintained their Gaelic and retained detailed knowledge of the island landscape. On several occasions I was told of exiles who had returned to Carnan, sometimes several generations later, who were able to go to specific locations – ruins unrecognised by locals today – on the basis of information which they had passed down in their families. Such stories support notions of connection to the place but also serve as something of a reproach to local people who may compare their own relative lack of knowledge about the past unfavourably with that of the exiles.

Alongside the positive nostalgic images of home, however, emigrants, exiles, incomers and the media may also make less flattering comparisons. Emigrants' and incomers' remarks about the relatively restricted range of goods in the Island shops, and the lack of cinemas and other amenities, may cast 'home' – and its inhabitants – as rustic and backward. On one occasion I was present when a recently returned emigrant visited an old friend, Effie, in Carnan. The emigrant was complaining about the price of fruit and vegetables on the Island and comparing this to markets that she was used to in London where she could 'buy a whole bag of avocado pears for a pound'. Effie, however, became tired of the emigrant's complaints and what she later described to me as the woman's attempts to show how 'fancy' she was. After politely enquiring as to the taste of avocado pears and various other exotic fruits mentioned by the emigrant, she remarked matter-of-factly 'Well, I think you'd have done better to stay in London'.

As well as being a label for what are perceived as significant cultural differences, 'away' is also used to refer to values which are seen as not local. For Effie, her ex-friend would be 'better off away' not simply because she could buy avocado pears galore but because her attempts to show off her sophistication were part of a way of behaving 'away' which Effie judged to be inappropriate locally. Often, 'away' refers to practices or values which are locally perceived as strange or morally dubious. News reports of drug-taking in Edinburgh or child-abuse in the South of England would elicit comments like 'it's bad away' or 'that's away'. And even things happening on the Island to islanders – an unmarried couple living together or a girl suffering from anorexia nervosa – might be accounted for in terms of 'that's the way away'.

However, while the contrast between 'home' and 'away' is able to depict island life favourably through drawing upon a contrast between the country and the city which has roots in disaffection with modernisation (Williams 1973) and a local constellation of sentiments about place, this is not unequivocally held. Although 'away' is often depicted as a world in which people pass one another on the street without so much as a nod and do not even know their neighbours, it is also the 'land of opportunity'. For young people in particular, 'away' may offer a more exciting way of life and an opportunity to escape the networks of gossip which they see as a claustrophobic feature of rural life. The phrase 'you have to get out to get on' is widely used and casts the locality as socially static by contrast with 'away' (cf. MacLean 1983). If you have not managed to 'get away' the implication often is that you have not done well. Kay MacLean from Carnan writes that she has been asked the question '"What is there for you here?" . . . a hundred times' (ibid.). The ambivalence surrounding 'away' is also characteristic of attitudes towards 'home,' and is described by MacLean as a 'combination of conflicting emotions — inferiority/ superiority or love/hate' (ibid.). It is an ambivalence related on the one hand to the salience of ideas about emotional connection to place, and on the other to ideas of progress and backwardness, of 'getting on' or of 'being left behind'. Both have their place in the local cultural repertoire; and for some individuals these are, at times, experienced as problematic and contradictory.

Despite the contrasts drawn between 'here' and 'away', and between 'locals' and 'incomers', the majority of Carnan's inhabitants live 'away' at some point in their lives. In the central three townships where I carried out a survey, almost half of those aged over twenty-five had lived on the mainland for at least five years; and many more had been away for seasonal work. Amongst those over sixty, 66 per cent had lived away for at least five years and 27 per cent had lived away for more than twenty-five years. They had gone, they said, to work and or train — there being few opportunities for either on the island, especially at professional levels. Emigrants, then, are not so much a distinct group of people as a stage in the life cycle. However, those who leave do not always return; and emigration is thus a liminal, 'betwixt-and-between', state whose outcome is uncertain. It is for this reason that it is regarded with such an ambivalent mixture of achievement and disappointment by many.

Incomers

The 'home' — 'away' distinction is also mapped onto a division between 'locals' and 'incomers', talk of 'locals' and 'incomers' (by both locals and incomers) being widespread in everyday speech. When used as part of a general contrast 'incomers' or 'strangers' referred to those who have come to the area with no, or few, previous connections. These are the incomers like Sheila who also warrant the label 'white settlers' who come, mostly, from mainland Scotland or England, who are unlikely to have relatives in the area, and who do not speak Gaelic (except perhaps for a 'smattering' picked up at classes). 'Being part of the place' is for some of these incomers, like Sheila, something of a preoccupation.

About a third of Carnan's residents had moved into the area within their lifetime (without having lived there previously); and half of these were 'white settlers' with no kinship links to the locality.[5] 'White settlers', even more than exiles, bring something of 'away' to the locality, and indeed, they constitute the predominant 'awayness' through which 'local' or 'native' identity is affirmed. 'White settlers' may also be referred to in Gaelic as *Goill* (sing. *Gall*) meaning 'foreigners'; and sometimes as *Sasunaich* or 'English folk'. The latter term is used even though many of these incomers are from mainland Scotland. The sense that they are especially numerous, as Edwin Ardener observes, is matched by the perception that they are 'invading' and greatly increasing in numbers (1989: 218). On return visits to Carnan I would often be told 'There's so many incomers coming in, you'll hardly know the place now Sharon', 'It's all white settlers and bed-and-breakfasts now, right the way through the township', 'There's nothing but English coming in. You'll not be finding much Gaelic now'. Incomers too would sometimes lament the number of incomers arriving: 'I don't think the place will remain the same for much longer' said one. Yet when we went into our usual detailed conversations about who was now living where, it often turned out that the overall proportions had not changed much, for many of the white settlers had moved into properties vacated by other white settlers. Indeed, the tendency for white settlers not to stay long in the area seemed quite marked. When I began fieldwork none had been there for more than three years, and many have since moved on though a few remain.

Many of the white settlers can be described by Forsythe's term 'urban refugees' (1980). They had often visited Skye or other parts of the Highlands for holidays for many years and then – perhaps because they were made redundant or unemployed, or their children had grown up or they had simply become 'sick of all the pollution and everything' – had moved to the Island when they got the opportunity. Many local people made a distinction between two sorts of these white settlers: as one man put it, 'the ordinary incomers and the hippies'; and indeed these two groups were generally keen to distinguish themselves from one another. In Carnan, the former were mostly from non-professional backgrounds and had not had higher education. Their past and present jobs included bus-driver, taxi-driver, book-keeper, caretaker and electrician. They had come to the Island either as couples or as families. In talking of 'the hippies', Carnan locals usually meant one particular household of young incomers, mostly from middle-class backgrounds with higher education, who had bought an old shooting lodge up on a hill. The number of 'hippies' in Carnan fluctuated as friends came to visit, sometimes for months on end, and as some members of the original collective either left or spent periods of time living elsewhere, though there was a fairly stable core of about eight adult members and four children – all but one born since their mothers arrived in Carnan.

There is a good deal of variation among all of these incomers in the number of contacts which they have with 'locals', though for the most part the hippies are seen as more separate than the others. The 'ordinary incomers' are, however, more likely to forge contacts with families in which either the husband or wife is not from Carnan; and they do quite a lot of 'networking' with each other. They visit each other socially, to consult on matters of home-improvements, to dine, and to play games of bridge or *Trivial Pursuit*. The 'dinner-party circuit', as one incomer described it, is relatively exclusive to the ordinary incomers and the families where the wives have come fairly recently from Glasgow. This is not because these incomers have purposefully set up an exclusive institution, but simply because there tends to be greater willingness to participate and mutual understanding of the 'rules of the game'. Barbara, from Birmingham, told me of how she had invited a local family for a meal but, although she and her husband knew them well, the whole event had been rather uncomfortable and formal, and had only accentuated difference rather than broken it down as she had hoped. The family had turned up in their smartest clothes and had eaten virtually nothing despite the fact that Barbara had gone to great trouble to make things which she believed they liked. They had also spoken very little and left rather sooner after the meal than she had considered polite, though no doubt their intention had been not to put her to any trouble.

White settlers seem to find that they simply have a lot in common with one another, and conversations often centre around the problems of getting particular shades of emulsion paint on the Island; the ravages of the elements on their horticultural efforts; the expense and poor quality of fresh fruit and vegetables; and the extraordinary difficulty of local naming practices. *Was* Iain Bàn also the one they called Blondie, or Iain Culna-beinn, or Iain Donald Angus, or Iain MacDonald, or Iain Dòmhnallach?[6] Discussion is also often about 'them' – 'the locals' – and their habits. Sometimes this confirms the images of community and exotic difference which attracted them to the Hebrides. The number of 'Get Well' cards that Sheila received when she was taken into hospital was an example of the caring community which she would never have found on the mainland; the time that Donnie Sheorais had spent helping Roy mend his car was an example of neighbourliness alien to the city; the Gaelic conversations between passengers on the bus told them that despite appearances this really was 'a foreign country'. For some incomers, however, there seemed to be disappointment that there was not more exoticness. They often tried to press some from me, questioning me about keening at wakes, clan-feuds and belief in fairies. For some, there was definitely a suspicion that locals were hiding these things from them in an irritating pretence at normality. Some visible aspects of daily life which had not, perhaps, been evident before incomers arrived were built into a reconfigured sense of the exotic nature of their local neighbours. The Sabbath and the Highland churches, and drunkenness, were particular subjects through which difference was discussed (Chapter 6). Often, however, this conversation centred around ways in which local people failed to live up to images that incomers had once held of them. Drunkenness was the dark reality of the conviviality they had hoped to find; Presbyterianism and Sabbatarianism the dark reality of Hebridean spirituality and belief. Belief in the area as a 'community' was also questioned by some, who described 'petty backbiting' and quarrels between locals; and who saw that locals too could be 'out for what they can get'. The lack of participation in organised leisure activities – often described by incomers as 'apathy' – was also a contradiction to their expectations of community (Chapter 7). Even the physical environment which they sought seemed sometimes to be in danger from locals. The old Rayburns, agricultural implements, and car wrecks that surround many croft-houses were one of the most topical subjects of incomer conversations. For incomers, these were ugly blights on a beautiful and quaint landscape; for locals they were simply old things which had to go somewhere and for which they might just find a use one day.

Most 'ordinary incomers' attempt to integrate themselves into local life and indeed there sometimes seems to be a degree of competition among them to be 'accepted'. Almost all have at some point attended Gaelic evening classes or the local history society. However, these in themselves did not seem to help their integration much. Having already established English-speaking relationships with local people, incomers felt embarrassed to try out their classroom Gaelic, and in most cases their experience in the classroom merely confirmed the difficulty and inaccessibility of the language. In the case of the local history society, set up in Carnan in 1984, the fact that incomers attended made some of the local organisers rather annoyed and they blamed incomers for the fact that other local people had not become involved, arguing that incomers' presence had made locals think that it was something for incomers. Morag, who was something of a local activist, complained bitterly to me about the 'English folk' who came along knowing 'dashed all about the place'. She told me that they had 'created an atmosphere' in which Gaelic could not be spoken and that their presence – coupled with a lack of old people from the area – meant that the society did not manage to 'get off the ground'. The local history society suffered a lack of local history.

Figure 5.1. 'Useful Rubbish': van used for storage (by Julie White)

For Morag, as for several other local activists, incomers were a threat not just to Gaelic speaking but to the whole character of the locality. She explained to me:

> It's not that we don't want them ['English folk']. I mean, they're very nice some of them and one or two are okay. But more than that and they change everything. *Tha iad a milleadh an àite* – they spoil the place.

Other locals, however, seem to welcome incomers, especially if they are young and may bring up children in Skye, so helping to avert some of the problems of a declining community, such as the closure of local schools. And others seemed to switch from one position to the other in the face of what is, undoubtedly, a dilemma over the maintenance of the locality and its population.

The Hippies

For many local people, the hippies seem to epitomise 'strangeness'. Unlike Carnan's other incomers, they dress in ways perceived to be strange: their clothes are often colourful and baggy, with holes and frayed edges seemingly purposefully on show. Most of the men have beards and some have pony-tails; and the women mostly have long hair which is allowed to fall untied. The formerly grand house in which they live is surrounded with numerous brightly painted vans and cars, some with rainbow motifs, in varying states of disrepair, something which even local people complain about, comparing the present state of the house unfavourably with its grandiose past as an elegant house for gentry. I lost count of the number of times that I was told of the polished brass ornaments that used to stand in its lobby in contrast to its state today.

If local people articulate their own social and moral codes through contrast with 'incomers' and others from 'away' in general, they do so much more actively through contrast with the hippies. The hippies do likewise. Notions of order and disorder, cleanliness and purity, are one of the means through which difference is expressed (Douglas 1966). The hippies are often regarded as untidy and dirty. 'Can't they find a hairbrush?' and 'There used to be running water at the House' were typical comments. When one man described them as 'breeding like rabbits' he expressed what he perceived as promiscuity. A woman who seemed to dislike them particularly, but who was unsure of my contacts with them, told me: 'They're all vegetarians you know. It's very bad – cheese is terribly constipating'. They used a similar, culturally appropriate idiom to express what they perceived as her social inadequacy: 'She's on Valium'.

In some respects the classification of them as untidy is one which 'the hippies' accept for theirs is a rejection of established notions of order. Their choice to live on a Hebridean island is part of an attempt to escape the constraints of what they see as a narrow bourgeois lifestyle. For the hippies the idea of 'order' is devalued relative to that of 'nature', and purity is associated with the latter. The emphasis is conceptualised as a shift from the external or superficial to the internal and meaningful. The philosophy is applied both to society and relationships, and also to matters like diet or dress. Thus spontaneity is valued above discipline; 'natural' fabrics above man-made; wholefoods above processed. This alternative pattern of values is sometimes misunderstood by local people. For example, the fact that the hippies were not married was taken by many as evidence of unabandoned sexual permissiveness. In their early days in the area, the women told me, they were pestered by a group of local men who on one occasion arrived in the middle of the night supposing that 'free love' would be available. Most of the hippies, however, live in fairly conventional couples within their household.

Contact between inhabitants of the House and their local neighbours often seemed to provoke such cultural 'mismatches' (McDonald 1987). For example, the eldest of the children at the House sometimes visited a local family nearby to play with their children. But although they seemed to get on well the local mother expressed exasperation to me about what she saw as the child's lack of socialisation. 'I want to pee', little Kaya would announce, a healthy open attitude towards bodily functions from the House point of view, rudeness from the local. 'I see no reason why she can't say "please may I use the toilet"' said the mother. On one occasion I was visiting a local couple who were employing two of the men from the House to do a little building work. During a tea-break they came in to chat with me and Iain. The subject of education came up and Iain began to bemoan the lack of corporal punishment in schools today and went on to tell an anecdote about his wife's experience as a teacher in Glasgow. She had given a boy the strap for swearing in class. The boy's mother had then come along to the school to complain. When told what her son had said she retorted, 'Well, I can't think where the hell he got it from'. At this, Iain guffawed loudly and, after a few seconds of silence while trying to get the joke, the hippie men and I laughed nervously. Corporal punishment and indeed any sort of reprimand for using 'down-to-earth' language would, of course, be alien to the House philosophy (which I certainly shared at least in part). Paradoxically perhaps, the reason why this mismatch occurred was that Iain had decided that we were okay and would share his view. Alternatively, he might have been having his own private joke by telling a story which we would not easily appreciate.

The fact that the hippies are well-educated seemed to increase local wariness of them. In 1984 they put in a bid to purchase a section of river near their house (from a company based some distance away). Unknown to them (I presume) was that this section of river was used for poaching by local people. Of course, locals could not openly give this as the reason why the portion of river should not be sold, and had to resort to various excuses, such as that it was a place to tip ashes (an excuse not likely to appeal to those at the House). I was told at the time: 'You've got to be careful of that sort, they're clever enough when it comes to it. They've all got educations behind them. They're educated drop-outs'. It seemed to me highly unlikely that the hippies would have prevented poaching. However, as Isobel Emmett has argued for Wales (1964), poaching is also a means through which locals express their opposition to authority and 'the powers-that-be' (which in Wales means 'the English') and there-fore the assent of incomers – especially of the hippies – would detract from the meaning of the activity and might mean an unwelcome involve-ment in it.

In many respects the hippies' expectations of local people and life were not realised in Carnan. When I asked them why they had come and what they had hoped to find, all said that they had expected to find 'more going on' and that they would be better able to participate in local life. Instead, they tended to find themselves excluded and had come to feel a much greater chasm of difference between themselves and locals than they had anticipated. What they found in Carnan was not the alternative healthy cultural identity which they sought. One said: 'There's no get-up-and-go. It's a dying culture. Any people with any go have left'. He went on to describe how local life seemed to him to be 'typical of all dying cultures', and pointed particularly to 'alcohol abuse' ('and I've never seen alcohol abuse like you see it here') and 'the dying language'. Carnan people were, in his terms, a clear example of a culture which had not remained true to itself and was showing the pathological symptoms. He contrasted this with the House saying, 'We're a self-contained community', clearly indicating that he thought that if Hebrideans had followed the same pattern they would not have succumbed to the ills which he saw them to be afflicted with. Others talked of their expectations of finding a lively 'folk culture' with, perhaps, folk music clubs like in Ireland and better attended ceilidhs.

The hippies were also disappointed that many local people seemed so 'conventional' and 'bourgeois'. None of the House children was old enough for school but Kaya's mother told me that she did not want her to attend the local primary school because she thought that the educational principles there seemed to 'be all about killing natural expression and just getting them to behave', and because she disapproved of 'all this girls should be in pink sort of stuff'. They seemed genuinely surprised that many locals regarded them so warily.

Unlike in some other Celtic areas, Carnan's hippies do not seem to have tried to appropriate a Gaelic identity.[7] Beyond wearing jewellery with Celtic designs and attending Gaelic evening classes in the local school, none have become involved in Gaelic linguistic and cultural developments. Partly this is because they had no previous involvement that I know of in Gaelic or Celtic activism, and were not from University Celtic departments. It is also, however, because the Gaelic world which presents itself in Carnan is not particularly attractive to them. Rather than being tied in with mystical Celticism, it seemed much more closely associated with the local Presbyterian churches, whose whole aura and dogma are antithetical to House philosophy. One woman, Marsha, described her own religious stance ('I have my own religion') which was embedded in sentiments of personal freedom, nature and disassociation from institutions and said of Presbyterianism: 'It's not even Celtic really'. The Celtic world, like the healthy folk-culture and self-contained community, was simply not present. Not surprisingly, perhaps, the collective was disbanded in the late 1980s and the house sold. Partly a matter of internal disagreements, it was also a consequence of the mismatch between their expectations and what they found locally. They could not easily belong.

Place and Community

The idea of belonging to a place is very strongly articulated in Carnan (as in the Highlands more generally, cf. E. Ardener 1989: ch.14). Visitors such as myself would be asked — often before we had been asked our names — '*Cò as a tha thu?*' — 'What place are you from?' It was a question which always threw me into a stuttering confusion. Where *was* I from? Having moved often it was not a question with an obvious answer. Sometimes I simply ventured 'England' but that was too unspecific. 'But *where*?' I would be pressed. I suggested 'Oxford', where I currently lived, but as I had only been there since becoming a student this was dismissed as the place where I was *from*. 'Where are your people from?' I was asked, but neither the place to which they had recently moved, nor any of the places which they had left, seemed to be of sufficient permanence to constitute my place of belonging. In the end it was my place of birth that seemed to come closest to what was required, though as I have no memories of Newcastle-upon-Tyne (which I left as a baby) nor any enduring connections with it (no relatives, no reason to return) I felt most uneasy when one man composed a song about it which he would sing whenever we met: *Caisteal Nuadh, Caisteal Nuadh . . .*

Placing seems very important in local conceptions of identity – people must be *placed* – where you are from is a key part of who you are. These geographical locations are typically very specific: a particular township or island. Terms such as *Sgitheanach, Leodhasach,* and *Niseach,* which indicate individuals from Skye, Lewis and Ness respectively, are widely used; though for answering the question 'Where are you from?' they will often be specified further. Such placing typically locates individuals not just in a particular geography, but in a set of kin and neighbours. Locals often specify clearly where incomers are from – 'Sheila and Roy are from Oldham. Do you know it?' – partly, it seemed, in the hope of eliciting further information which could 'place' them more fully, but also as a reminder of their non-localness. For those versed in the genre, conversations which begin 'Where are you from?' move swiftly through a discussion of place, in which island is narrowed down to township, and then perhaps to the croft itself ('By the jetty?' 'Is that near the Wee Church?'), and draw in neighbours, relatives, church ministers, and perhaps tales of visits to the place. The place of belonging is, then, also a social network; it is the place of the family croft – passed down over the generations; the place to which relatives exiled to the mainland return for holidays, family weddings and funerals, and even to be buried themselves. Indeed, when I was trying to deal with the question about my own placing I was once asked 'Where will your remains go home to?' 'Place' is a place of return – an enduring location which outlasts all the sites in which a person may temporarily reside.

This conception of 'place' is neither the romantic vision of the Hebrides that attracted those such as Sheila and the hippies, and nor is it simply part of some widespread cultural localism or post-modernist development of 'place myths'. Places are considered important for identity not because of the aesthetic qualities of the landscape, nor because they *have* a particular 'culture' or 'heritage', but because of the social relations and knowledge which they entail. The kinds of stories recounted in 'Where are you from?' conversations are more likely to be about particular individuals than distinctive 'culture', or about the success or failure of some recent industrial experiment than about the older history of the area. Nevertheless, at the same time, the emphasis on place may be informed by ideas about the connection of people and land forged in the Land Wars, and by the practical fact that the inheritance pattern of crofts set up in the 1886 Crofting Act tends to mean that the same families do stay in particular areas.

Carnan

'Carnan' was not often given by local people in answer to the question of where they were from. Instead, if from the area, they tended to specify the particular township; or, if from further afield, the parish, or estate or island. The lack of reference to Carnan was not just a matter of scale, however. For although the fact that Carnan was generally seen by outsiders as not just a significant geographical entity but also a particularly 'strong' or 'thriving' 'community', it was not much used locally and many were unsure of its boundaries, though as I describe in Chapter 8 this was rapidly changing during the 1980s with the appearance of new bilingual signposts indicating both the limits of the area and various 'Carnan' institutions such as the primary school and the community cooperative. An account in 1963 notes that 'There is widespread confusion as to the application of this name [i.e. 'Carnan']' (Gordon 1963: 101) and suggests that it has only recently come to be used to refer to the area of settlements around the bay, and is still 'rarely used at all by Gaelic speakers' (ibid.: 102). The bay, however, is recorded as *Loch 'Carnan'* in eighteenth-century maps (ibid.: 101), a name that is used by local people. In fact, the use of the name 'Carnan' to refer to a number of the settlements around the bay can be found in police and newspaper reports of the Land Wars in the 1880s, a usage which is in some ways surprising given that the area had no particular autonomous interest in the Wars: opposition was articulated in terms of the crofters, cottars and squatters of the Highlands as a whole, or more locally in terms of the occupants of the estate or of particular townships bordering farms. Ironically, the single most important reason why the area found its way into history as 'Carnan' seems to be that the police authorities, who generally arrived in the locality via Carnan Bay, had called their police station 'Carnan constabulary'.

If the name Carnan, and the idea of the area as a 'community', are relatively new to local people, however, this does not mean that they will not be able to become meaningful, as we see further in Chapter 7. Moreover, the language of place, localness, relatedness and belonging is readily available to source articulations of Carnan as *a community*, though as we shall also see, these do not always match up with other expectations of what it means to be a community.

On Kinship and Belonging

Sheila is in a minority of Carnan residents who have no kinship links to the place. The great majority of the population (72 per cent) was brought up in the locality, and almost all of these have at least one parent also brought up in the area (71 per cent) and at least one grandparent (69 per cent).[8] This seems to imply a remarkable consistency of belonging based on kinship: those defined as locals were not simply born in the area but also can claim kinship links over at least several generations. Thus locals are different from incomers not just by place of birth but also by the fact that they have relatives 'going way back' (as one incomer described) and are very likely to have other relatives living in the area. Certainly this appears to be a very firm empirical boundary to many incomers who often remark upon the relatedness of Carnan's inhabitants: 'Everybody's related to everybody else. You really have to watch what you say here', 'They're clannish when it comes down to it', ' The next thing you know, you'll have said somat and it'll turn out they're a second cousin', 'The locals can be pleasant enough to you, but in the end it's not what you do or what kind of person you are that matters, it's whether you've got relatives going way back over the generations'.

However, although at one level there was a clear-cut distinction made between those with kinship links to the locality (locals) and those without (incomers), among locals there was also a good deal of flexibility in ascribing degrees of 'incomerness' or 'strangerhood' and relatedness could be invoked here too. As Edwin Ardener has observed of the Hebrides, there is 'a wide definition of "strangers"' (1989: 218) − those from neighbouring parishes can be so dubbed as well as the 'white settlers' who come from the Lowlands or England. Moreover, 'the stranger remains "marked" for longer, perhaps for ever, so that the residue of strangeness accumulates' (ibid.). Those who had married in − virtually all of whom were women − were sometimes referred to as 'incomers' even if they only came from a neighbouring parish. Moreover, while nearly all of those brought up in Carnan also have at least one grandparent from the area, more than 40 per cent have a parent from elsewhere and two-thirds have a grandparent from elsewhere. So although locals could claim belonging through kinship, the fact that they had relatives who were 'strangers' (generally from other Highland areas) might also be pointed out and this taken as evidence that they are somehow not fully local. So when one man grumbled to me about a local member of the community council not doing things 'for the good of the locals' he observed that his father was from the mainland, ignoring the fact that his mother had been brought up in the area. Nor are such classifications only ascribed by others. Gaelic-speaking Ruaridh, a crofter who I found it impossible not to think of as a 'local', described himself to me as 'a kind of incomer', his father being a non-Gaelic-speaker from the mainland (though himself with parents from the area). Likewise, when Jean tried to persuade me that she was unsuitable to answer my questionnaire because she was 'not of the place really, an incomer you could call me', she was referring to the fact that her mother was from the Scottish Lowlands and had married in. Jean's mother spoke no Gaelic and although Jean was fluent in the language she told me that she did not always do so out of a kind of solidarity with her mother who had felt very excluded in Carnan: 'I don't always speak Gaelic you know. I like to keep up my side of things'. Claiming a degree of strangerness was a means not only of trying to avoid the attentions of the anthropologist (despite my claims of interest in 'everybody') but sometimes also of attempting to stand outside what were perceived as some of the circumscriptions and foibles of localness. Jean, for example, after telling me what a waste of time she thought crofting was, again reminded me that she was 'a bit of an outsider' – as a way perhaps of reminding me that what she said was not to be construed as part of the local world view, and perhaps too that her comments were more dispassionate and clear-sighted than those of a local might be.

Alongside the apparently firm boundary between locals and incomers, then, there is also a relativity of strangerhood. That Effie from another part of Skye, or Fiona, one of whose grandparents was a Lowland shepherd, could sometimes be classified as 'strangers' (Gaelic: *coigrich*) shows how fine the scale on which strangerhood is drawn may be. Because kinship is reckoned cognatically – through either mother or father – there is a good deal of flexibility in drawing up lines of 'belonging' or of 'strangerhood'. However, although there is a relativity of belonging, there seemed to be no special status accorded to those who, on genealogical criteria, might be said to have the strongest connections to the locality (i.e. those with four grandparents from the area). Unlike in the English village of Elmdon, as described by Marilyn Strathern (1981, 1982), there was in Carnan no sense of 'core' families who were thought of as representing the 'real' community. Perhaps this is partly because those who can make genealogical claims are not in a minority as in Elmdon.

Although 'locals' might not, then, be thought to be equally local when particular individuals were considered, they are likely to be so in contrast with 'white settlers'. In response to questions about whether some people are thought of as 'more Carnan' than others, I received replies like the following:

> No, we don't think of any families as more [Carnan] than others, because in
> all the townships, excepting the white settlers, they are descendants of [Carnan]
> folk who occupy the crofts. (Written reply to a letter)

This kind of formulation of belonging casts local people as equals on the
basis of descent, and both feeds into and supports the idea of an egalitarian
'people'. It presents the occupancy of crofts and the distinction between
locals and 'white settlers' as immutable matters of 'blood' (*fuil*) and
inheritance.

This construction is also supported by some of the other ways of
expressing relatedness. In Gaelic, the same terms can often be used to
mean either those who are directly related by descent or a less specific
category of 'people', perhaps associated with a particular place, as works
also with the term 'people' in English (and as this is used in the Highlands).
For example, *mo mhuinntir*, 'my people', are either consanguineal relatives
or a set of people associated by location, e.g. *muinntir an Eilean*, 'people
of the Island'. The terminology collapses place and kinship together in
an assumption that those who live in a place are likely to be related.[9] This
kind of collapse is more explicitly made in contrasts that local people
make with 'away'. They say that 'Most folk here are related in some way
or other', and may use this to account for other qualities of 'here', such
as the low rates of reported crime. Despite these general statements of
relatedness, however, when asked if a specific individual is related to
another, the answer is often that they are not – or 'Well, I suppose that
they might be some way or other, but only far out'. A distinction is drawn
between kin who are 'far out' or 'distant' (*fad as*) and those who are
'close' (*cairdeas dlùth*). It is at the level of 'far out' relations that Carnan
folk might all claim to be related. For most practical purposes, however,
these distant kinship relationships are not invoked or even reckoned (many
people having difficulty working out who their third cousins are). 'Close'
kin generally means relatives no further 'out' than first cousins; and these
are those who there is a sense of obligation to see at New Year (unless
they live away) and who would be invited to a wedding. Today, few people
would feel obliged to invite third cousins, though older people said that
this was formerly the case.[10] Even 'closer in', however, very little of social
life beyond the household is organised on the basis of kinship. Recruitment
to boat-crews – of which there were few – in Carnan was not on the basis
of kinship (unlike in Whalsay, Cohen 1982a); and the formation of work-
groups (for, say, picking potatoes or bringing home peats) was only
occasionally organised on the basis of relatives beyond the household. One shopkeeper told me that he had some obligations to buy from

particular retailers because of his kinship links with them; but in general the household seemed to be much more significant in the ordering of daily work routines than did any wider kinship links.

Localness, Relations and Politics

One domain where the idea of kinship links and localness seemed often to be invoked was in relation to politics, both local and national. As has often been noted of the Highlands, who a particular candidate is, and whether they are from the area, is often seen to be more important than the party to which they belong (but see Chapter 7). Skye is part of the Ross, Cromarty and Skye constituency; and since 1983 has had the Social Democratic Party (later to become Liberal Democrat) Member of Parliament, Charles Kennedy. Charles Kennedy himself has no particular personal connections with Skye but even so many of those in Carnan expressed his suitability as a candidate in terms of local connections and ideas of genealogy. The previous Member of Parliament was Russell Johnston who had been brought up in Skye and attended the island High School, and this connection was often spoken of as particularly important: 'You see, he was from the Island so he knew what the people wanted – he knew without having to be told. A stranger – well – an incomer just wouldn't know the same'. Although Charles Kennedy had no similar connection (and in 1983 his share of the vote was less than that of Russell Johnston) his suitability as an MP was often expressed in terms of the fact that Russell Johnston had given him his blessing: 'It's a continuation of support for Russell Johnston really – he was from Skye you see'.

While local connectedness may be valued, however, it is not enough. A candidate also has to be seen to be successful by the codes of 'away'. The fact that Charles Kennedy was 'a good scholar' was one quality which was frequently remarked positively upon.[11] In local politics too, where the language of relatedness and localness is still more ramifying, those who take up political positions (e.g. community and regional councillors) have to negotiate between evidence of 'belonging' to the locality and of experience in dealing with 'away' and 'the powers-that-be'. This is not to say that a candidate who mediates these two will always be preferable: as we see in Chapter 7, there may at times be greater swings towards one or the other. Those who held positions of power in Carnan often complained that they were pressed for favours by relatives. More generally, sometimes to the despair of those in political positions, there were often rumours that kin were being preferred. Such rumours themselves could have effects on who was willing to stand, whether they would be elected, how they would deal with the requests and rumours and, in some cases, whether incomers might even be preferred.

Inheritance, Households and Marriage

Relatedness also has a rather specific significance in the Highlands because of the fact that croft tenancies are inherited; and this affects the likelihood of an individual being able to remain in a township, or even on the Island at all. In theory it is the eldest son who inherits the croft.[12] However, where there is no will it is the widow (or, in unusual circumstances, widower) who will legally inherit; though this tends to be conceptualised as 'filling in' until the widow dies and the son inherits. If there are no sons, daughters will inherit; and parents sometimes choose to assign the croft to a particular relative (often one who has stayed at home to look after them) rather than simply pass it on to the eldest son. The fact that in general only one child inherits can on occasion lead to family disputes and a good deal of bad feeling among siblings. An anthropologist in Lewis was told that 'no one could properly understand the Hebrides unless they knew that it was possible for two brothers to sit at the same fire hating one another' (Condry 1980: 241). The inheritance patterns and crofting legislation have the consequence that many children will be bound to leave the Island; and it is partly for this reason that 'scholarship' and 'making one's way' are encouraged as a means of providing those children who will not inherit with an alternative future – though one which is almost inevitably 'away'.[13]

Despite the problems of a shortage of housing, and despite the extent of kinship links and the romantic assumption that households in the Hebrides will surely consist of extended families (i.e. more than one generation in the same household) rather than nuclear families (which are sometimes depicted as symptoms of a more alienated way of life), 85 per cent of households in Carnan's central three townships consisted of a nuclear family, married couple or single person. Moreover, the remaining 15 per cent would in all cases be better classified as 'supplemented nuclear families' rather than extended families, because all involve a nuclear family together with the man's widowed mother who is generally described as 'staying on in the house'. Even this, however, is often thought unsatisfactory. According to the Gaelic proverb: *Dà chù le aon chnàimh, dà chat le aon luch, dà mhnaoi 'san aon tigh, chan fhaca riamh sùil ri sùil* ('Two dogs with one bone, two cats with one mouse, two women in one house, they'll never see eye to eye') (cf. Walker 1973: 121). Antipathy will arise between wife and mother, I was told, because the woman who was formerly 'in charge' now finds herself 'having to bite her tongue and do as she's told'. I was struck in several such houses that I visited that the widow was reluctant to answer my questionnaire, telling me that they were not the householders, and in one case that 'the lady of the house is not at home'.

The reluctance to share housing, the relative scarcity of it and the fact that crofts are often not inherited until an individual is into their late thirties or older means that marriage is often late and sometimes the subject of inter-generational conflict. I was told on a number of occasions that until recently boyfriends or girlfriends would not visit the home of their future in-laws until the marriage was actually planned, and in some cases not even then. This was usually dismissed as 'ignorance' but even so many young people did seem to feel that they should hide their dating from their parents. One woman in her twenties told me that she had been 'going with' her boyfriend for seven years before she let her parents know, and that her father would 'have killed me likely as not!' if he had found out. She seemed rather surprised that I should find her secrecy unusual. As in this case, it is lack of housing and the fact that young people may be forgoing the opportunity to make a good living for themselves 'away' that parents object to particularly. However, if marriage to an islander may mean housing and financial problems, it also has what most parents see as the advantage that children and any potential grandchildren will be close by. Annag, when talking about her nineteen-year-old daughter, would frequently switch from complaining that she wasn't taking up that nursing course in Glasgow where she could have the sort of fun that Annag herself had had in her young days, and telling me how much she liked having her daughter around and hoping that she might marry 'a local' and remain on the Island.

If there are worries about sons and daughters marrying too soon, there are also worries that they may be too late and may even 'miss out' altogether. After the death of his father is seen as a time for a son to marry even if his mother is legal heir to the croft. She is regarded as simply holding the croft in the interim period, though local people approve of the legislation for they say that it safeguards the widow against a prodigal son or other potential inheritors. In the family gathering after one funeral that I attended there was a good deal of light-hearted joking about the eldest son's marital prospects and the widow said very pointedly that it was now time for him to find himself a wife. In the days which followed, a woman who was locally said to have been 'chasing' him for years (though who I had never seen before) visited the house every day. She was made very welcome by the widow, though to her exasperation Donnie Sheorais usually disappeared out onto the croft for some apparently urgent task or other after a quick greeting.

Households, which in Gaelic are referred to by the word *teaghlach* which can mean household or family, are regarded as distinct units in Carnan and are generally more important in local social organisation than other kinship categories, and are one of the many divisions which may cross-cut the idea of 'community'. They typically operate as economic units and much day-to-day crofting work is carried out on a household basis. Moreover, while kin who are not of the same household may take different sides in disputes within the locality, it is generally expected that the household will present a unanimous 'front' or 'face' (*aghaidh*). The household is also a nexus of gender relations and acts, I suggest, as a microcosm of what are seen as some of the most significant cultural alternatives within the local repertoire. It is within the household, as we will see further below, that various wider identities – and their ambivalences – are played out and brought home.

Gender and Belonging

Marriage is often talked about as something that men – especially long-time bachelors – have to be coerced into. It is mainly women who are described as doing the 'chasing' and as 'catching' the men; and marriage and incorporation into a household is described in terms of socialising men and curbing their unbridled participation in the community of men. This is depicted particularly in the idea that men will give up any heavy drinking when they marry. Indeed, marriage for older bachelors may be described in similar terms to religious conversion, and there is always a good deal of gossip about such prospective marriages. Donnie Sheorais was the subject of much speculation and many neighbours said that it was 'time for him to face up to his responsibilities' and to take on the role of head of the household. He himself seemed to be deeply ambivalent about his future. For while he seemed to be running away from the woman who was 'after' him and from marriage more generally, and while he certainly maintained his old circle of drinking partners, he began to go out less often and not get drunk quite so much, and his mother told me that he had even said that he might go out to the morning church service as well as the evening one on the Sabbath. 'Well, perhaps he's making some effort', said one neighbour wryly.

If the household is a place where a man is 'caught', the obligations and roles are not wholly unwelcome, however, for in the publicly acknowledged role as 'head of household' (*ceannard an taighe*) a man's position in the locality 'counts' in a way that that of men living with their parents does not. As head of the household a man becomes part of a particular local conception of 'community' or 'people'. At some community events, most notably funerals, it is 'heads of household' who attend, and they constitute 'the township'. It is possible to say of a funeral that 'everybody was there' without there having been any women, younger men or children present at all. However, although within the household it is the man, in his role of head of household, who 'officially' represents the household within the community, his wife also has an important role in representing the household; though what she represents is, at an abstract level, fundamentally different from what men represent.

If men represent the egalitarian thread in Hebridean life, women represent, at the level of the household, status differences. Women are the 'improvers'. Marilyn Strathern has suggested that at the heart of the class system there is a paradox between what is fixed and what is flexible: between the apparent stability of the system and the idea of mobility (1981: 186). In Carnan, I suggest, there is a parallel paradox. Although Carnan people claim not to bother about class, they are concerned about the 'standing' of different families; and this is something which tends to be differentiated more (though not exclusively) in relation to women, and domains of social life with which women deal, than to men. In this way, women represent and may even effect social mobility; while men represent, by way of the complex of ideas about land and egalitarianism which is informed by the Land Wars, that which is (relatively) fixed.

The idealised inheritance system of land passing from father to son provides a further source through which men can be seen as relatively 'tied to' the land and the past. If place is important in identity, this is much more likely to be fixed for men than it is for women, as women are more likely to move at marriage; and indeed for women (and especially non-Gaelic-speaking women) who have moved in, the issue of being 'of the place' is often a matter of discussion.[14] Several such women expressed their feelings of exclusion to me, and often described the language barrier as especially significant. They tended to regard local people who chose to speak Gaelic with their husbands as engaging in purposeful attempts at exclusion or at least as being 'ignorant'.

Women's property is also more likely to be the stuff of mobility. Although there is no substantial transfer of property at marriage, wedding presents tend to be household goods (bedding, towels, electrical appliances, tableware) and these are thought of as being for the woman. One woman, Cathy, told me of how a bachelor uncle of her husband's, when he delivered their wedding present (a toaster) had said, 'I hope that's good enough for the bitch' (*Tha mi'n dòchas gum bi sin math gu lèor dhan ghalla*); a comment which indicates both his notion that the gift was for the wife and his understanding of the status possibilities of household goods, as well as his dislike of her. This dislike was not purely a personal matter, Cathy explained, but part of a more general dislike by men 'of the old school' of women in general and 'incomer' women in particular (though Cathy was only from the next township). The idea that women disrupt the status quo – that they are 'interfering' – seems to be part of the reason for the dislike. Women are seen as the ones who will use the household goods and more generally who will be in charge of household consumption, especially that which serves to differentiate the household. A household's 'standing' is often discussed in terms of material signs of well-being, particularly such matters as dress (how well 'turned out' the family, especially the woman, is). While men tend to dress alike in dark colours, women, particularly for special occasions such as weddings, will often have smart new outfits including hats, perhaps in bright colours. However, women are limited in the extent that they can express status: they run the danger of being thought 'fancy' or 'posh'. These terms, which are also used in Gaelic speech, are sometimes used jokingly, but they have an edge and sometimes blur into the more serious matter of being thought 'too proud'.[15] Anybody who is 'too proud' is in danger of being 'shown up' and 'shamed' (*air a naraichadh*), something which seems to be thought especially likely for women as they are the ones who negotiate the fragile boundary between the expression of social standing and being posh.[16] These boundaries are often alluded to in everyday speech, especially through the fairly common phrase 'I would be ashamed to . . .' ('*bhithinn air mo naraichadh . . .*').

Women, Materialism and Localness

In expressing social standing through material possessions, women express an alternative to the notion of the Highland people as egalitarian and non-materialistic. This non-materialist notion, which also meshes with romantic conceptions of rural peoples, is informed in part by ideas about 'the people' as formulated during and subsequent to the Clearances: it was the landlords who put trivial worldly possessions above people. Women, in being the ones to deal primarily with household possessions, find themselves defined as not fully part of 'the people'. Indeed, while at a general level they are subsumed under the category 'the people', at a finer level of differentiation, they find themselves representing cultural alternatives which may threaten to disrupt the ideals through which 'the people' is constituted.

The distinction also maps on to the 'home'/'away' distinction. When one woman said to me, 'Bed and breakfasts and world possessions and all that is now coming in. But it didn't use to be like that', she might have been speaking either the romanticised language of community or the local 'home'/'away' distinction. 'Away' is generally conceptualised as wealthy relative to the locality; and as bringing a set of values at odds with those of community: 'Now everybody's after his own'. Yet, as we see, the interest in material possessions and their capacity to express social standing is not located simply 'away': it is also thoroughly part of 'home'. If on the one hand, the acquisition and display of material possessions risks disrupting community egalitarianism, on the other, to forgo them could also risk being cast as old-fashioned: 'You've got to keep up with the times', 'We don't want them [outsiders] thinking we're backward', 'We don't want to be left in the byre'. This is the language of 'improvement'; and we see here how the gendered differences also map (though not absolutely neatly) onto the alternative ontologies of modernity: 'being' through improving, or 'being' through remaining true to a cultural core. In the constant juggling of these two, women tend to be regarded as the improvers, and men as those who are true to the demands of community. These are, of course, generalisations and there are, as we shall see, many exceptions. Nevertheless, this general repertoire, I suggest, has its effects in daily life and in the workings of Gaelic developments; though it is given local inflections and, as we shall see, does not necessarily entail the full romantic nationalist baggage of what it means to *be* 'a culture' or 'a people'.

The distinction between home-egalitarianism and away-social standing is also articulated in other domains of daily life. To take one example, it can be seen in the spatial organisation of the home. Most houses have a 'best room' which contains a glass-fronted cabinet (either of the older free-standing type or part of a whole wall-unit in a more modern design) where the best pottery, glassware and any silverware (often wedding presents) are displayed. There will usually be an upholstered three-piece suite, fitted carpet and fireplace. The suite and carpet are often fairly ornate and plush: the suite is generally large and covered with velvety fabric or leather, and the carpets are often Axminsters and Wiltons. No best room that I have been in was without framed photographs. Mostly these were professionally-taken posed pictures of relatives in what could be classified as events demarcating social standing: especially weddings and university graduations. Some of these would be large with surfaces like an oil painting. Many people only use their best room when they have visitors, especially visitors from away, on special occasions. In one family with which I stayed, for example, it was only used three times within a year. Once was during the communion season when a missionary and various other 'important' guests visited; the second time was when some officials from the Highland Board came; and the third was after a member of the family had died and the coffin was kept there.

Everyday visitors, those from the township who just drop by, will usually be received in the kitchen. This is not so much the room where food is prepared, as the 'family room'. The sink, cooker and fridge are often in a smaller adjoining room referred to as the scullery. The kitchen virtually always contains a Rayburn (a cooking range, like an Aga) – with a kettle constantly simmering – a table, chairs, the radio, and perhaps the television. Meals are usually eaten there; and it is from this room that individuals come and go to work on the croft. By comparison with the best room, the kitchen may be less smart – the furniture is less likely to be upholstered and the floor will be covered with lino and perhaps a rug or two. Washing hangs to dry near the Rayburn and the dogs and cats that are usually banned from the best room vie for the warmest place next to it. There may be photographs here, but they are more likely to be unframed snapshots of, say, young relatives at home on the mainland or on holiday. This is the family's everyday face; and here a visitor may be given a 'piece' (i.e. something to eat such as a biscuit or scone) in their hand rather than the amply-laid trays or plates of food that the best room calls for. And although women certainly spend much of their time in the kitchen, they may feel that they would prefer to be associated with the best room. In one house that I visited the woman, Bellag, ushered me through the kitchen into the best room saying (half-jokingly) 'I wouldn't want you judging me by the state of that [i.e. the kitchen]'. Later, when one of her sons put his head around the door she warned him 'You'd better not be coming in here with those big dirty boots', and turning to me, 'They can do what they want out there but I make sure they behave when they come in here!'

While the category 'locals' is often used to imply an egalitarian people and a set of shared values, it is also cross-cut by other divisions: those of gender, of social standing, and of household. Furthermore, 'localness' is not fixed: like strangerhood, it is a 'shifting concept' (Frankenberg 1989). At the same time, however, there are limits to the possibilities within the repertoire that can be achieved by any individual: neither localness or strangerness are equally open to all.

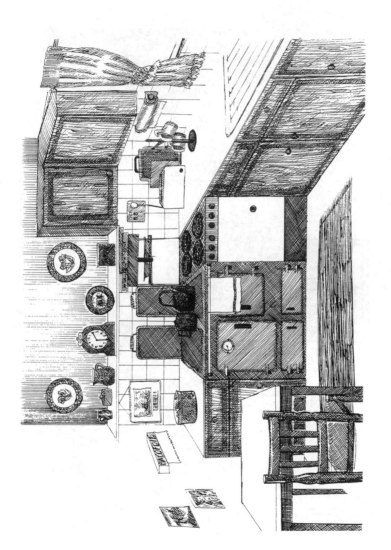

Figure 5.2. Everyday household space: a kitchen (by Julie White)

Figure 5.3. A 'best room' (by Julie White)

As we have seen in this chapter, oppositions, especially that between 'home' and 'away', express not just geographies and the movements or origins of people, but also moralities. Yet while on the one hand they may declare clear-cut counter positions, they are also regarded ambivalently and used variously in everyday contexts; and it is this quality of apparent clarity coupled with flexibility of use that makes them so apt for expressing the simultaneously closed and open nature of belonging. Moreover, while the label 'away' implies that which is not local, it would be wrong to regard it as therefore external to the locality. On the contrary, 'away' is constantly invoked in local discourse and mapped, if only partially, onto other differentiations, such as those of gender, of standing (including the people versus powers-that-be) and of 'ethnicity' (Gaels versus Galls – foreigners; Scots versus English); and as such it is very much part of the repertoire through which identities are articulated in everyday life. One consequence of this partial and multi-directional mapping is that categories such as 'away', 'foreigners', 'Lowlanders', 'England' and 'the English' are brought thoroughly home through being incorporated into everyday discourse and social relations.

The idea of attachment to place, and the contrast between 'home' and 'away', easily fit with a romanticisation of rural areas and the back-to-the-simple-way-of-life philosophy of 'urban refugees' (Forsythe 1980). However, the local notions are not simply versions of that externally produced imagery. Whilst the visions of Highland life which have been formed outside the Highlands may strengthen and even catalyse local conceptions, on other occasions there is a 'lack of fit' (Ardener 1975: xii) between the visions. Anecdotes local people tell about the urban refugees who buy up dilapidated croft houses with no running water or the tourists who cannot understand that a crofter may be in a hurry are testament to what local people see as the differences between their own attachment to place and outsiders' romanticisms. In the next chapter we turn to consideration of Highland Presbyterianism, a strictly Puritan and Sabbatarian form of Protestantism, which is felt by many incomers, including Sheila and the hippies, to be one of the most marked barriers to their being able to be thoroughly 'part of the place'.

Notes

1. Jane Nadel-Klein observes that it may have become the British equivalent of the Mediterranean honour and shame complex (1991: 502). I am particularly indebted here to her insightful discussion of these issues. Descriptions of distinctions between 'locals' and 'incomers' (or whatever the local rendering of the term may be) in the British context include Cohen 1982, 1986; Edwards 1996; Frankenberg 1966, 1989; Phillips 1986; Rapport 1993, Stacey 1960, Strathern 1981, 1982. Ethnographies of Scotland discussing the distinction include Cohen 1987; Condry 1980; Ennew 1990; Forsythe 1980; Jedrej and Nutall 1996; MacFarlane 1981; Mewett 1982; Nadel 1984; Neville 1994; Parman 1972, 1990; Payne and MacLeod 1993; Stephenson 1984. For an interesting discussion of the construction of discourses of localism in geography see Duncan and Savage 1991; and for some theorised discussions of anthropological discussions of 'the local' see Fardon (ed.) 1995.

2. Jane Nadel-Klein observes that the anthropological definition of 'localism' as resistant to homogenising forces is similar to the romantic definition (1991: 501). While this is the case to some extent, the romantic vision tends to cast localism in terms of a set of predefined qualities – non-materialism, neighbourliness, attachment to tradition – whereas the anthropological entails investigation into local specificities which might be at odds with broader romantic ideals (e.g. particular uses of mass produced objects, the rejection perhaps of certain traditions).

3. *A bhos* and *air falbh* are not, formally speaking, oppositions. The 'official' opposite of *a bhos* is *thall*, the terms having the sense 'here' and 'there' or 'hither' and 'thither' (Dwelly 1977). *Thall*, however, is not normally used in the particular contrast between the islands (or Highlands) and mainland. *Air falbh* is an adverb, though it is also used (as is the English 'away') as a noun. The 'home' and 'away' contrast is widespread throughout the islands (Mewett 1982; Parman 1990).

4. *Fuadach* is the word I was given in Carnan for 'exile'. *Fear fuadain*, 'an exile', has the secondary meaning of 'outlaw'. The Highland Clearances are also known in Gaelic as *fuadach nan Gaidheal*. Thomson (a Lewisman) gives *fògarrach* (1981) for 'exile'. Previous accounts of exiles have recognised the role they may play in local self-imagery. Susan Parman (1990) shows well how they may affirm positive images, while Peter Mewett takes the opposite stance to argue that they 'express . . . the negative evaluation of the esotery of island

life' (1982: 223). Mewett's argument that '*mainstream culture . . .* projects a derogatory rustic image of rural life' (original emphasis, ibid.: 222) is, however, surely too simplistic in that it ignores processes of romanticisation.

5. The others were mainly women who had married in.

6. For discussion of Highland naming practices see Dorian 1970; Parman 1976; Mewett 1982a; Macdonald 1987 Appendix 5B.

7. My comparison here is particularly with Maryon McDonald's work on Brittany where wholemeal-bread eating hippies are also Breton militants living out alternative lifestyles in rural areas (1986, 1986a, 1987, 1989); and also Rosemary McKechnie's work on Corsica (1993).

8. These figures are based on my survey data from the central three townships of Carnan and give findings for individuals born before 1970. I did not undertake systematic research beyond the level of grandparents, though it is well known that some Carnan families moved there from elsewhere on the estate at various times during the nineteenth century, and also came from the isles of Flodday and Rona earlier this century. Other families in Carnan can trace their families back in the area for as long as familial memory allows – usually up to about five generations (circa 1800).

9. See also Fox 1978. There are other interesting semantic features of Gaelic kinship terminology which I deal with more fully in Macdonald 1987. The term *càirdean* (sing. *caraid*) means both kin and friends; and the adjective *càirdeas* means 'friendship' or 'kindness' (Dwelly 1977). Likewise *cuideachd*, meaning relatives, is related to *cuideachadh*, meaning 'help.' This indicates a syncretism which is found in many societies (cf. Condry 1980: 230; Hastrup 1985: 75): the idea that relatives are friends, that it is relatives who will proffer help. Edwin Ardener has remarked in a seminar (November 1986) that this idea, together with its often unlived reality, is a central sociological problem in the Highlands. My comments below on inheritance bear upon this.

10. Some people told me that if they had not kept up relationships with second cousins then they would not feel obliged to invite them either, thus introducing an element of choice into what seems previously to have been a more prescriptive matter. For some older people this introduction of choice into the kinship domain is seen as symptomatic of a decline of moral standards: 'Nowadays they don't even bother to invite some of the close relatives. It's like "away". But it wasn't like that in my day. It would be the whole township and beyond'.

11. His Catholicism, by contrast, seemed never to be mentioned; though it may have accounted for some of the fall in the vote at the 1983 election.
12. Condry notes informants referring to this as 'patrilineal' (1980: 258). More generally, the kinship system has been described as cognatic as descent can be reckoned on either the mother's or the father's side (Walker 1973: 181; Fox 1978; Condry – with reservations – 1980: 258). However, there is an agnatic tendency within this (cf. Hastrup 1985: 72) in terms of a preference for sons to inherit; something which I suggest is related to the complex of ideas about the men, land and belonging.
13. Occasionally parents attempt some compromise as a way of providing for more than one child. Sometimes this means leaving other property (e.g. money) to those who do not inherit the croft; though one unusual compromise of which I heard involved a son being left the croft and a daughter being left the croft house (which she then sold to the son).
14. About a third of the women in my survey who had married in to Carnan were not Gaelic speakers.
15. The two most commonly used Gaelic words for 'pride' both have negative connotations. For *àrdan* Dwelly (1977) gives 'pride, haughtiness. 2. Anger, wrath'; and for *pròis* 'pride, haughtiness. 2. Flattery'. For *moit*, another word meaning pride, he gives 'sulkiness, sullenness, moroseness. 2. Pride. 3. short neck, as of a bird cresting up.'
16. There is a Gaelic proverb which suggests the importance of the idea of 'shame': *Is buaine na gach nì an nàire*, 'Shame is more lasting than anything'. Although the concepts of 'pride' and 'shame' or 'modesty' seem important in the Highlands, I would not argue that they are the same, or so ramifying, as the so-called honour and shame complex of the Mediterranean (see, for example, Peristiany 1965).

6

'The Last Bastion': The Highland Churches

S unday in North Skye. Little traffic passes first thing in the morning, only the odd tourist car in the holiday season. Murdo goes out to feed the animals. Mary Ann gets breakfast and puts the joint in for lunch, wearing an apron over her Sunday best. Around eleven thirty the cars begin to go past, first a few, then a more steady stream. Mary Ann puts on her heeled shoes, her brimmed hat, and picks up her bible (King James, Gaelic *Biobull*, New Testament translation 1767; Old Testament 1801) and the little brown envelope which contains the collection money. We are getting a lift from her brother today, so we go and stand outside. Several cars go by; and their occupants wave or nod to us. We squash into the back of the car with Mary Ann's sister-in-law. A male neighbour sits in the passenger seat. Both of the men have their hair greased back and are wearing dark suits and ties. They are scarcely recognisable from their workday appearances. We chat. It's good weather for the time of year. Who will be doing the service today? A visiting minister so it won't be in the Gaelic. That's a shame for you, Sharon. The morning service is usually in Gaelic; and it's for the Gaelic that you go isn't it? I say that I do not mind.

We pass the Church of Scotland and the Free Presbyterian Church on our way to the Free Church. All three are simple whitewashed halls, with no spires or steeples or stained glass. Their car-parks are practically full, as is ours when we arrive. We have to park outside on the road. We greet in Gaelic those we meet as we go in. The elders and missionary, standing by the little round table where the collection envelopes are laid, smile at us and say 'Good Morning' to me, though Mary Ann reprimands them '*Tha Gàidhlig gu leor aice*' ('She's got plenty of Gaelic'). We always sit in the same place in the church as does the rest of the congregation. Mary Ann describes it as 'the family pew'. The service begins with a Gaelic psalm sung in the characteristic metrical fashion which sounds so alien to ears used to hymns. There is no musical accompaniment but one of the elders, standing at the front of the church, acts as a 'precentor', singing a line before the congregation joins in. It is said that this is a pattern that was established when most of the congregation was illiterate and could not read the words. I find it difficult to make out distinct words in the cacophony anyhow. We sit to sing and then stand for the prayer. It is extempore and my impression is that this elder is struggling to keep it going for the minimum ten minutes or so that these prayers generally last. The minister, in the highest part of the pulpit (the elders stand in lower booths), gives the sermon which expounds on a verse of the Bible. Today it is in Gaelic after all, though the style is the same whatever the language: dramatic intonation in which the minister's voice rises to great crescendos and then falls into whispers. He repeats and repeats the key line – which today is *'Tha sinn uile 'nar caoraich air seacharan'* ('We are all lost sheep'). He probes the line from many angles, telling us that we are like sheep in that we are born sinful, and we are lost 'from the Lord our God'. He occasionally switches to English to jolt our attention: 'baser instincts get their grip'. During the sermon, we suck the mints that Mary Ann passes along to us. Three today as it is such a long sermon. Out of the service at last we greet various neighbours. Especially if there is anybody there who has not been for a while – perhaps because they have been ill or are just visiting – the men shake hands and the women kiss. In the car, Mary Ann remarks how good and strong the first precentor's voice was and asks 'Did you feel the service long?' She says that she hopes that I managed to get something out of it given the difficulty of the *'Gàidhlig na cùbaid'* (lit. 'pulpit Gaelic,' or *'Gaidhlig na h'Eaglais'*) and the minister's *'blas Leodhasach'* (lit. 'Lewis flavour,' 'Lewis accent').

Back home, Murdo – Mary Ann's son – has prepared lunch. By the look of him, he has been round to Donny Ewen's for a drink too, though Mary Ann appears not to notice. We make the final preparations for lunch. It is always the same: packet soup, followed by a joint, potatoes (boiled, served in their jackets and peeled at the table), tinned peas and Bisto gravy. For desert we have Cremola with tinned raspberries. Archy mutters grace. It is English, though I cannot tell. He is annoyed with Murdo for being drunk but Mary Ann begins to sing to keep the peace. Nobody speaks. After lunch, Mary Ann and I clear up and then we sit and listen to the Gaelic service on the radio. Today it is from Barra – a Catholic service. I wonder whether Mary Ann will switch it off but she continues her knitting, remarking that she likes the *clàrsach* (Gaelic harp) and *'sin mar a tha e'* ('That's how it is'). I stay at home and write some notes while Mary Ann, Archy and Murdo go to the evening service. Then I visit a neighbouring Church of Scotland family for a while. They are watching David

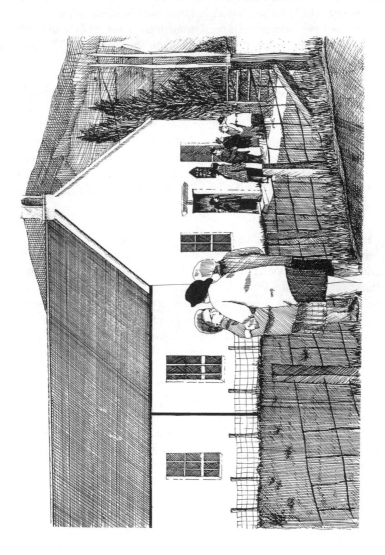

Figure 6.1. At Church on the Sabbath (by Julie White)

Attenborough's *Life on Earth*, which sparks a discussion of how marvellous the photography is, and how did they manage to get the camera down those holes. I have heard that evolutionary theory is not taught in the secondary school on the Island because the churches object. They don't seem sure but Norman tells me that there is no use for evolutionary theory – 'You've got to say it's God when you see something like that [the nature programme]'.

After spending some time by myself I go round to see Mary Ann, Archy and Murdo again at about nine-thirty. We have a cup of tea, cream crackers and cheese and then sit round to read a chapter of the Gaelic Bible. As it is Sunday, we take it in turns to read a verse each – it is something they started when the children were young. Today we read from the Book of Job. Archy doesn't really hold with the New Testament. I take my turn too, which always makes Archy chortle, though he insists that I read it well. What is funny, he says, is to hear me speaking the antiquated Bible Gaelic 'like a minister'.

For many outsiders the Highland Presbyterian churches, with their Puritan Calvinist doctrine, are one of the most difficult features of contemporary Hebridean life to reconcile with romantic images of community and Celticness (cf. Chapman 1987: 25). Yet, they are also different and even 'exotic'; and seem in many ways to be bound up with the Gaelic language. They are problematic for revivalists. On the one hand, in many parts of the Hebrides they are one of the few regular social gatherings where Gaelic is spoken. On the other, the churches are unwilling to see themselves as agencies for reviving the language; and their own position is that they will use whatever language best reaches the congregation: their view of the overwhelming importance of the word of God leaves no space for the romanticisation of linguistic specificity. Also problematic for revivalists is that the archaic nature of *Gàidhlig na cùbaid* is sometimes thought to put young people off the language; and the churches may oppose renaissance developments if they consider them 'sinful', as in the case of the community hall (Chapter 7).[1] Historically, as we have seen, they also occupy an ambivalent place. They are bound up with the development of 'the crofting community' in the Northern Hebrides, having grown out of opposition to landlordly patronage and having played a part in articulating the notion of 'the people' with equal access to 'the Truth'. Yet they also created divisions within that 'community', divisions both between the different churches and between church adherents and members. These ambivalences still play themselves out.

Carnan is not unusual in the Northern Hebrides in having three different

Presbyterian churches: the Free Presbyterian Church, the Free Church and the Church of Scotland. All three are fairly similar in their form of church government and doctrine, and in the conduct of their services. The Calvinist doctrine that they follow is that of the Westminster Confession of 1643 (Burleigh 1960) and involves an eschewing of elaborate ritual and ornamentation, and regards the individual as inherently sinful and dependent upon God's grace for salvation. Although the Church of Scotland is the most liberal of the three – and most likely to have services in English – in the Hebrides it follows the Highland pattern of singing metrical psalms and shunning musical accompaniment that is characteristic of the other two churches. It is only different in that here the congregation sits to pray and stands to sing; that the service is shorter (it lasts an hour rather than an hour and a quarter or hour and a half); and the minister is more likely to relate an anecdote from his hill-walking experiences or even tell a joke (though, as in the other churches, there is rarely even a flicker of a smile on any face). The Free Presbyterian Church is the strictest of the three and is the one that is locally referred to as 'Wee Free' (*An Eaglais Bheag*, lit. 'The Small Church'), though outsiders often refer to the Free Church, and sometimes all of the Highland Presbyterian churches, as 'Wee Free'.

The stereotype of the Wee Free is familiar throughout Britain on account of publicity given to cases such as that of Lord MacKay who was reprimanded and removed from religious office for attending the funeral of a Catholic friend (MacLeod 1994). Regularly in the Highland press there are articles about Sabbath observance and church strictures: the Lord's Day Observance Society objects to plans to allow a swimming pool to open on Sundays; a Free Presbyterian minister is dismissed for becoming intoxicated and another for something cryptically referred to as 'a family matter'; AIDS is denounced by an eminent minister as 'God's law enforcement agencies at work'; the Princess of Wales is condemned for meeting the Pope; and the Moderator of the Free Church refers to the Catholic church as 'the Scarlet Woman (the Whore Church)' (*West Highland Free Press* 23.5.1986).

At one level, the strict Presbyterianism of the northern Highlands marks a significant cultural and social difference from 'away'. The churches see themselves as a kind of last bastion of true Christianity in a morally beleaguered world; and the Highlands as in constant danger of the infiltration of the liberalisms and laxities of 'away'. At this level, the churches tap into and reinforce a notion of 'the Highland people' as culturally and morally different from those on the mainland. At another level, however, the three churches disrupt the notion of community solidarity through their differences with each other and through the differences of horizontal social relations which they make within the church-going population between Members (those who have been 'saved') and Adherents (other church-goers), and between the ecclesiastically, but not spiritually, recognised distinctions between congregation, elders and ministers. These differences are themselves articulated through the division between 'home' and 'away': the Church of Scotland being cast as closest to 'away' and a possible source of laxity within the islands, and the Free Presbyterian as 'most uncompromising' ('uncompromising' being a term that they willingly use themselves). However, none of these matters is uncontested; and although most local people say that they 'belong' to one church or other and the majority 'turn out' for church at least once or twice a month, religion and the power of the churches is the source of a good deal of ambivalence within the area. In this chapter, my aim is to describe something of the often indirect contestation of 'Highland' moral and religious identities that is made through activities and talk – and especially the charge of 'hypocrisy' – surrounding the churches.

Fieldwork

As for most of Carnan's incomers, Wee Free Presbyterianism initially filled me with trepidation. My own religious upbringing had been within the atheism and agnosticism of home, the liberal Anglicanism of school, and the guitar-strumming Methodism of chapel Sunday school. The stereotype of Highland Presbyterianism, with its emphasis on sin and iniquity, seemed dark and forbidding. I had heard stories about how women who cut their hair or wear trousers are regarded as depraved, and anthropologists elsewhere in the Hebrides had told me that they were initially thought to be Vatican spies. With this rather melodramatic picture that I had assembled, I worried that my attendance at church might be questioned or even denounced. In fact, I was always greeted warmly and some people even encouraged me to record a service – 'for the singing'. Part of the reason for this acceptance was surely Mary Ann's friendship and the degree of respect she commanded locally.

Although I had thought that people would not assume me religious at all, my behaviour conveyed rather mixed messages. Attending all three churches was not something that any local person would do and showed, I thought, that my interest was academic. However, for an incomer, and even for a local of my age, I attended church fairly frequently, usually turning out for at least one of the services on the Sabbath and attending services during the communion season and even occasionally weekday services known as 'prayer meetings'. Mostly I went to the Free Church as it was Mary Ann's church, was most likely to have Gaelic services and had the largest congregation locally. Like other women, I wore a hat (usually a beret) and carried my Gaelic *Biobull*. I also sometimes joined in family worship with Mary Ann and her family. Each night, between ten and eleven, Archy, Mary Ann's husband, would read a psalm and a chapter aloud from the Gaelic Bible and I often stayed, and sometimes arrived, for this. This, together with the fact that Archy enjoyed spreading the tale of my reading the Gaelic Bible 'like a minister' mixed the message about me further. Occasionally, people would ask me indirect questions about where I stood: 'You like the Gaelic don't you?', 'It's the Gaelic you go for, isn't it?', 'You were out today [i.e. at church], you must be a good church-going girl'. I was never sure how to respond to these and usually would try to make some joke about how I had not understood a word of the minister's Lewis accent. On two occasions I was asked by strict Presbyterians '*A bheil thu a' creidsinn ann an Dia?*' ('Do you believe in God?') and rather dishonourably pretended that I had not understood the question and changed the subject. On two other occasions I was asked the same question in English. Once was by the Church of Scotland minister who, when I apologetically said that I was afraid not, told me that he was very pleased with my reply for nobody in Carnan would have ever said such a thing to a minister. I was not quite sure what to make of this. The other occasion was after an elderly communicant had described his conversion to me in detail. To have replied simply that I did not believe would have been to dismiss his account. I told him that I was not sure. 'But you're not totally against it then?' he pressed. I assured him (honestly enough) that I was not, and after lengthy discussion he concluded that I was a rationalist who would have to think things out, rather than be in his privileged position of having simple faith.

Here and Away

If outsiders see the Presbyterian churches as a unity, at one level so too do local people. They contrast the churches '*a bhos*' ('here') with those '*air falbh*' ('away'). These contrasts are typically made through reference to the detail of practice, such as the liberality of churches away in granting communion or their use of hymns and musical accompaniment. While these details may simply be remarked upon without further comment, they may also be implicated into the more general moral distinction between 'here' and 'away' – a distinction in which the Highlands are generally cast as closer to a proper Christian morality. Psalms, for example, are favoured above hymns because they are regarded as having been directly dictated to David by God.

The articulation of moral difference between 'here' and 'away' can be made through apparently trivial matters too. The eating of sweets in church is a case in point. For all its apparent triviality, it is remarked upon as a cultural difference between 'here' and 'away' by local people, and incomers are often rather shocked that even Free Presbyterians eat sweets in church, so contrary does it seem to strike them relative to the image of Presbyterian austerity.

Sweets in Church

On the morning of my own first visit to church in Carnan with Màiri and her mother, Màiri made various comments about 'sweets' on the way to church: 'Have you got the sweets mother?'; 'Now, Sharon, I hope you're not averse to a sweet?' She was obviously finding the matter rather funny and her mother kept muttering: '*Shioraidh* Màiri, don't. What will Sharon be thinking of us?' I was baffled by the comments and assumed this was some joke; and was surprised when a sweet was pressed into my palm and it became evident that this was part of a wider congregational practice. As I was to discover, sweets are eaten in all of the churches and the pattern is the same in each. Sweets – the most popular being the Pan-Drop (a large oval mint) – are passed along the rows, mothers in families generally being the stock-holders. It is played out as a covert activity: knuckles are kept upwards, hands well down, eyes remain ahead, smiles and nods of thanks restrained. However, as the sermon begins there is a perceptible rise in noise levels created by the removal of sweet wrappers and some-times rather noisy sucking. Incomers who had joined Carnan's Church of Scotland told me of their discomfort with the practice: 'We'd never do that back in England', 'I hate it when you feel this hand, and then a sweet. I don't know how they dare. We just put them in our pockets . . . I couldn't do it, I just couldn't'. When they heard that 'even the Wee Frees' eat sweets, they thought this at odds with their stringent moral reputation and, therefore, hypocritical.

Local people are aware that outsiders may view the practice unfavour-ably. However, perhaps because they view their own churches as morally superior to churches away, they may be dismissive of criticism. On one occasion when I was helping at sheep dipping a joke was told that illustrated the point. It was a township fank and we were taking a break and sitting with our backs to the corrugated iron of the enclosure, drinking tea and whisky. The men present were mostly regular church-goers, though none were communicants. Sandy, the teller of the joke, related how, when he was staying in Wales, he went to chapel with the people he was staying with. (Whether this related to his own actual experience I do not know but doubt.) Apparently, they told him that they did not eat sweets in chapel: 'It's bad for the singing, not that we're trying to put you off', he mimicked in Welsh-accented English to great guffaws of laughter from all present. Highland Presbyterian identity is affirmed through the embarrassed reaction of the Welsh (one category of 'away') to this 'foreign custom'. The feeble excuse – 'It's bad for the singing' – is a further source of mirth, partly because Highlanders sometimes claim that it is good for it. The humour also stems from the fact that such a trivial matter can be taken seriously.

Outsiders and incomers expect that locals who attend church – especially the Free Presbyterian Church – will strictly adhere to its tenets. In part, this expectation stems from an application of models of choice to religious behaviour: incomers tend to regard church membership and attendance as matters in which individuals act in accordance with their own desires and religious feelings. However, for local people church-membership is an ascriptive matter: you join the church of your parents, and, if you are a woman, move to your husband's church on marriage. Very occasionally, as we shall see, individuals may choose to change church, but this is never done lightly. Although attendance at church varies widely among individuals and it is becoming increasingly common for younger people to choose not to attend, older people tend to regard church-going as something which one simply does. 'Everybody went to church when we were younger. You didn't question it really', said Archy, 'But it's like everything now. Questions, questions. Do as you please'. While it is uncommon for local people to openly criticise their own churches, this does not mean that they follow the stricter Calvinistic strictures rigidly. Indeed, I was told 'very few people are Calvinistic round here'. By this was meant that few people insist upon not cooking on the Sabbath or not listening to the radio. To outsiders, however, the fact that church-goers do not keep absolutely to the rules, or that public rules are broken in private, easily seems hypocritical. Incomers tell stories of Wee Frees who object to teenagers playing football on the Sabbath watching television after church; and of a strict FP woman being 'caught' doing the vacuuming before the minister comes for Sunday lunch. Yet, although local people themselves employ the charge of hypocrisy in relation to one another, some of those gaps between public and private that seem hypocritical to incomers are not regarded as such by church goers. Respecting the public observance of the Sabbath is as much a matter of respecting neighbours and what has become part of the 'Highland way of life' as it is about personal morals. Televisions and vacuum cleaners in the home do not infringe the public sanctity of the Sabbath in the way that, say, a football match does.

The Bible and the Bottle[2]

Perhaps the aspect of local life that strikes outsiders as most contradictory to their image of Wee Frees is the apparently high incidence of drunkenness.[3] This easily leads to speculation about how the two are related; and many incomers and commentators conclude either that 'heavy drinking' (as it is usually called) must be a rejection of religion, and even 'anti-religious'; or, perhaps relatedly, that heavy drinking is a pathological outcome of the imposition of such a dour religion upon a Celtic people; or that both are symptoms of cultural decline.[4] Such explanations, however, overlook local understandings and contextualisations of both drinking and religion. In particular, they fail to appreciate the way that both may be harnessed to ideas of 'the people', and seen as positive dimensions of local social life. Few heavy drinkers would themselves perceive their drinking as a rejection of religion or themselves as 'anti-religious'. They might be 'sinful' but so are all but the elect minority; and they are as likely to unexpectedly receive God's grace (*gràs*) as anybody else, it being a tenet of Calvinism that no worldly state rules out this possibility. Donny Ewen, who probably spends more man-hours drunk than anybody else in Carnan, is 'a great man for the Bible'. He can quote the whole of the book of Isaiah from memory; and is even said to have once acted as a Free Presbyterian lay-preacher. On Sunday mornings, groups of local people – mainly bachelors, but also a few women and married men – gather to share a dram and some cans of lager in hay-lofts, caravans and down at the shore. Many of these participants, however, attend the early evening church service, which again suggests that they should not be classified as 'anti-religious' or 'non-believers'.

Although Presbyterianism is widely thought by outsiders to be 'tee-total', the churches expect temperance rather than abstinence. Local people do not regard all forms of alcohol consumption – nor all alcoholic drinks – as equivalent or indeed as related to 'heavy drinking' and alcoholism. Incomers relished a story about a Free Church minister taking a drink at a wedding and a Free Presbyterian district nurse who would regularly prescribe a stiff dram. However, both were behaving in ways that would have seemed unremarkable to local people and quite unconnected from the local 'drink problem'. Taking a drink as part of a wedding toast is an integral part of the proceedings; though it is unlikely that the minister would drink whisky (classified as 'strong drink'). Instead, he would probably drink a 'ladies' drink', such as sherry, which, like other ladies' drinks (including 'Bacardi and Coke' and 'vodka and orange'), is widely thought to be scarcely alcoholic at all.[5] Drinking for medical purposes is also classified as a separate kind of drinking from 'heavy drinking', and whisky is believed to have helpful medical properties, particularly in the treatment of colds and flu. The district nurse's own negotiation of these categories was evident when I visited her shortly after New Year, when it is customary to offer any visitors to the house a drink. She mixed together whisky, cream and condensed milk, and told me 'It's not really a drink – more of a tonic really'. Most other 'Wee Frees' would take a drink too, especially on 'social' occasions such as New Year and at weddings; and several told me that they encouraged their children to take sips of drink from an egg cup. The idea involved here was that drinking should be undertaken in a controlled way within specified social contexts. Problem drinking, by contrast, is uncontrolled and often solitary, and not within contexts governed by rules of hospitality and sociability.

Nevertheless, drinking can act as a symbolic rebellion against the authority of ministers and elders. In this, it draws upon the connotations of male camaraderie and 'peoplehood' that are widely associated with drinking. It is at this level, perhaps, that we might relate drinking and Calvinism. The imagery of drinking offers individuals a sense of community and belonging in the face of Calvinism's emphasis on the lone individual. This is also expressed metaphorically through the idea of 'warmth' (*blàths*) – a property of both whisky and congenial people. Homes too are ideally 'warm' (*blàth*), preferably with a real fire burning; and hospitality typically entails entreating a visitor to come out of the cold and into the warmth. Although communicants often seemed to me to be warm and hospitable people, it was not unusual for some of them – and for some ministers – to be referred to as 'cold' (*fuar*). Such people were also those most likely locally to be cast as hypocritical, one Gaelic word for which is *fuar-chràbhach*, which literally translates as something like 'coldly pious'.

None of this is to say that heavy drinking is regarded with equanimity. On the contrary, the problems that it aggravates in individuals and families – unemployment, poverty and domestic violence – are well recognised. However, this 'problem drinking' does not throw into question the more positive understandings of drink. What is problematic is solitary drinking and 'uncontrolled' drinking. One man, who was locally known as a heavy drinker, emphasised to me that he never drinks alone – 'that's when you've really got to worry'. His implication was that his drinking was social and therefore not a 'problem'. Because of the community associations of drinking, and the fact that drunks are generally also neighbours and relatives, drunks are rarely shunned or even persuaded to sober up. Indeed, there seems to be little attempt to keep drink out of their way. Thus, in Carnan, the already drunk Donny Ewen will be given a lift to the bar; and children will talk politely to a drunken neighbour who has wandered into their house, and when he pulls out his 'carry-out' their father takes a dram too.

Community and Hierarchy

The establishment of the evangelical Highland Presbyterian churches played a part in articulating notions of 'the people'. As we saw in Chapter 3, the evangelical revivals of the eighteenth century and the split with the Established Church, were part of a rejection of the ecclesiastical power of landlordly patronage. The evangelicals preached a message that differences of social standing and education were irrelevant before God and that 'the Truth' was equally accessible by all. While this message could be, and was, linked into the idea of the people as a social unity, Calvinist egalitarianism is not itself allied to a sense of community or togetherness. On the contrary, according to Calvinist doctrine, individuals stand alone before God and even their behaviour towards one another in life has no relevance to the question of their salvation.

The distinction between those who have received God's grace – those said to have been 'saved' or 'converted' – and those who have not is the only distinction given spiritual significance. Those who have received grace are known as the 'Elect' and become Members of the church; other church-goers are known as Adherents, and although they 'believe' their spiritual status is no different from that of non-believers. Although the churches recognise several levels of ecclesiastical organisation, these are fairly minimal and do not imply greater or lesser degrees of power or proximity to God. A minister is not an intermediary standing between congregation and God, but on a parity with other church Members. Of those church Members some may act as missionaries (lay-men who are financially supported by the churches to spread the word of God), deacons or elders. Elders are elected by the Kirk session and carry out much local church organisation. Unlike ministers and missionaries, who often come from the Outer Isles, especially Lewis, elders are local men. (The Church of Scotland permits women to stand for any office but women do not take on any such roles in the Highlands.) As their name implies, they tend to be well on in years. Within the elders there is further differentiation with the institution of 'leading' or 'ruling' elder.

Local church government is carried out by the Kirk session, which consists of the elders and the minister, who generally acts as the Moderator (Chair). It acts as a local court, deciding upon matters such as the stance the church is to take upon the community hall or whether particular individuals should be allowed baptism. There are several further courts to which matters may be referred and which are responsible for formulating wider policy. These are the Presbytery, or district court; the Synod, or regional court, which is the highest court of the Free Presbyterians; and the General Assembly, the national court. Each of these consists of equal numbers of elders and ministers, and the moderator of each is elected by popular vote (though only ordained ministers are eligible). Although the position of moderator is designated as an organisational one,[6] moderators of the General Assembly are perceived by the general public as leaders and spokesmen of the church.

Despite the democracy of Presbyterianism, the churches are often perceived as hierarchical and authoritarian within the community. In particular, the distinction between Members and Adherents is sometimes sharply felt – despite the fact that Adherents may at any time be 'saved'; and church officials are seen to exercise a sometimes domineering authority. Elders, who are mostly local (unlike the majority of ministers), are often influential in the affairs of the community, where their authority to act as a moral force derives from the axiom of 'localness' or 'Highlandness' as well as their spiritual and ecclesiastical position. In all three churches elders tend to take a fairly 'hard-line'. For them, a 'strong' and morally upstanding church is one that resists the influences of 'away' and of liberalism. In the Church of Scotland there are some elders in Carnan who have been made elders away and who take a more liberal view. However, their voices tend to be muted. 'It's not that they don't let you speak . . . but you might just as well not be there for all they listen' one told me. More liberal Church of Scotland members often feel that there are local people who are 'disinheriting themselves' because they dare not 'put themselves forward' as communicants for fear of being denounced by the 'hard-line' church officials.

However, liberal attempts to broaden the appeal of the Church of Scotland locally, even if supported by a minister, are generally resisted by local elders. For example, one evening the Church of Scotland arranged a meeting at which local people could come and put religious questions to a panel of church Members. At this, a liberal visiting minister said that there were times when he too, like anybody else, had doubts about God. On the way home in the car (as he told me later) it became evident that the elder who was accompanying him was extremely angry. According to the elder, the minister had been quite wrong to voice doubts: 'We don't say things like that here'. In the elder's strict framework, true belief is logically divorced from doubt: belief is absolute, and divisions between those who have and have not received grace are clear-cut. Because being 'saved' is in theory something that comes suddenly – Saul on the road to Damascus is the archetype – there is no twilight of half-belief and belief intermingled with doubt. This means that nothing other than total belief can be talked about. The elder's words also reveal another dimension of his concerns, however: 'We don't say things like that *here*'. Within the locality, the authority of the Church of Scotland elders will be weakened if they are seen to be more liberal. The moral high ground in Carnan is occupied by those who are 'hard-line' – and this is a position which is bolstered by the distinction they make between 'here' and 'away'. Localness, strictness and authority are intertwined.

The problem for the Church of Scotland elders here is also the two other Presbyterian churches in the locality in relation to which the Church of Scotland is perceived as most liberal. Unwilling to appear morally lax in the face of these churches – and especially the FP which is strictest – there is a pull on the Church of Scotland Kirk session to be much stricter in the Highlands than in other parts of Scotland. In effect, there is a hierarchy of churches in the area – though as with other hierarchies it is contested. Because the stricter Calvinist forms of worship are now much more common in the Highlands and Highland congregations in Scottish cities, these forms are often conceptualised as 'Highland' or 'Gaelic'. This link substantiates the idea of the Highlands as a 'last bastion' of true Christianity and also fosters the more general idea that the Highlands must resist the onslaught of 'the outside world'. Features which are not themselves scriptural have become part of the stricter churches' claims to belonging to the Highlands. For example, the fact that the Church of Scotland rarely has services in Gaelic is interpreted as it lacking such a strong affinity with the area.

Such associations could be seen in debates at the Free Church General Assembly in 1986. The Free Church is positioned between the Church of Scotland and the Free Presbyterian Church. As such, it might be seen as lying on a continuum not only of spiritual values and ecclesiastical practices, but also of 'Highlandness'. Maintaining three different Presbyterian churches is costly, especially in a time of declining congregations and fewer individuals joining the ministry, and union of the churches is sometimes suggested. In a highly controversial speech in 1986, the Moderator of the Assembly argued:

> To unite with the Free Presbyterians seems logical, but to unite with the Church of Scotland is impossible on scriptural grounds as it means a compromise. You can hold the highest office in the Church of Scotland, reject ninety-nine percent of the Bible, and not be disciplined but even feted (*West Highland Free Press* 23.5.1986)

There was much disagreement with this as the summing up to the debate on 'Public Questions, Religion and Morals' implied:

> We have to face the fact that the supply of migrants from the Western Isles to the mainland . . . is tending to dry up. The question which poses itself in consequence is urgent and unavoidable. Must the role and identity of the Free Church be based on the Gaelic/Highland ethos as the main thing? (*West Highland Free Press* 30.5.1986)

The 'Gaelic/Highland ethos' is that of the Free Presbyterians and 'hard-liners' like the Moderator.

Divisions within the churches — Members, Adherents, Elders — and division into three separate churches within the locality, all disrupt the notion of 'the people' as an egalitarian community. This tension is one that is negotiated — though mostly implicitly rather than overtly — in everyday events within the locality. It is a tension which, as we have seen, is also a feature of the churches historically. The past sources contemporary ambivalence by setting up the debate between 'the people' and hierarchy, and linking Presbyterianism with both.

History in the Present

As we have seen in Chapter 3, the evangelical revivals in the Highlands articulated a model in which 'the people' and the evangelical church were opposed to landlords and the Established Church. However, the evangelical church soon underwent many realignments and fissions itself, so disrupting the notion of a homogeneous 'people'. Between 1900 and 1929 Carnan, like many other Highland areas, had four churches: Established, Free Presbyterian, United Free and Free. The divisions were often rancorous and certainly disrupt any picture of a harmonious community. A local schoolmaster, William MacKenzie, in a book published about the area in 1930, referred to the 'waste of energy and wealth' that divisions had caused and the 'bitterness' that was felt between the churches, though suggested that by 1930 there was 'more tolerance apparent' (MacKenzie

1930: 29). I was told in Carnan that in the past the Church of Scotland was referred to as '*an Eaglais Dhubh*' ('the Black Church') by some of its opponents. How many of the local population were involved in the theological debates and dissensions is difficult to say, though MacKenzie comments that 'this zeal for "principle" is not marked by more regular church attendance' (ibid.).

All churches and their members seem to share an interest in depicting the divisions between the churches as longstanding. This is the case both for those who wish to assert peoplehood today and deny the relevance of the divisions as well as those whose interest lies in depicting their own church as inevitable and traditional. Through different interpretations of ecclesiastical history all three contemporary churches can claim to be the most traditional or 'truest' Presbyterian church – notions which they closely associate. However, although the Church of Scotland might claim to be oldest, the Free and Free Presbyterian churches can lay claims to being the true heirs of Thomas Chalmers' Disruption Church, and therefore of the Reformation.

Although divisions are depicted as longstanding, those whose interest lies in asserting peoplehood prefer not to talk of divisions at all.[7] Placing them in the past and 'forgetting' them denies their contemporary relevance. I was told by several people words to the effect of 'All that's of the past now – we really are not bothered with it'; and an elder told me: 'I don't know about it at all, and quite honestly I don't want to'. Such people will, however, more willingly talk of the early evangelical period and in particular of characters such as *Maighstir Ruairidh*. Through their different interpretations, all of the churches lay claims to him; and all can talk of this period rich in images of community and people, prior to ecclesiastical fissions.

Another reason for not talking of church divisions, however, is part of the more general reluctance to talk of the past in its specifics because of its implications for individuals today. On one occasion, I had come across some published religious poems (*marbhrannan*) written by a deceased uncle of a local man in honour of *Maighstir Ruairidh*. *Marbhrannan* are a mix of scriptural reference and eulogy (MacDhòmhnaill 1989). Initially, he offered to show me more such poems but suddenly changed his mind and said 'I don't think that I should be showing you these'. Perhaps it was because I was a stranger. Perhaps, however, it was also connected with the fact that the uncle who wrote these texts seems to have been involved in the type of social climbing which many local people – especially their relatives – like to 'forget'. At the time that the tacks were being broken up to make new crofts and farms, this uncle changed church several times. He ended up with a farm, something which some local people hinted was connected with his changes of church, though I have been unable to find any historical material which would support this.

As with other aspects of crofting history then, as discussed in Chapter 4, remembering history in its detail can be disruptive of contemporary community relations as of visions of the past. Church history is particularly problematic, for the history of division is visibly etched into the present in the form of three different churches in this one locality. It is problematic too, in that the churches' role both in the formation and perpetuation of the 'crofting community' and in the maintenance of the Gaelic language are ambiguous.

Hypocrisy and Resistance

The authority of the elders is not absolute and nor is the moral superiority asserted by the FP church uncontested. For some local people – the young in particular – the rhetoric of tradition and Highlandness are unappealing or at least ambivalently viewed. More specifically, the association between old men (the elders), tradition, Gaelic and the church makes for a package that may be rejected as a whole.

Just as incomers use accusations of hypocrisy to question the moral superiority of the Highland church-goers, local people use such accusations to question the superiority of the stricter members of their churches. For local people, it is just the 'strict' and 'Calvinist' members of local churches who are referred to as 'Wee Free'. These are the people who would probably not even cook or watch television on the Sabbath; who would attend both Sabbath services and possibly a prayer meeting during the week; who would, if women or girls, not cut their hair or wear trousers. Not all such 'Wee Frees' are equally liable to be accused of hypocrisy. Those who seem to be aloof or disapproving of others are the most likely targets. All 'strict' or 'hard-line' Presbyterians – and especially the Free Presbyterians (the FPs) – risk such accusations, however, because of the social divisions which their behaviour expresses. In doing what is sometimes referred to as 'putting themselves above other folks' or being 'holier than thou,' they cut themselves off from 'the people'. As one Free Church adherent told me:

> Well, some of the FPs are awful narrow you see . . . and they're putting themselves above other folk. If they're real God-fearing people then they don't need to be shouting about it. It doesn't matter what church you're in . . . what matters is your faith.

As with the accusations of hypocrisy levelled by incomers, it is the emphasis on outward signs rather than genuine religious conviction on which charges of hypocrisy rest. Often anecdotes highlighting hypocrisy tell of an overemphasis upon outward appearances. I was told of FPs who worried more about the colour of the cover of their Bible than its contents; and of church-goers who spent more time thinking about what they would wear for church and commenting on the outfits of others than upon 'their own sins'. One adherent of the Church of Scotland, told me a story about a 'lady visitor' (a holiday-maker) who attended the FP church wearing trousers and no hat:

> And she was probably a good church-going woman away . . . but she was just having a holiday, and they don't mind about things like hats away. But you should have seen the looks she got . . . and the minister preached against her from the pulpit. Imagine! And she just got up and said "I think you're a load of hypocrites" and walked out, and I don't blame her . . . Just because you're not wearing a great big hat and a tweed skirt doesn't mean that you're not a good person.

During my fieldwork I acquired a whole catalogue of such stories. As in this case, they were sometimes told partly to highlight the liberality of the teller's church relative to that of the FPs. Another type of story concerns church-goers who are more in the thrall of the minister than spiritually inspired. They tell, for example, of FPs who would go for a walk on the Sabbath while carefully avoiding the area of the minister's residence, or who would never go to a dance locally but who would do so in more distant places. Such behaviour is condemned not only because of its emphasis upon outward appearances, but also because of its subservience to the 'powers-that-be' in the form of the minister's authority.

A particular body of stories around these themes concerns a character called 'the Wee Doctor', who is identified as a specific person who lived in Carnan between about 1880 and 1950. In one story the Wee Doctor is taking hay out to his livestock on the Sabbath. A minister stops and tells him to remember that the Sabbath is the day of rest. The Wee Doctor asks: 'Do you feed your dog on the Sabbath?' 'Of course' replies the minister. 'And I feed my cattle' replies the Doctor, leaving the minister stuck for words ('He didn't know what to say to that!'). In another story, the Wee Doctor has been to a Free Presbyterian service. When he returns, his wife asks whether he enjoyed the sermon. 'Well, it wasn't based on the Bible at any rate', replies the Doctor, 'I think it was from Great Mills [clothes catalogue] – all the minister talked of was women's clothes'. As with other such anecdotes this is told with great relish for the Wee Doctor's cheek and 'wittiness'. Even the telling of these stories might be said to constitute a kind of opposition itself to the authority of ministers, though it is rather indirect. Take for example the circumstances in which Archy told me the following Wee Doctor story. It was a Friday during the Free Church communion season.[8] Friday is Question Day (*Latha na Ceist*), a day when male prospective communicants must speak to questions before the congregation and I had attended the service with Mary Ann. It had been a very long service as each of the three candidates had stuttered his way in Gaelic to give long scripturally based answers to the question of how the Godhead can be one and three (during which I began to wish they would answer as succinctly as a Holy Fool about whom I had been told who in answer to this question rumpled the fabric of his shirt into three ridges and then let it fall back flat). We had been away for about three hours and when we returned Archy was annoyed about the length of the service: 'It's not right keeping folks so long', he grumbled, 'there's not even a lavatory in the church. It's the ministers trying to get the upper hand on the people and it's not right'. Mary Ann, a communicant, ignored him and busied herself making a meal. While she was out of the room Archy told me the following Wee Doctor joke:

> The Wee Doctor had been taking a drink and he was going along the road when he met the minister coming by in a trap. The minister looked down at him and said, 'You're drunk Ewen'. Ewen replied, quick as a flash, 'You're drunk yourself, you bugger'.

At this point Archy fell into peals of laughter and repeated the punchline several times in English and Gaelic: *Tha deoch ort fhein, a' bhugair.* I confess that I did not find it that funny but Archy's amusement was infectious. He went on to say how 'the men were so witty in those days', the spontaneity of reply always being a highly valued quality of the Wee Doctor's performance. Archy also stressed the 'moral' of the story: 'They didn't let ministers get the upper hand in those days'.

A more direct instance of opposition to church authority in Carnan concerned a conflict over the removal from office of a Free Presbyterian minister by the Church Synod. Although the minister had left before I began fieldwork, the matter was still not fully resolved until an out of court settlement was made in 1986. There was disagreement over the factual details of the case (which have not been published) and local people were divided between those who objected to his removal and those who did not. Those who did not object argued that the Church Synod would not have removed him without good reason and as the details were not fully known it was wrong to question church authority. Those who did question it, however, claimed that the church was overstepping the proper limits of its authority and dealing with areas beyond its remit. It was, they claimed, 'a family matter which should never have entered the church'. They claimed that the real reason for the minister's removal was not really to do with the case anyhow, but was because he was rather liberal for a Free Presbyterian minister. 'He would go round in jeans and a sweater . . . and he wasn't a proud man . . . it didn't matter what church you were from, he'd still stop and have a chat'. To some people it was precisely this liberality that was really at issue: 'They had him earmarked . . . they were just waiting for an excuse'. After he was removed a petition was started by some FPs to have him reinstated. I heard very different estimates of the number of people who had signed though it was clearly not just a single family. The division often ran between siblings and generations; though in no case was a household openly divided. Although it was seen as centrally 'an FP matter' other local people also showed their support for the minister by 'turning out' to help him when he returned to the manse to collect 'his belongings' and by attending a 'farewell function' held at the local school for him later. Many FPs attended, though mostly adherents rather than communicants. One communicant, however, was debarred by the FP church from continuing to take communion for his participation at the farewell function. On account of this affair, about four families left the Free Presbyterian church altogether, some when the minister was first removed and others when he himself finally left the Church to join the Church of Scotland. Unlike the minister, these families all joined the Free Church, as though to state that their disapproval was limited to the specific case rather than to the principles of the stricter churches as a whole. The majority of families, including those who had started the petition, remained in the church, however. They explained their decision to remain by saying that the matter was not serious enough to warrant 'leaving the church that you've always gone to and that your parents went to before you'.

Negotiating Individual Religious Identities

Church membership and attendance, and religious practice more generally, are articulated with the expression of other social identities. On the one hand, the churches are one possible expression of being 'Highland' and of resisting the influence of 'away', on the other, however, becoming a convert may remove an individual from 'the people'. Individuals may have difficulty in reconciling their religious feelings and preferences with other social identities; and these difficulties may be compounded by the

Calvinist ideal of sudden and total conversion, and the changes in life-style which follow from this. The other difficulty for individuals is that, as several local people put it, 'religion is not something we talk about here'. By this, they meant not that people do not talk about church attendance or make Biblical references (as was fairly common) but that individuals have little opportunity to talk about religion except in terms of absolute faith or rejection.

All local Carnan people are affiliated to one or other of the three churches, and people often talk of their church adherence in a kinship idiom – e.g. *eaglais mo cuideachd* (lit. 'church of my side', 'church of my people') – which naturalises the churches as part of the local repertoire. This is partly what makes at least occasional church-going seem inevitable for many people. This is coupled with a local expectation of such attendance. As one Free Presbyterian woman explained: 'It's knowing what people would be saying more than anything. There's plenty that won't bother when they're away'. However, despite the acknowledgement that people may be attending 'for the wrong reasons', non-attendance is usually remarked upon, and those who do not attend may feel that not just their spiritual status but their whole moral status is in question. As another woman put it: 'Some people might think badly of you if you don't go – think you're a bad person or something like that'. Non-attendance may well upset family members. A man in his twenties described himself as 'the black sheep of the family' for not going to church ('I think they accept it now, but they're not pleased'). However, just as attendance may not necessarily indicate strong religious belief, non-attendance does not inevitably entail an atheistic or agnostic position. One non-attender told me that she had simply 'got out of the routine' of going to church on Sundays.

Many people maintain a middle, and largely verbally unexplicated, position on the churches. They go to one – but not both – of the Sunday services, or perhaps attend alternative weeks; and they may attend some but not all of the services during the communion season. In this way, they avoid cutting themselves off from the church and giving offence to relatives and neighbours, but nor do they show themselves ready to become communicants and cut themselves off from many aspects of their worldly lives.

Only a small minority of church adherents become communicants. According to Calvinist doctrine, God's Divine Will can never be truly known. This notion is forcefully expressed in Gaelic through the fact that the same word – *rùn* – is used to mean both 'secret' and 'Will'. Although it is, therefore, unknown whether a person has really received God's grace or not, it is accepted that there are outward signs of 'grace' (*gràs*). The communicant is expected to renounce all vain worldly pleasures such as going to dances, cinemas and the like, to pray and study the Bible regularly and to generally follow an upstanding life-style. The communicant does not, however, renounce worldly life altogether, and indeed it is expected that members of the Elect will follow some worldly 'calling' ordained by God. In Carnan, the more pious religious families are for the most part fairly well-off: their homes are smartly kept and sometimes fairly expensively furnished, and they are 'well turned out' for church. This appearance of evident but restrained wealth is seen as evidence of hard work and following a calling. As a member of one of these families said to me: 'I'm not against people who are poor – I'm not against them at all – it's just if they don't try to better themselves'. Improvement, is seen as a key feature not just of personal identity but of morality, the two being closely intertwined (Taylor 1989).

This emphasis upon improvement is in tension not only with the egalitarian emphasis upon community, but also with the fatalism inherent in Calvinism. If salvation may come to anybody at any time then worldly actions become irrelevant. Certainly, fatalistic expressions, such as 'That's the way it is' (*Sin mar a tha e*) and 'That's the way of the world' (*Sin mar a tha an saoghal*), are used frequently in everyday speech and stricter Presbyterians avoid planning ahead and may preface any comment about the future with the phrase 'If we're spared' (*Ma bhios sinn air ar cùnadh*). However, in practice, the emphasis upon 'improvement' and 'outward signs' means that fatalism is held in check; and individuals negotiate the repertoire of possibilities.

In theory, conversion comes suddenly in life. An archetypical conversion described to me by one man emphasised the fact that he had been 'a drunkard and a blasphemer' until he had a horrifying vision of hell: 'I was right on the precipice, I could have gone over. I just thank the Lord that I was allowed to choose between the Kingdom of Darkness and the Kingdom of Light'. Immediately, his bad habits ceased: he stopped smoking his daily twenty Capstan and ounce of hard tobacco 'just like that' and has never touched a drop of whisky since. An important theme in his account was that even he, 'a simple man,' could receive God's grace:

> And the Lord said, 'all those who have faith in me will be delivered unto the Kingdom of God'. I'm glad I'm not one of those professors who can't understand it because of all their arguments. It's too simple for them . . . I'm glad that I'm simple so that I can understand.

This idea that God's message is, perhaps especially, open to those who do not rely upon reason is sourced by the history of *Na Daoine* in

Presbyterian evangelism and its stories of Holy Fools (Chapter 3). A wall plaque in one Carnan Free Presbyterian home used a Biblical passage to make the same point: 'Trust in the Lord with all thy heart and lean not to thine own understanding' (Proverbs 13). This idea provides, perhaps, one way in which becoming a member of the Elect may be at least partially reconciled with localness, ordinariness and affiliation to 'the people'.

But whilst simplicity and faith may be idealised, individuals need to have a good knowledge of the Scriptures if they are to 'put themselves forward' for communion. All potential communicants are questioned before the Kirk session when they first apply, and men must be prepared to speak to scriptural questions before the congregation on 'Question Day' in the communion season. I was told that men's greater ordeal accounted for the fact that only a third as many men as women are communicants. Also, however, women's lives, which are not so much part of the comradely crofting community as are those of men, are less 'worldly' and require less change of lifestyle. Despite the ideal 'Saul on the road to Damascus' type of conversion, in most cases it is much less dramatic. Communicants tend to be well on in years, and are unlikely to be partaking in many unsuitable activities. After they have been accepted by the Kirk session they will be issued with communion tokens (like coins) to ensure that only accepted communicants partake of the Sacraments.

Each church holds communion twice each year, with two services each day from Thursday evening to midday on Monday. This is known as the communion season or *orduighean*; Each day is named according to the particular stage of preparation or thanks, Sunday being the day on which communion is actually taken (Owen 1956; Parman 1990a). Communicants and non-communicants attend the services, with visitors often attending from other localities. Attendance at communion services makes Adherents aware of belonging to a particular and distinctive way of life and of the possibilities of salvation (Parman 1990a). At the same time, however, they are also made aware of within-community difference, hierarchy and exclusion. For many, it is a time of intensely ambivalent feelings. As one woman told me, 'Yes, I rejoice for those that are saved. But I do feel sad myself for I want to go forward but, well, I don't know, but somehow I am held back'.

This woman was not unusual in feeling reluctant to 'put herself forward'. Her reluctance was not a matter of belief: she was sure that her faith was strong enough. Ministers are well aware of the reluctance of individuals to present themselves for communion. As one put it in a sermon, they are 'backward in coming forward'. Modesty (*nàire*) is a quality instilled from childhood and this makes it difficult for individuals to think themselves 'special' and better. The spatial metaphors that are used to describe becoming a communicant – 'coming forward' – evoke the sense of separation that is involved. 'Putting yourself forward' is equated with 'putting yourself above other folks' which is generally frowned upon and seen to run counter to the ideals of peoplehood. Communicants risk being charged with being aloof and hypocritical. For many individuals, this sets up a tension between modesty and belonging to the people, and finding themselves 'disinherited' (i.e. not 'saved') which they undoubtedly experience as perplexing.

The individual in the Presbyterian Highlands negotiates their own route between the tensions, or different codes, that religion sets up in relation to other dimensions of identity. He or she negotiates the alternative possibilities of self-improvement and of not being 'pushy' or ostentatious; between being 'worthy' through humility or 'worthy' through 'going forward'; between the worldly life of the community and the individual, spiritual life of the Elect; between maintaining the social 'face' of acceptable behaviour and avoiding charges of hypocrisy. He or she also negotiates the line between rejecting church authority and asserting the democratic ethos of Presbyterianism; and between rejecting 'hard-line' Calvinistic principles and rejecting the place of the Highland Presbyterian churches as distinctive of Highland identity.

If Presbyterianism poses dilemmas for individuals, this is not because it is somehow 'alien' to the Highlands as some commentators have suggested. For local people, Presbyterianism is a given in the local repertoire; and individuals inevitably define their own identities in relation to it. What is more, religious identity is thoroughly intertwined with other aspects of identity, and like them is neither uni-dimensional nor contradiction-free.

This is not to say, however, that the 'localness' of the churches and the attempt of so-called 'hard-liners' to speak on behalf of 'the community' is not questioned locally. On the contrary, as we shall see in the next chapter, this may well be contested. However, the fact that there is such contestation, and its means of expression, must be seen as part of the repertoire available for creating new possibilities.

Notes

1. There has also, though more recently, been criticism of some of those involved in Gaelic renaissance — referred to as 'the Gaelic Mafia' — by those who regard them as, among other things, forsaking the Highland churches (MacLeod 1994).
2. This subtitle is taken from the title of a chapter in Parman 1990 which gives further discussion of this subject.
3. This is mainly supported by official surveys on the matter, see Macdonald 1994 (especially fn.15).
4. Some anthropologists make such assumptions too. See, for example, Peter Mewett's labelling of drunkards as 'anti-religious' (1982: 117). Parman discusses ideas about alcoholism and mental illness (1990). See also, Condry 1980 and Ennew 1980.
5. I comment on this further in Macdonald 1994; and include an example of a man who claimed he had not been drinking after consuming several glasses of Bacardi and Coke.
6. The Moderator of the Church of Scotland does have a more exalted position. He is called 'Right Reverend' and ranks for precedence in Scotland next to the Lord Chancellor (Highet 1950: 6).
7. An exhibition about Skye history, called 'The Skye Story,' created by young Gaelic revivalists from the Island, which opened in 1993, contains no substantial reference to the churches despite the fact that it gives a large part of its attention to the nineteenth century. Its aim, however, is to foster a sense of united peoplehood, continuous with the present. See Macdonald 1997 for an analysis.
8. See below for some additional comment and Parman 1990a for a detailed description and discussion of communion in the Highlands.

Part III
Cultural Renaissance

'Culture is not an organism, nor a totality, nor a unity: it is the site of a dialogue, it is a dialectic, a dialect. It is being between' (Cairns Craig, commenting on the Gaelic poet Sorley MacLean, 1996: 206)

In Part I of this book I explored some aspects of Highland history that have been mobilised in the Gaelic renaissance; and argued that these representations of the past configure 'identity' and 'culture' in specific ways. I also argued here, and more fully in Part II, that these are not the only ways in which those living in the Highlands today think about and represent to themselves who they are. These previous chapters have already touched on a number of developments which may be seen as part of the Gaelic renaissance – the *Airigh Shamhraidh* (Summer shielings project), the women's waulking group, the Gaelic media; and Part II has more generally been concerned with the relationship between images of Highland life and self understandings in Carnan during the 1980s Gaelic renaissance. In this third part of the book we turn more explicitly to a number of projects intended to promote the 'revival' of Gaelic language and culture. Chapter 7 considers developments intended to revive 'community': a community hall and cooperative; and Chapter 8, projects intended to foster Gaelic: Gaelic playgroups and Gaelic medium primary education.

In this part of the book I draw on the previous parts to try to show how and why the projects were received as they were. I consider why those in the locality who became involved in revival projects did so, and why some opposed or felt uneasy about them. Gaelic renaissance, and ethnic revival and community development more generally, have often been subject to a good deal of heady optimism from outsiders, and sometimes a sense of disappointment when those who are being 'empowered' in 'their own culture' seem not to welcome the developments with open arms or when the projects do not seem to follow the expected course. My aim here, from the position of an anthropologist, is to try to highlight some of the misunderstandings that were sometimes involved. In doing so – and in voicing some of the sentiments of those whose views tend not to reach a public stage – I hope that this study might be able to help promote a more informed and sensitive dialogue.

7

'From Strength to Strength': Community Revival

Scenes in the life of Carnan community hall:

Inauguration of new Free Church Minister. This is the most packed that I ever see the community hall. Row upon row of tables run across the entire space. At a 'high table' running the length of the hall sit the new minister, the former minister, the elders, the ministers from the other churches and various Free Church elders and their wives. The chairs at the high table are upholstered with orange velvet, those at the other tables are stackable plastic. Not only Free Church members but a few members of the Church of Scotland (though no Free Presbyterians) are there too. There are not enough table places for everybody, so some must sit at the edge of the hall with their plates on their knees. The tables are laid with individual place settings and plates of sandwiches and cakes (scones, butterfly buns, foil-wrapped Swiss rolls) all prepared we are told by 'ladies of the congregation'. Local women, the younger ones dressed in black and white like waitresses, serve tea. There are speeches and prayers given by various of those on the high table. The atmosphere is more that of a wedding party (with the speech about the new minister, recalling some of his wayward habits as a student, highly reminiscent of a best man's speech) than a prayer meeting: jovial rather than pious.

Children's Christmas Party. Nearly twenty children, ranging in age from toddlers to young teenagers, attend the Christmas party. They are dressed in their party best – girls with white tights and glossy ribbons, boys with ties. The hall is chilly and a bit bare, the balloons strewn around look rather lonely, and the music from the tape-recorder is faint and tinny. Perhaps this is why the party seems restrained. Or perhaps it is because the children have been told to be on their best behaviour and not spoil their clothes. Or perhaps it is because the games – pass-the-parcel, musical chairs – are not familiar to all of the children, especially the younger ones, as there is no strong local tradition of children's parties. Or perhaps it is because they are in awe of the beautiful, wealthy and rather famous woman who is running it. She is an incomer though with 'strong Highland ties'; and she regards the party as an opportunity to 'do something for the kids – especially at this time of year'. Christmas is not officially celebrated by Presbyterians[1] and she is aware that an outsider – and one who is 'looked up to, in a way' – is 'more likely to get away with it'. Several local people say that they expect that it will 'go the same way as the Christmas dinner for the old folks' which was held only once. She is unsure whether or not to try to make it into a 'regular thing'.

Ladies Keep-fit.   This evening class is run by an incomer and attended by about a dozen women, mostly middle-aged. We generally stick together in one corner of the hall near to the heaters doing our various exercises in a circle around the tape recorder which plays Jane Fonda. We stretch when we are told to stretch, and look intently at the floor when it comes to squeezing for 'those most important exercises a woman can do'. About half of the women at the group are Gaelic speakers and the others are incomers of various degrees. The latter nearly all wear tracksuits or leotards, whereas none of the former do so. The Gaelic-speaking women also seem more self-conscious and tend to group themselves together, to laugh and to speak Gaelic, in a kind of affirmation of togetherness. When I first arrive – tracksuitless and a bit bedraggled – one of the Gaelic speakers turns to me and says in Gaelic: 'You can come along with us'.

Country Dancing.   The country dancing evening class is held by an elderly quiet Gaelic-speaking man, who learned the dances while away in Glasgow. The majority of those attending are schoolchildren in the older reaches of primary school, though there is a fair smattering too of older people – both incomers and some locals who have spent time away – making about thirty people in all. We charge around, doing our reels and square dances, clapping our hands, and bruising a few toes.

Annual General Meeting of the Community Council.   A table has been set up at one end of the hall for the Committee, and there are also several rows of stackable chairs set out. Alasdair, the leader of the Council is there, as are four of the five present members of the council committee. There should be seven members in all but two posts lie vacant. Unfortunately a quorum of fifteen is needed, so, after noting the apologies and waiting for a while to see if anybody else will turn up, the meeting is disbanded.

The Festival Ceilidh and the Disco. The festival is held for the first time in July 1986 and consists of a week of various activities, such as Highland dancing classes, mostly directed at children. The *Ceilidh* is the *grande finale*, and is hosted by a well-known Skye doctor who is something of a Gaelic-scholar and a great teller of jokes. It features an Irish folk group who have some difficulty with their acoustics, as well as various well-known Skye singers (mostly singing unaccompanied and in Gaelic with lovely clear voices) and players of the clàrsach (mini-harp) and bag-pipes. The hall is about half-full, mainly of tourists, especially back-packers, and of children visiting for the *Airigh Shamhraidh* – a Gaelic holiday for children from the Lowlands. Some of the latter have been persuaded to do a piece in the show. There are a few local people there, mostly those who are related to one or other of the singers, but they are sufficiently few in number for the local press later to lament the fact that 'not a single adult from the Carnan area was there'. Later, after the Ceilidh itself has finished, the disco begins. Big trestle tables, brought by the mobile disco company, are mounted with disco lights and record playing gear. 1970s and 1980s rock begins to pound out. At first, the floor is mainly occupied by younger teenagers, running across the hall, laughing, and now and then breaking out into rather self-parodied dance. Older teenagers and those in their twenties arrive later, some coming from other parts of the Island, and they hang round in the car-park, sharing carry-outs (alcoholic drink purchased from a bar to take away). Inside, they tend to cluster in groups near the walls as there are not enough people to fill the large space of the hall. Couples form and slip away; there are skirmishes in the car park and a car window is broken. The next day older people tut at the sight of the beer cans and shattered glass and there is talk that the hall will not be used for such events again, that the noise and litter are causing 'disturbance to the community', that it is attracting 'trouble-making elements'; and that instead of being a 'public amenity' it is more of a 'public nuisance'. But younger people say that it was a good night, that there was just an accident, not trouble, that it is great to have a place in Carnan itself rather than always having to go further afield, that it is about time that there was something for young people in the area.

Carnan community hall was opened in 1983 and the scenes above briefly describe just some of the activities that the hall was venue to in its first two years. In addition there was the Burns supper, badminton, the youth club, a Highland dancing class, a whist drive, men's keep-fit, several sales-of-work, and the playgroup. Some of these were short lived. Others seemed like they might become a regular part of the social calendar. The number and range of these activities on offer, and the fact that Carnan had seen the building of such a spacious community hall, certainly seemed to be evidence that it was the 'thriving community' of which the media repeatedly talked. Yet in the circumstances and arguments surrounding the construction of the hall, in the practices and arguments surroundings its uses, and in debates about its future, there was also much evidence of community divisions and different ideas about the proper uses of a hall, and of the nature of community, and of Carnan and its people. While on the one hand the hall was an important symbol of community, on the other it was also an arena for playing out divisions within the locality and ambivalences about it.

In this chapter I look at the developments that led to the construction of the community hall and at a number of other community developments, particularly the community cooperative. My aim here is to explore the ways in which the idea of 'community' was mobilised in Carnan; and to look at some of the contrasting visions that this entailed. I argue that the community hall and community cooperative, like the community council which predated them, are not simply *products of* a community but in important ways helped to instantiate the idea of community – and the idea of Carnan as a community. This is not to say, however, that they are forceful impositions from outside nor that the idea of community is somehow alien to local people. On the contrary, there is a complex inter-play between the state and its policies and the locality; and between ideas which have their roots in nineteenth-century romanticism and more local conceptions of belonging as outlined in the previous section of this book. My aim in this chapter and in that which follows, is to try to chart some of this complexity – the varied assumptions, the social differences and tensions, the players, and the ambivalences – involved. Through this, I hope to show that community and Gaelic revival developments in the Highlands should be seen neither as simply products of 'the grass-roots' nor as 'invented traditions' imposed from outwith. Moreover, as in the scenes from the life of the community hall above, and discussed further below, there is by no means a uniform 'response' within the so-called 'community'.

On Being a Community

As I have noted in the introduction, there has been a significant current in the anthropology of Europe which is critical of the use of 'community' and its implicit or explicit contrast with 'society'. Communities, according to this critique, have been conjured up in the academic as well as the romantic and popular imagination as places of close face-to-face relationships free from the stress and alienation of 'modern society'. Communities have been assumed to 'be traditional', to 'have' 'culture', 'heritage' and 'authenticity', to be 'integrated' and homogeneous, and to be 'meaningful' to their members. Within such a set of assumptions, it is then easy – and often incorrect – to assume that local practices are necessarily traditional, and that diverse views within the community and disagreements, as well as 'modern' practices, are a consequence of the malign hand of modernity.

Alongside, and partly inspired by the romantic conception of communities as part of a fast disappearing traditional way of life is a community development conception of communities as authentic 'grass-roots' social groupings. Communities, according to this conception, are not necessarily traditional but they are 'authentic' social groupings in so far as they are assumed to share a common set of characteristics based upon a common experience which place them in a position of structural disadvantage relative to the state. It is in this sense that labels such as 'the Black community' or 'the gay community', as well as 'rural communities' or 'the Gaelic community', are used. Like the traditionalist conception of community, however, this 'grass-roots' conception tends to assume that communities will have a common viewpoint and that, given the means, they will naturally campaign to improve the position of their whole 'community'. The fact that communities recognised by community developers are not already campaigning is regarded as evidence that they require 'empowerment' to act as such. Providing the barriers to effective action are removed, communities are usually expected to want to be self-governing and to be more effective providers for their members.

In this chapter I look at the way that such conceptions of community play out in relation to community developments within Carnan. While I am in broad agreement with the anthropological critique of community argument that we need to avoid reifying nostalgic and idealist assumptions about 'community' I do not believe that the answer is to avoid the term, and anything which might possibly constitute a 'community' altogether. On the contrary, I argue that we need to recognise that 'community' is an extremely salient and powerful notion in the modern world, and to explore its appropriations and effects. Also, as I have been arguing throughout this book, in attempting to avoid assuming rather than analytically exploring romantic notions, we must beware that we do not also disregard the locally specific or features of local life which might previously have been characterised by terms such as 'community'.

As I have noted in Chapter 5, the idea of Carnan as a 'community' or indeed even as a bounded geographical area, was a fairly recent one to

Carnan people and many of them still expressed uncertainty about it and rarely used it to refer to themselves. At the same time, however, Carnan was increasingly frequently mentioned in the local media – the press and radio in particular – not just as a geographical area but as 'the Carnan community'. In the mid-1980s when I began my research these phrases did not slip easily off most Carnan tongues, though the local activists who were invited to speak on the radio seemed increasingly to use them with facility particularly when they were discussing new developments such as the community hall and community cooperative.

Officially, Carnan had been a recognised community, with designated geographical boundaries, since it gained its own community council in 1976. This was an outcome of an Act of Parliament of 1973 and was intended to provide a forum for expressing views within the community and, although the council lacked any statutory powers of its own, the idea was that it would be able to initiate action at the district or regional level where appropriate. However, while the community council was envisaged by the policy-makers who devised it to be closer to the grass-roots of the community, I found that most people in Carnan were unsure of its remit, of its members (with the exception of its leader), of how many committee members it had, or of how and how often representatives were elected. Nevertheless, the community council was often consulted by outside agencies over development plans in Carnan – for example, plans for a new road, and for the community cooperative – and local people did sometimes attempt to get the council to initiate action, as in the case of the community hall described below and as it did over such matters as getting an extension for a burial ground. As we shall see, however, the community council was by no means an unproblematic representative body of 'the community'.

While the official designation of Carnan as a community was fairly recent, it did make sense as a geographical entity for, although long and straggling and far from the image of a clustered nucleated community, it represented a fairly discrete collection of settlements and as numbers of people living in the townships declined and car ownership increased it made increasing sense to share services (e.g. the primary schools, the churches, the doctor's surgery, a petrol station and several small shops and post offices). Indeed, this concentration of services was something which had been underway for some time: in the 1940s, for example, there were nineteen shops within the area, but by the early nineteen-eighties there were only two. During the 1980s the creation of the community hall with the community shop (providing Carnan's first supermarket style shop), craft shop and cafe all run by the community cooperative, gave a considerably strengthened sense of a centre to the area. Proposals, since realised, to amalgamate Carnan's two primary schools into one which would be located near to the hall reinforced this further. Moreover, the many events and clubs held in the community hall came, often by default, to be regarded as belonging specifically to *Carnan*, e.g. in relationships with other youth clubs, that run in the community hall became Carnan Youth Club.

Carnan, then, was rapidly gaining a sense of itself as a community and the terms in which the media spoke of the area – e.g. '*the* Carnan community', 'a thriving community' – were beginning to slip into everyday self reference. This was a spiralling process in which the idea of being a community was invoked in order to argue for more facilities to operate *as* a community (it was this kind of argument which was of great rhetorical force in arguments for a community hall), and this in turn furthered the realisation of the area as a community. Yet this realisation was by no means complete and it did not entail the full baggage of either the traditionalist or the grass-roots conception of community, though there were various attempts to activate both of these. Alongside the growing use of the term 'community' was also what is probably its inevitable *alter*: a sense of the area as a 'failed' community, as one which somehow did not manage to live up to the community expectations. Such views were part of the more general ambivalence about the locality and belonging which we have outlined in earlier chapters, ambivalence which might be voiced by a single speaker.

Below I look in more detail at the campaigns and arguments which surrounded the development and running of the community hall and the community cooperative. I attempt to show here the contrasting views of 'community' which were invoked, the social cleavages and alternative understandings which these encountered, and local conceptions of social relations – as discussed in the previous part of this book – which played a part in this 'meeting'.

Agitating for a Hall

The 'meeting' between the state and the locality is also one that involves particular individuals, especially those who I refer to as 'local activists'. These are the people who are sometimes regarded in community development literature as the voice of 'the grass roots'. However, this is not necessarily the case and instead of being fully part of or representative of everybody else within the community, they may well be 'set apart' in

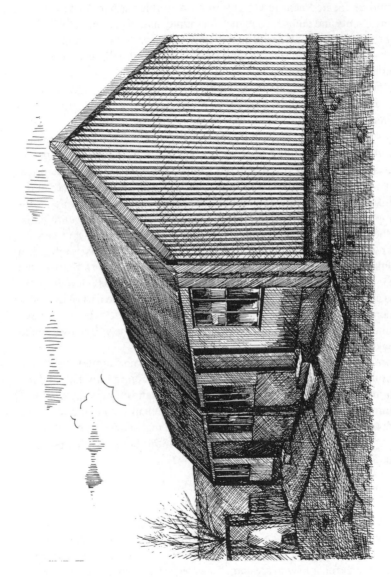

Figure 7.1. General store (by Julie White)

various ways and their action may serve to both further set them apart and bring them into conflict with others within the community.

In the developments leading to the construction of the community hall a local Gaelic-speaking woman called Catriona was particularly active and the following is a description of events leading up to the construction of the hall based on her account. Catriona had married into the area from a neighbouring part of the Island and, now in her early forties with two teenage children, had spent some time away in her late teens and early twenties training at catering college in Glasgow. Catriona's involvement in the moves to develop a hall stemmed from her involvement in the youth club of which her children were members at the time. The youth club met in the school but were encountering problems over the use of the room because of alleged 'vandalism' (which Catriona said were minor breakages due to forty teenagers being crammed into one old domestic science room) and disagreements with elders in the Free Church and the Free Presbyterian Church over the running of the youth club. The community council which administered the use of the school on behalf of the education department were asked by some elders to stop the use of the school for the club. Catriona, herself a member (by marriage) of the Church of Scotland, was very annoyed about the interference and what she saw as misconstruals of the youth club activities. In particular, a youth club visit to Aviemore had been seen as 'inappropriately' bringing together boys and girls, although Catriona claimed that they were in separate dormitories and the churches had entirely misinterpreted the trip. The school room was also 'too small, with no facilities, and we wanted somewhere of our own'. It seemed to Catriona quite obvious that 'we should have a community hall. It was a real lack not to have one. Just look around and you can see even little places like ... with a place for meetings and that'.

Catriona also discovered that there was already a fund which had been started with money left by a school headmaster in the 'early 1900s' for some kind of community hall. She talks about this, in tones which echo those discussed in Chapter 3 in particular, as a 'time of great community spirit'. However, opposition from the churches had stopped the developments, though they were resuscitated again in the early 1930s when 'there were halls being built all over the island' and initial plans for a hall were drawn up. Again, however, opposition from the churches prevented the actual building of the hall and the outbreak of the Second World War put everything on ice. Catriona's account emphasises the longstanding nature of community and desire for a hall, and the repeated opposition from the churches. Also, however, she regards the provision of a hall as a sign of development: 'Ever since I can remember, people talking about it felt backward because they didn't have a hall'. After the difficulties with the youth club Catriona determined 'I'll get a hall for Carnan if it's the last thing I do'.

She went to the community council to ask them to act on the matter. According to her account she was told that it was 'nothing to do with us' because, she thought, 'they didn't want to be involved in any come-back'. We should note that several of those on the community council at that time were church elders and had themselves been involved in the concern about the youth club trip. However, the council agreed that she could hold a public meeting about the matter. She contacted the Citizens Advice Bureau, the secretary for Social Services in the Highland Region and the community education officer for advice. Her meeting was attended by about a hundred people 'all in favour' and a committee was formed to organise fund-raising. The following Sunday, however, the Free Presbyterian minister 'preached against it' and referred to the prospective hall as a likely 'den of iniquity' and to 'the influence of Satan'. Four of those on the committee who were Free Presbyterians resigned from the committee but they were replaced and fund-raising began. Within a year £7000 had been raised.

It was at this point, late in 1980, that the committee was contacted by the HIDB with the suggestion that they couple their plans for a hall with a community cooperative. This would mean that the Board would match local funding 'pound for pound'. This was an attractive proposition financially; and various plans were drawn up, with the assistance of the HIDB, for 'economically viable projects'.[2] These included a restaurant and a craft shop and later an agricultural supplies shop. In addition to fund-raising via sales-of-work, sponsored walks and even a clay pigeon shoot, those living in Carnan were invited to buy shares in the cooperative (as was the case in other cooperatives) and by May 1983 a shareholders' newsletter stated that £28,000 had been raised, and 150 people had become shareholders; a higher *per capita* amount than in any other cooperative area (*MacTalla* [shareholders' newsletter] May 1983; cf. Breathnach 1984: 4). By now the enterprise had spiralled well beyond original intentions and the Scottish Education Department and Highland Regional Council, as well as the HIDB, contributed substantial sums to what had become a £160,000 project.

In 1983 the hall was opened and a manager – to be paid for by the HIDB for the first three years – was appointed to run the community cooperative. This manager was a young Gaelic-speaking local man who had undertaken management training away. His appointment was highly symbolic of the sense of the hall and cooperative as a marker of the revitalisation of the local community for he was a member of a group of educated young Gaels who had nearly always in the past ended up leaving the area in order to find employment. Not only had he been induced to stay, however, he was also a former member of the youth club whose troubles had first sparked the moves leading to the construction of the hall and the cooperative.

The coupling of the plans for a hall with that of a community co-operative transformed the project from a campaign for a local amenity into an enterprise which was much more thoroughly part of the Gaelic renaissance. While the cooperative movement in the Scottish Highlands did not foreground Gaelic language issues nearly so strongly as was the case in the Irish *Gaeltacht*, it was seen as part of a package of developments which might play a part in helping to stem Gaelic language decline. In Ireland, Gaelic language activists, often from outside the areas, played a large part in instigating the development of cooperatives (Breathnach 1984).[3] And while in the Scottish Highlands language activists were not so much involved and the development of cooperatives was more likely to come at the initial suggestion of state agencies (i.e. the Board) than from activists 'on the ground', cooperatives were widely seen as *Gaelic* developments; and it was on this basis in part that the Scottish Education Department was induced to contribute to the hall and cooperative funding. Indeed, in Carnan the cooperative was virtually always referred to by its Gaelic name of *co-chomunn* in both Gaelic and English speech. Yet the 'Gaelicness' of the project – and practical matters such as whether those employed should be Gaelic speakers or not and whether Gaelic events should be specifically sponsored – was ambivalently regarded and became one of the sources of tension surrounding the hall and *co-chomunn* as I discuss further below. First, however, I look further at the persons, events and cultural practices involved in the campaign for the hall.

Actors and Actions

Catriona's activism and the success she had in mobilising local people was very unusual in Carnan as she, and a number of other people, pointed out. 'Most can't be bothered' she told me, and – in words echoing those used of religious adherents – 'they don't want to put themselves forward'. Many social and political activities are poorly supported locally and are often short lived for this reason, and at elections candidates are often uncontested and returned time after time. Why should people generally be unwilling to be politically active and what made Catriona and the case of the community hall different?

Very often those who are elected to political positions are 'strangers' within the community in some sense: if not necessarily incomers they may be 'set apart' for some reason, such as having relatively few kinship links in the area. To some extent, this 'strangerhood' is a quality that may be evoked *post hoc* (cf. Frankenberg 1989: 18) – evidence for it only being sought out and expressed when local people wish to disassociate themselves from those who have accepted political positions. For this reason, complaints about local (including district and regional) political figures were often accompanied by statements about them being 'out of touch' and 'not really of the place'. At the same time, however, those participating in politics did seem to be particularly likely to be 'set apart' in some sense, and, moreover, to have some alternative domain of life from which to derive their authority. In particular, those who stood for public office were unlikely to be fully part of the crofting world of men, as described in Chapter 4: for example, those who stood as councillors were often church elders or professional men. These are people who have already 'put themselves forward' and separated themselves from other local people to some extent. That is, they have already put themselves into a position which might be interpreted as an attempt at social climbing and pride (*pròis*), which brings with it the danger of 'falling' and being 'ashamed'. Another reason for reluctance to stand for public office is that those who come to take on positions of power or responsibility readily find themselves accused of matters such as favouring relatives or one section of the 'community' over others; and they know that they are likely to be objects of suspicion and gossip (many of those involved in such positions made comments to me such as: 'I know there's talk behind my back but I've grown thick-skinned, you have to'). Those who take on political roles within the locality, then, are generally not regarded as straightforwardly representative of the 'grass-roots' and are likely to be seen, and to see themselves, as not necessarily thoroughly 'of the community'.

Most public positions are held by men. In the first eight years of the community council only one of its seven positions had been held by a woman, and the district and regional councillors were both men. Given that it is men who are not fully part of the crofting world of men who are more likely to stand for public office, and given that women tend to be conceptualised as not thoroughly part of this crofting world and even as more likely to be the agents of social mobility, we might expect women to take on public roles. However, they do not do so for a number of reasons. First, the social mobility with which women tend to be associated is regarded much less favourably than the rhetoric of egalitarianism. As we have seen, the former is inclined to be mapped on to ideas about 'away' and the latter to the more noble source of 'the people' and the crofting wars. In many ways, the very fact that women are more readily associated with mobility forms a greater barrier to their participation, for their actions are more likely to be interpreted as not fully 'for the people'.[4] Second, women will only be 'the head of the household' (*ceannard an taighe*) where there is no adult man; and, as we have seen, households are expected to have a united 'face' in public and the head of the household to speak on behalf of its members. Significantly, the one female member of the community council was a single parent and, therefore, herself a head of household.

Catrìona's actions, then, were unusual both in the extent to which she succeeded in mobilising local people, in the fact that she was an Islander, and in the fact that she was a woman. However, her participation was made more acceptable by the fact that her activism had emerged from her involvement in an issue concerned with children, i.e. the youth club. This was the case too for other women, including the community councillor above to some extent, and the women involved in the Gaelic playgroup discussed in the following chapter. These women's actions, insofar as they were concerned with children's welfare, could be seen as an extension of their domestic role, and indeed this was something which they all seemed to be keen to stress. Catrìona often talked of the cooperative running a café where there would be 'good plain home cooking', so again linking her participation to domestic and even traditional concerns. At the same time she was particularly animated by her frustration with the stricter churches and the criticism which she felt was being made of her in relation to her running of the youth club. Her strategy was to mobilise a notion of community which projected back into the past and had long had to do battle with the stricter churches. In so doing, she used the past and the idea of an earlier 'great community spirit' to legitimate her efforts in reviving community, and to imply that this, rather than the strict churches (which as we have seen often made their case through the idiom of 'trad-ition') was more authentic to the locality. This vision of community drew in part on the language of the community development officers and others with whom she consulted but it was also informed by ideas about 'the people' and local ambivalence about the churches. And in articulating and projecting this vision, Catrìona was very adept. On one occasion, after she had told me of her own worries about the direction in which the hall and cooperative were going, I later heard her on the radio talking very engagingly about how successful Carnan community cooperative was and how it was going 'from strength to strength' (a phrase which, in English and Gaelic, seemed to become especially associated with 'Carnan community' and with the cooperative in particular).

Others within the locality were mobilised by Catriona no doubt partly on account of their shared view that there should be a hall, but also because she so successfully managed to present it as something which local people had a right to and were 'backward' without. In formulating it in this way, Catriona tapped into local people's longstanding concerns that they might be seen as less advanced than others. A community hall, then, was effectively articulated as both a link to a past 'great spirit of community' and also to modernity.

Catriona was also well aware of the local reluctance to take a lead in community action but understood that this did not mean that local people could not be enlisted to participate. Helping out with fundraising was a well-established part of local life and Catriona managed to present the campaign for the hall as a *charitable* concern: 'doing something for the youngsters', as many people expressed it. Fundraising also became a matter of somewhat competitive local pride and here again this linked in to existing practices, in this case of charitable giving. The Presbyterian Hebrides as a whole pride themselves on the way in which their church collections are always considerably higher *per capita* than elsewhere in the country, and at the way in which in national collections for charity, such as the *Children in Need* appeal, they generally raise exceptionally large sums. Individuals often spend large amounts of money at sales intended for charity: one crofter, for example, told me that he had spent over £300 at one sale-of-work alone. Such high levels of spending were described to me by a government official as 'like a potlatch', and indeed it does seem that personal status and prestige can be enhanced by generous giving. Contributions to charity are one of the few forms of conspicuous consumption in which local people can freely indulge, for unlike individual consumerism this is not restricted by the taint of immorality. Moreover, giving is much more public than it is in many places: when door-to-door collections are made in Carnan, contributors are asked to sign their names in a notebook together with the amount of money that they have donated. Likewise, in the Church of Scotland and Free Church, contributions to the collection are made in individual envelopes, named or numbered for each household. Large donations to charity are usually widely discussed and admired. Fundraising in Carnan was so successful, then, not simply on account of the fact that all those who gave money were especially motivated by the prospect of a community hall and community cooperative, but also because the organisers managed very effectively to draw on an existing practice of charitable concern and competitive giving.

Figure 7.2. Carnan Co-chomunn (by Julie White)

'Grass-roots' and 'the powers-that-be'

Given the extremely large amount of money raised and the extensive work put in by the organisers, it is not surprising that the Carnan effort was widely taken as 'a fine example of what can be achieved' (*Community Enterprise*, n.d., no. 1: 15). With the exception of the Free Presbyterian Church, which was dismissed in a shareholders' newsletter as 'a small but vocal minority', the project looked as though it commanded widespread support and enthusiasm. Perhaps because of high expectations surrounding it, perceived difficulties over the hall and *co-chomunn* soon arose and these were the subject of much discussion locally during the period of my fieldwork. Rumours and allegations of financial crisis, of 'underhand' operations, and of 'disruptive' uses of the hall (such as the disco) were widespread, and some locals began to suggest that the co-operative had 'lost its way' (*MacTalla* Winter 1983), and even to argue that 'the Board should step in and sort it all out'.

My intention here is not to try to evaluate the success of the project or go into detail about the organisation and disputes surrounding particular developments but to look at some of the perceptions of the different groups involved, perceptions which were often rooted in past experience. This highlights some of the misunderstandings about the nature of the cooperative and of the community which led to a sense of the hall and cooperative as less successful than they had originally seemed to be.

For the HIDB, Carnan had looked in many ways like a model community: the fundraising had been impressive and there seemed to be a good deal of youth and dynamism in the area. A scheme for founding community cooperatives had been begun in the Highlands and Islands by the HIDB in 1977 (Storey 1979: 1). Modelled on the Irish community cooperative movement, the Board was aware that the Scottish case was different in various respects and that therefore the development should be 'experimental' and continuously open to feedback (Storey 1979: 10). Crucial to the scheme, however, was the idea that as much of the impetus and input as possible should 'come from the communities themselves': community cooperatives were not to be imposed from outside. The role of the Board was not to run the cooperative or to try to direct its affairs but to act as an 'enabler' for the community. Indeed, from the perspective of the Board, effecting a cultural change among local people seemed to be as significant as the possible economic benefits of cooperatives. As the Chairman of the HIDB remarked in 1978:

I believe that the value of such community activity lies as much in what it can do for morale and self-confidence as in its direct economic impact . . . A collective or community approach to development can foster self-confidence and a spirit of independence within the community by demonstrating that progress can be made under local leadership and need not lean so heavily upon outside influence and help (Alexander, quoted in Hunter 1991: 170–1)

Many local people, however, seemed to regard the Board and its role very differently. Many indeed seemed to regard the *co-chomunn* not as a 'grass-roots' enterprise but as a Board project. In doing so, they drew upon their longstanding perception of the Board as part of 'the powers-that-be', and a longstanding perception of the Highlands as subject to experimental enterprises by such outside powers.[5] Like other 'powers-that-be', the Board was mostly conceptualised as opposed to 'the people' – as part of an interfering bureaucracy emanating from 'away'. At the same time, however, in a relationship also shaped by the history discussed in Chapter 3, the Board was envisaged as a patron; and, as such, there was a degree of expectation among local people that the Board would act as a provider. This was not simply a matter of a lazy local passivity, however, as some outside officials bemoaned ('they sometimes seem to just expect everything to be done for them' complained one), but out of a sense of historical and contemporary justice – reparation for previous failed promises (that soldiers returning from the war in the 1940s had not been given crofts as they believed they had been promised was still often given as an example of the untrustworthiness of the powers-that-be), and because they saw other parts of the United Kingdom to have much better amenities by comparison with their own.

The Board was seen by local people not as a changing organisation but as a continuous entity; and as dissatisfaction grew in some quarters over the *co-chomunn*, instances of what were perceived as past 'favouritism' by the Board were cited as evidence of the partisan nature of the project. Some Free Presbyterians, for example, claimed that the Board was 'against' the church and what they referred to as 'forces of tradition'; and they substantiated this with an example of the Board failing to give a Free Presbyterian hotelier financial assistance because he would not open his hotel on Sundays or serve alcohol. From the Board point of view, the decision would have been made on the 'objective' criteria of the economic viability of the proposal; but by those involved it was seen as reason for the Board to be considered 'underhand by God-fearing people'. Likewise, a family of shopkeepers who were angry at the *co-chomunn* starting up a shop which competed with theirs, after they believed they had been assured that the *co-chomunn* would not do anything to damage existing businesses, argued that the Board was only interested in large-scale enterprises or those suggested by incomers; and as evidence they cited both the large costs that the *co-chomunn* and hall had incurred and their own experience of failing to be supported in a proposal to build holiday chalets (whereas incomers had succeeded in this elsewhere previously). Of the latter, a Board official told me: 'But chalets might be the flavour of the month one month and out of fashion the next'.

The Board, then, regarded itself as an evolving organisation which would constantly review its practices and change them where necessary. That it behaved in one way in the past was not seen as a reason why it should necessarily act in the same way in the future and indeed this would probably have been at odds with the notion of a dynamic and successful development agency. Moreover, those working within the Board were also much more likely to see particular development policies as linked to specific internal organisational directives and members of the organisation at particular times. This all contrasted markedly with local perceptions of the Board as a single and continuous agency and with local people's reasoning in terms of previous instances creating future entailment. The Board also saw itself as 'objective' in its treatment of proposals. 'It makes no difference to us whether it is locals or incomers' one Board member told me, while acknowledging that incomers often seemed to be more likely to come up with proposals which looked more viable. Local people, however, were more likely to regard the Board's decisions – because they did not seem to necessarily follow from previous practice – as linked to social decisions about the applicants. Incomers they saw as being favoured *as incomers*, Free Presbyterians disfavoured *as Free Presbyterians*. That is, they interpreted the Board's actions in terms of social judgements and entailments; and therefore they were on the look-out for social patterns in the decisions made by the Board in terms of, for example, favouring particular families or particular segments of the population. Such accusations were mostly surprising to the Board who tended to regard themselves as trying to help the whole *community*; and who often seemed to despair over the social divisions and disputes that they encountered. Describing local people, one Board official told me: 'They're like the Mafia. Turn around for one minute and there'd be a dagger in your back'. His analogy depicted local people as foreign and secretive, and motivated by feuds which were often opaque to outsiders. An incomer made the same analogy to me, complaining that local decisions were often made not on the basis of 'objective' criteria but in terms of social connections: 'round here it's not what you know, it's who you know'. The Board and incomers, then, tended to expect matters such as the allocation of funds and jobs to be disconnected from social relations; local people, however, were much more likely to perceive events as entailing such relations.

In the dealings over the *co-chomunn* the Board was particularly keen to take what one official described to me as 'a hands-off approach' as far as possible. This was, after all, a key part of the idea of community empowerment. However, partly because the *co-chomunn* manager was funded directly by the HIDB, many local people seemed to regard the Board as ultimately in control and the manager as in effect working for the Board. When the *co-chomunn* decided to set up a grocery store, then, this was seen by some locally as a decision probably instigated, or at the very least supported, by the Board, and accordingly it was to the Board that they made their complaints. The Board, however, was reluctant to 'step in and sort it all out' as the plaintiffs wanted because they were operating with a model in which matters should be resolved at a *community* level. To those who felt damaged by the grocery store, however, the Board seemed to be dragging its feet because it was in favour of the *co-chomunn* store and was probably just waiting for the family store to go out of business.

The other major local cause of concern over the *co-chomunn* concerned its finances. According to the financial returns of 1985 there was a deficit of £28,000. This was widely seen as disastrous by local people; though I found that the Board regarded it as a fairly small 'operating deficit' and as not at all unhealthy by comparison with other *co-chomuinn*. However, the deficit occurred at a time too when many of the social activities that had previously been held in the hall had been withdrawn: after various instances of 'vandalism' (or 'accidents' by youths 'messing about') the hall ceased to be freely available throughout the day and evening to young people in the area and pool tables were removed; dances were held only infrequently; events such as the Christmas dinner of 1983 were not repeated; and charges were levied for the use of the hall to the protest of various local groups. Altogether, this created a good deal of fear about the future of the hall and a sense that it had failed to live up to its original expectations. Even some of those who had originally played a part in campaigning for the hall, such as Catriona, expressed concern that the project had got 'out of hand' and had lost track of its original objectives. Catriona began to say locally that the locality had never wanted a *co-chomunn* or a hall which would have to make money and that they had been unduly pressured along this path by the HIDB (though at the same time she 'spoke up' the *co-chomunn* when invited to speak on the radio or when interviewed for the press).

Alongside the withdrawal of activities, were also complaints – particularly from incomers – about local people failing to participate in many of those which did run, especially some of those which seemed more specifically directed at regenerating local *Gaelic culture*, such as the Gaelic festival and its ceilidh. Accusations of local 'apathy' seem to be quite common in rural areas (cf. Frankenberg 1989, Strathern 1981), especially from 'incomers' who are often likely to try to initiate social activities which they perceive to be lacking. In part, this sense of community *manqué* is a consequence of expectations that people are particularly likely to participate in activities within a rural area both because it is assumed that participation is linked to a sense of belonging and sometimes too because it is assumed that people living in rural areas have more time on their hands to fill with social activities. One incomer woman whose society had foundered told me: 'You'd think they'd want to be involved. It's not as though people don't know each other... I really don't know what they all think they're so busy doing that they can't find the time to come along'. Yet given the size of the population and the number of social activities available, participation is not particularly low. Moreover, some activities – such as the ceilidh – are often regarded by locals as more directed at outsiders and tourists, sometimes on account of such matters as the time at which they are run. Of the festival ceilidh, I was told that it was ridiculous to expect local people to be sitting inside listening to 'some youngsters playing the pipes' at a time of the evening when it was still light enough to be getting the hay in.

In the frustrations over the hall and some of the attempts to deal with the financial crisis, incomers seemed to become a particular target. One incomer who worked part time in the *co-chomunn* shop felt that she was being personally hassled by the youths who had been debarred from the hall after the vandalism. They would, for example, come and ask to have the toilets unlocked and then not come out for ages. They would also speak Gaelic, she said, in a way which she felt was to highlight their difference from her and to make it impossible for her to understand them. Another incomer was sacked, supposedly because of the financial deficit; but shortly afterwards a more local man was employed in his place. A member of the *co-chomunn* committee told me that she was fed up with incomers coming in and taking the jobs and that the point of the cooperative was to employ 'locals not incomers'. Incomers were, then, rhetorically useful to blame for the difficulties. But the employment of local people was not without its difficulties either, mainly because of accusations of favouring relatives. And while the favouritism of relatives was viewed critically at one level, at another it was assumed – and to some extent even seen as acceptable – that it would go on. The hall manager told me that he had grown tired of people coming to him with requests on the basis of their kinship relations: 'You just can't operate a business like that', he told me, 'But, yes, I know I've put a few backs up'. Not acceding to a request was always likely to be interpreted as a personal offence even if he emphasised his aim to be 'objective'; and, of course, emphasising the latter could also support local people's suspicions that he was really being directed by the Board. He clearly felt that he was in something of a no-win situation for he would be criticised whether he was partisan or not. In 1986, then, when his initial contract came to an end, he decided to move on. Significantly, the *co-chomunn* shareholders selected an outsider – a Lowland Scot – to fill the post. This was explained to me as 'a new broom – a clean sweep', somebody who would not be involved in any of the previous disputes or in local kinship networks. It might also be speculated that here was somebody who, as an incomer, would be more easily expedient if there were criticisms to be made than was a young, local Gaelic speaker.

The filling of the post by an outsider was, however, something of a blow to the ideals of a 'grass-roots' 'local' 'community enterprise' that the cooperative movement had been intended to foster. Yet it would be a mistake to see it as evidence, therefore, that Carnan was somehow especially 'dysfunctional' or that it had lost touch with the kind of values which had once motivated 'a great community spirit'. In a way, as Franken-berg argued long ago in his study of a Welsh village (1989 [1957]), the appointment of 'strangers' to positions of responsibility is rather an effective strategy for dealing with the dilemmas of leadership within a community and should not, therefore, be taken as a sign of community pathology. So too, the identification of 'incomers' with the problems the *co-chomunn* was encountering was not so much evidence that incomers were the *cause* of the problems as part of a longstanding means of arti-culating and affirming 'localness'. Moreover, many of the social divisions which came to the fore in the disagreements over the *co-chomunn* were ones which had been part of the dynamic of local social life for a long time: divisions between churches and between households. And while there was talk, as from Catriona, about a 'past great spirit of community', this should be seen – as should her talk on the radio of the community going 'from strength to strength' – not so much as an unproblematic statement of fact, as a rhetorical strategy to *produce* community.

In the mid-1980s, then, Carnan was very much seen as a community undergoing revival; and developments such as the community hall and *co-chomunn* were a key part of this. Yet, while the developments were shaped in many respects by often longstanding local perceptions and practices, *revival* was not simply about 'awakening' an already existing but slumbering 'community'. It was also about creating something new; which in this case included the notion of this particular area as a community.

The revival or renaissance process was one which involved an interplay between external state agencies – especially the HIDB – and local aspirations and practices. It was also a process in which particular individuals – 'local activists' such as Catriona – played an important part; and in which locals mobilised the notion of 'community' as a means of acquiring amenities. To 'be a community' was, without doubt, of considerable strategic advantage for a locality in dealing with external agencies. As we have seen, however, the different players involved often held different visions of 'community' and expectations of the revival projects; and these visions were themselves sometimes a source of the difficulties which arose.

The fact that Carnan was a strongly Gaelic-speaking locality was frequently remarked upon in media commentaries on the success of the *co-chomunn*. Carnan was not simply 'a community': it was a 'Gaelic community'. In the following chapter I explore this in more detail through focusing on some of the developments aimed at reviving Gaelic use, particularly among the young, in Carnan.

Notes

1. Though people with children almost always do celebrate Christmas by having Christmas stockings for the children. There are, however, no church services at Christmas or celebration of Christmas as a Christian festival.

2. The HIDB has acted as a channel for various European funding in the crofting areas of Scotland. That available in this case was not from such a source though at the time there was speculation that this was the sort of project for which European funding might become available. Indirectly, therefore, a looking to Europe was involved here. See Hunter 1991: 167–72.

3. The Irish situation was also different from that of the Scottish in that in Ireland there was a much stronger 'degree of politicisation and

popular conscientisation' (Breathnach 1984: 3) associated with Gaelic and the *Gaeltacht* civil rights movement; also, priests often took on leadership roles in the establishment of the cooperatives (ibid.; McDyer 1968).

4. We should note that this is not simply an opposition between public and private in which women are restricted to the latter. Rather, both the domestic arena and the world of crofting are regarded as distinct from the world of public office, which tends to be associated with 'the powers-that-be' rather than 'the people'.

5. This has been commented on by various anthropologists writing of the Highlands: e.g. Parman 1972, 1990; Condry 1980; Ennew 1980; Ardener 1989 (ch.14).

8

'Saving the Gaelic': Language Revival and Identity

Seumas is about forty years old and was born in Carnan. He began school with 'scarcely a word of English' and most of his daily conversations – with family and friends – are in Gaelic. He listens to the Gaelic radio every day, chats in the local shop and post office mainly in Gaelic and generally attends the Gaelic church services. Seumas himself might be thought of as a kind of 'last bastion' of Gaelic for he is somebody who has had ample opportunity to switch to English but has not done so. He was brought up at a time when there were no pro-Gaelic policies in the area, when there were no Gaelic playgroups or festivals, when English was the medium of all schooling and Gaelic only taught as a minor subject of study, when there was no Gaelic television and very little Gaelic radio. Gaelic then was not fashionable 'away', Gaelic speakers on the mainland were derogatorily called 'teuchtars' and, even in the island capital, Gaelic was regarded as *an cànan an t-sitig* – the language of the midden. Seumas himself has spent a good deal of time away from Carnan, working in the merchant navy and then on the oil rigs, sometimes for stretches of several years at a time. He is fully proficient in English and reads and writes it more easily than he does Gaelic. Nevertheless, Gaelic is the language that he speaks for much of the time.

One day, after Seumas and I have chatted for a while about how the new road is coming along, and I have asked him about his various times of working away from the Island and about whether he got much chance to speak Gaelic, he talks of the changes that he perceives with regard to Gaelic and his own views on the matter:

Now it's becoming the in-thing to have the Gaelic – it's becoming posh. . . And now, you see, there's people like yourself learning it and coming here. And there's others from the universities and, well, people like Iain Noble in Sleat – they go all in for the Gaelic. But you see, they're extremists don't you think? It's all right for them. But for me, well, Gaelic hasn't held me back but

217

it hasn't helped me any, and I wouldn't have got far with nothing but the Gaelic.

He goes on to say that in 'university circles' it is becoming 'the done thing' to try to get your child to speak some Gaelic: 'it's becoming middle-class and posh'. He tells me about a radio item he heard about a Gaelic-learner couple in Edinburgh who, after having been learning Gaelic for about five years, had apparently brought up their child with nothing but Gaelic. This had been given a good deal of publicity recently on the Gaelic media as evidence of what could be done with dedication. However, Seumas was very uneasy about it, as were some of the others who mentioned it to me. Seumas explained:

> I speak the Gaelic here with my parents and when I go up to the [Hotel bar]. I speak it not because I have to but because it is what we speak. I like the Gaelic. But if it is going to become something artificial, then, well, I won't feel like speaking it at all. I don't want Gaelic to be kept alive by making it artificial . . . For myself, I'd prefer it if it died.

This is a very strong statement, especially from somebody who uses Gaelic so readily and who, on another occasion, tells me that he prefers to speak Gaelic than English. Nor is he alone. There are others, especially among men over about thirty-five or so, who – while not voicing their sentiments in quite such stark terms – express a similar matter-of-fact attachment to Gaelic alongside negative attitudes towards pro-Gaelic policies. Archy, for example, who enjoyed telling me of 'the people', initially refused to speak Gaelic with me and would declare that it was 'a waste of public money'. He was scathing about 'that *sgoileag* thing' (meaning the *cròileag* – the Gaelic playgroup), Gaelic road signs – 'it's ridiculous – just confuses the tourists', and the new Gaelic College – 'Waste of time. Waste of public money'. Yet at the same time he himself spoke Gaelic in his home and with others in the area, and he grumbled bitterly when children spoke to him in English rather than Gaelic and at the fact that teenagers who used to congregate near his croft conversed in English: 'They can't be bothered with the Gaelic and they have good Gaelic-speaking parents too'.

In this chapter my aim is to explore some of these apparent ambivalences over Gaelic and Gaelic renaissance policies. Through a focus on various Gaelic developments, I highlight different positions which local people adopt and the concerns and cultural notions which inform these. The analysis draws upon earlier chapters to argue that local constructions of identity are not necessarily fully cognate with the romantic-nationalist conception which informs many 'minority' linguistic and cultural developments; and to show how the local identity repertoire is enacted in relation to pro-Gaelic developments.

Language, Identity and 'Naturalness'

As we saw in Chapter 2 the idea of languages not only as means of communication but as the central source and marker of 'peoplehood' is part of the romantic nationalist discourse of those involved in language revival and of most ethnonationalism more broadly. What we might call 'heritage languages' − i.e. languages with which a person should particularly identify on account of their ethnicity, which usually would be the mother tongue − are seen to lie at the heart of a deep-seated identity from which individuals and peoples should not be estranged. Within this model, language use is conceptualised not so much as a pragmatic matter as an affective, symbolic and political one; and the decline in 'a people's language' is seen as evidence of alienation and perhaps even repression. The loss of a heritage language is seen as synonymous with the loss of identity.

We might argue that Seumas' claim that he would prefer Gaelic to die than to become 'artificial' is evidence of him suffering some kind of alienation from the language and from his 'real identity'. Indeed, this was suggested to me by some language activists to whom I mentioned the fact that some local people seemed to be not wholly in favour of pro-Gaelic policies. They told me: 'It's not surprising. All their education has been in English. They don't really see Gaelic as a living language. They've lost touch with what it really means'. And when I asked: 'What does it mean?' I was told: 'Being part of something − you know, a history, a culture. Being Gaelic'. While they certainly have a point that the education system plays a part in constructing evaluations of Gaelic, as I shall discuss further below, it seems to me that Seumas' words, and those of Archy too, are precisely about what Gaelic 'really means' in their own terms. Indeed, I suggest that their words are a very strong statement of identity. However, this is not an identity in which a language in itself is regarded as the key repository and marker of self. It is not quite the romantic nationalist conception of identity.

Seumas talks of his Gaelic as being simply what he speaks. It just *is* the language of interaction with his family and friends. When I talked to others over the age of about thirty (i.e. born before the mid-1950s) in Carnan this was the way in which they usually expressed their Gaelic use. Indeed, many older people were rather amused that I should ask them about what language they used at home, so inevitable did it seem. In the words of one:

Aye, it was Gaelic we had at home right enough. Not a word of English. *A Ghàidhlig fad an t-siubhail*. It was just natural to speak the Gaelic you understand. You just wouldn't think of blethering away in English. Folks would be wondering what you were playing at.

Gaelic was the *natural* language of the home and of the locality in general. To use English would have been 'artificial' and caused social comment. The obvious motive for speaking English at home would have been social mobility, or as one woman told me 'putting yourself above other folks'. To use English would have been 'snobbish' (cf. Parman 1972: 136) or 'posh'. It would have a been a repudiation of notions of egalitarianism and 'peoplehood' which, as we have seen, are highly valued locally, even if they ignore other aspects of social relations. This strong sense of Gaelic as the language of 'here' (*a bhos*) and English as the language of 'away' (*air falbh*) maintained the use of Gaelic in the locality during the years when Gaelic was widely negatively valued outside and there was little official support for it.

Seumas' words draw upon this same repertoire of notions: naturalness and artificiality, here and away, and being part of the locality or being 'posh'. What he suggests, however, is that it may be Gaelic that is taking on the mantle that formerly applied to English – it may be Gaelic use that is increasingly artificial, posh and bearing the values of away. For Seumas, the Gaelic language has been, and is, important to him in that it is the language in which many of his valued social interactions take place. It is the language he speaks at home and with his mates in the bar. This is not to say, however, that Gaelic is only a pragmatic matter to him – his linguistic choice is based not only upon so-called rational matters of the number of speakers with whom he can interact or the material benefits that might be derived from certain language use – it is also a matter of the meanings which the languages hold for him. However, he does not regard these as absolutely fixed but as themselves shaped by changing social and cultural configurations; and he fears that the values that he formerly associated with Gaelic may be subsumed by others. For Seumas, then, Gaelic is not *in itself* necessarily the fundamental source and marker of his identity. He can envisage ways of being part of 'here' rather than 'away' which would not rely upon using Gaelic, and which might even involve avoiding doing so. He does, however, very clearly define himself in opposition to the values of 'away' and to this extent is making a statement of identity – of who he is. This is an identity which is bound in to his everyday social relations and local cultural values. It is not an identity premised upon having a fixed package of distinctive language and culture.

Changing Patterns of Gaelic Use

According to Census figures, the proportion of Gaelic speakers in the Highlands has been declining since the first Census was taken in 1891 (with the exception of 1971 as discussed in Chapter 2). However, certain parishes – including that of which Carnan is part – showed considerably less decline than average. Between 1921 and 1961 its proportion of Gaelic speakers remained fairly stable, to be followed by greater decline between each of the following decades than in the whole of the preceding period. It remained nevertheless one of a minority of Highland areas with over 75 per cent of the population reported as Gaelic-speaking in 1981.

My own survey and life-histories also showed a decline in Gaelic use amongst those born since around 1960, i.e. those who in the mid-1980s were aged under about twenty-five. There is, of course, an irony in the fact that it is in this period that Gaelic has seen such decline in its heartlands for it is in the same period that there has been an unprecedented introduction of policies and institutions designed to promote Gaelic (Table 2.1), and of minority and ethnic languages and cultures more broadly. The decline is not, however, a result of local people shifting their evaluations of the languages as a consequence of 'university circle' interests in Gaelic in the way in which Seumas suggested he might consider, though it is inflected by the same repertoire of notions about language use and identity on which Seumas' account draws.

As I have noted, for those born before the 1960s, Gaelic was invariably the language of the home and much social interaction in the locality (e.g. visiting neighbours, in the post office, in the shops). Those in this age-group nearly all began school with little or no English; and Gaelic was, for the most part, the language of the playground. Few of those under twenty-five, however, reported beginning school with no English, though many – especially at the upper end of the age-range – said they were not fluent in it. For this generation, Gaelic was rarely used in the playground. While Gaelic continued to be used in the home, local people of all ages reported an increasing pattern of children passively understanding Gaelic but using it only intermittently themselves, and of first-born children speaking Gaelic but subsequent ones comprehending and using it less. Among the children in Carnan primary school, although *all* had at least one Gaelic-speaking parent and more than half had both Gaelic-speaking parents, only about a third of the children were fluent in Gaelic (according to their teachers' estimations), though probably about half would be good enough by the time they reached secondary school to study Gaelic as 'native-speakers' rather than 'learners' (which constitute separate streams, and separate O-levels and Highers). However, when asked which language they used at home only three of the school's twenty-two children said 'Gaelic', and two 'Gaelic and English'; and the children themselves almost always spoke English when playing together.

Accounting for Gaelic Decline

There are a number of contextual changes that have largely occurred since around the mid-1950s which appear to play a part in the declining use of Gaelic. However, these alone cannot fully explain the shift. We need also to understand the local repertoire of possibilities in which language use and language transmission are embedded in order to see how new developments are appropriated locally.

Television. This first came to Carnan in the mid-1960s, though it was not for another ten years that the majority of homes had a set. When local people talk of children's altered language use television is often the main reason they perceive for the switch towards English. However, many families who watch English-language television have maintained the use of Gaelic and there seems, therefore, to be no necessary reason why English-language television in itself should cause a decline of Gaelic. Nevertheless, in that television actually *enters* the home it is undoubtedly important in altering the assumption that the home is unquestionably a Gaelic domain. Indeed, even some predominantly Gaelic-speaking families told me that, if they had been watching a television programme in English they might well talk about it afterwards in English – something which I witnessed myself on occasion. What happens, then, is that it becomes possible for English to enter the home other than for reasons of social climbing and snobbishness. It becomes part of the *natural* linguistic environment of the home.

Direct Contact with English-monoglots. In Carnan people's accounts of linguistic shift these too were seen as particularly significant, many noting the arrival in the late-1950s of two English-monoglot children to the school as the beginning of a shift to English as the playground language. Again, however, this was not a sufficient cause, for earlier examples had shown English-monoglot children becoming fluent in Gaelic. However, coupled with other factors, this too could help shift the inevitability of Gaelic as the language between peers.

Secondary Education. Until 1972 most Carnan children received their secondary education in Carnan itself, but afterwards all attended the school in the island capital. Here Gaelic seemed to be strongly associated with rusticity and a lack of sophistication by the children of the capital; and most young people from Carnan described themselves as having been keen to speak English so that they would not be 'looked down on'. Moreover, with the greater number of English-monoglots in the island secondary school, English seemed like the 'natural' lingua franca. While some Carnan teenagers continued to use Gaelic at home, others told me that they became more likely to use English, especially with siblings: 'you just got into the habit. And sometimes, well, you weren't wanting to be like your parents and that'. Again, this helped to naturalise English as the language between peers.

Work Away.   Many older Gaelic speakers, especially those over about forty, had worked away in at least partially Gaelic-speaking environments, especially in Glasgow. Many told me about how they would gather every Saturday or Sunday evening under *An Drochaid*, the bridge on Jamaica Street known as 'The Hielandman's Umbrella', how they would attend ceilidhs in Over Newton and tend to live in particular areas of the city such as Partick. Several Carnan couples had met their Gaelic-speaking spouses here. However, this 'home-from-home' environment, as one described it, largely disappeared in the late-1950s; and this has meant not just that those who work away are less likely to continue to speak Gaelic themselves while away but also that they are less likely to find Gaelic-speaking partners.

All of these changes, then, provided contexts in which English might be spoken without 'folks wondering what you were playing at'. The shift was a result not so much of outright 'oppression' by English or of teachers 'beating out' Gaelic, and nor of local people becoming alienated from their 'true identity' as Gaels, but of a combination of external changes and particular local notions.

Autonomy, Pushiness and Identity

Also important in helping shape language use and transmission from one generation to another are local notions about children's language learning. When I spoke with parents of children reluctant to speak Gaelic they repeatedly phrased the situation in terms such as the following.

> *Chan eil i a'bodraigeadh idir leis a'Ghàidhlig* – She just does not bother with the Gaelic

> I don't know why it is but Donald just didn't seem to take to the Gaelic. John

[his elder brother] got on with it fine, but Donald, he's just not bothered with it at all

She just does not have the Gaelic

Such comments were recounted matter-of-factly but with a sense of puzzlement. As Edwin Ardener has observed (personal communication) such statements are analogous to saying 'He does not eat potatoes'. They are not phrased in terms of matters of learning but imply that what is involved is an individual, internal matter, to do with the child's own particular disposition. The child is conceptualised as an autonomous agent, not as a product of cultural work by its parents.

Initially, this notion seemed to me to be at odds with many local people's criticism of parents, and especially mothers, of children with little Gaelic. It was said: 'It's the parents I blame', 'It's the mother, she's got fancy ideas' or 'They're too proud'. However, the criticism was made not because it was thought that such parents ought to have taught their children Gaelic, but because it was suspected that they had 'pushed' them into English because of their 'fancy ideas' or 'pride'. In other words, it was suspected that parents had been trying to be 'posh' through English use in the home. The parents were blamed not because they had failed to teach their children Gaelic but because they had failed to provide the kind of home context in which Gaelic would have been the language which the child would autonomously and naturally have acquired. And as mothers were the ones most closely associated with the ontology of improvement, it was mothers who were thought most likely to have 'pushed' the child from what would have been their 'natural' route.[1]

The view of the child as autonomous is related to other local ideas which have been mentioned earlier. In particular, it resonates with ideas about 'natural ability' and scholarship discussed in Chapter 4, and the related Calvinist sense of individuals having a 'calling' in life which they should follow (although I should note that comments on children's language use were never related to religious notions directly). However, although there is resistance to parents 'pushing' children as a means of social climbing, this does not mean that school education is in any sense regarded negatively, for this is seen as providing a context in which natural talents can emerge, albeit through hard work. The 'problem' – the socially unacceptable – is when individuals are led in directions which are thought 'unnatural' to them, which remove them artificially from the course which they would otherwise have followed.

In some ways these ideas seem to fit well with the notion of 'expressive individuation' – of individuals having an inner core which should be properly expressed. Insofar as Calvinism played a part in forming this feature of the 'modern identity' (Taylor 1989) the congruence is not surprising; but it is important to note that the local expectation that children act of their own accord, and that each individual has their own path in the world, is not accompanied by the same degree of urgency to express 'the self' – and to do so through certain culturally accepted markers – as Taylor describes of expressive individuation. Individuation, and the notion that individuals act primarily on the basis of their own dispositions (which may in turn be guided by God), is taken for granted rather than elevated into a calling in itself. Nor need this idea of individuation necessarily be coupled with the strong sense of individual identity as deep, singular and coherent that we find in some modernist accounts (see Chapter 1). Indeed, in parents' accounts of their children's language use they did not talk in terms of aspects of the child's personality, and nor did they try to account for a child's linguistic shifts in psychological terms. The fact that a child had, say, spoken Gaelic earlier and English now, would be described to me simply as a fact; and while it might be regarded as a puzzle, and perhaps as 'a shame', nobody that I spoke with ever made any suggestions that it raised problems of identity for the child or for their autonomy.

These ideas about language differ in many respects from those expressed in Gaelic renaissance literature. In this literature, Gaelic is conceptualised as a deep feature of the most important identity of the Highland people: their ethnic identity. Moreover, the language use of children is not regarded as a matter of their particular personal dispositions but as a moral and educative responsibility of parents, particularly of mothers. Clearly, if local people are likely to regard teaching pre-school children as 'pushing' them, and if this is against local codes of conduct as I have suggested, then this has repercussions for strategies for language revival. Below I consider two major examples of language revival in Carnan – a Gaelic playgroup and bilingual-medium primary education – to explore further local responses to Gaelic developments.

Portrait of two Playgroups

Since the 'new' Gaelic playgroup opened in early 1986, Carnan has had two 'Gaelic playgroups'. The 'old' playgroup has only recently decided to call itself 'the *Gaelic* playgroup', and has done so in response to proposals for the 'new' one. As Ellie Sheumais, organiser of the 'old' group, tells me: 'Well, I suppose we were trying to stake a claim really, to say we got there first, not that it's worked'. Ellie is annoyed because the old group had been running for some time and she had wanted to make it eligible for funding from the HIDB supported *Comhairle nan Sgoiltean Araich* (Committee of Playgroups) set up in 1982–3 ('Then we could have bought some Gaelic books and tapes for one thing'). Instead, however, the funding has gone to the new playgroup, which is usually referred to by its Gaelic name of *cròileag*.

The old group was not originally set up with Gaelic in mind and even now the social function of the group, giving mothers the chance to get together and 'catch up' rather than be 'cooped up at home', seems to be seen as more important that its linguistic function. Ellie tells me: 'We don't want to be sectarian, saying you can come but you can't. And the same with what language people speak there, it can be Gaelic or English. We are not in the business of policing – unlike some'. At the playgroup, where about half the mothers are native Gaelic speakers, other women echo these sentiments: 'You can speak what you like here. We try to encourage children to speak the Gaelic but we're not going to say that's all they can speak. And how could you do that? They'll do what they want anyhow'.

The playgroup meets in the community hall. A typical scene is one of children hurtling around on tricycles while most of the mothers sit together, nursing babies, drinking tea, fending off requests from their children to tell Wee Rory to get off the mini tractor, and chatting – mostly in English, though Ellie says that if no English speakers happened to be there, 'We would probably be blethering in Gaelic, though that's not likely to be very often, right enough'. There are occasional attempts to provide more structured activity and to introduce some Gaelic, for example, trying to get children to talk in Gaelic about the colour of the plasticine with which they are playing or telling a story in Gaelic. One child sometimes replies in Gaelic but most of those whose language is identifiable seem to be speaking English, though much of the vocabulary is 'bilingual' or even 'international:' 'Bang!', 'tractor', 'baby', 'dolly', 'Bow wow'. Other than '*Glé mhath*' (Very good) for the paintings and Duplo guns which the children come to show off, and 'Ishht' ('Shhh'), the mothers' responses to the children mostly seem to be in English ('No', 'Wait a minute, can't you?', 'Do you want the potty?').[2]

The *croileag* meets on Thursday mornings in a rather cramped room in the school. When I visit, in its early days, there are usually about six children there, three who were also at the old playgroup, and two play leaders. They had wanted to meet in the community hall but were told there were problems with the timetabling and the heating. They suspect that really the problem was with the other playgroup and 'somebody influential' trying to prevent the new group starting up. They are well aware of the opposition but Kirsty, a local mother who has been a main instigator of the new group, insists that it is essential to have a different kind of group 'if we're serious about the Gaelic'. At the *cròileag* there is a much more structured routine than at the old group. First, Anna, a part-time Gaelic teacher, takes the lead and we all try to follow her in various Gaelic action songs. The children are fairly quiet as most of the songs are not yet familiar to them; though a catchy song about a kangaroo gets an enthusiastic hopping around and chorus of 'kangaroo oo-oo-oo'. We then have juice (*dius*) and the children colour in photocopied sheets of people which have Gaelic labels for parts of the body. Anna and Kirsty comment pointedly in Gaelic about the colouring and pass crayons. Kirsty's daughter chatters cheerfully in Gaelic about her picture though the other children's replies are mainly monosyllabic. Occasionally the children ask questions in English and the adults reply carefully and slowly in Gaelic, pointing and using gestures to convey their meaning.

The establishment of a *cròileag* in Carnan was locally controversial. A development framed within the HIDB general remit to foster rural communities and to support Gaelic, it showed clearly that Gaelic was not necessarily a cause which would unite the local community. The way in which differences were articulated, however, deserves attention for while it helps us to understand the reasons for the dissent, it also reveals a good deal of shared cultural assumptions in which the arguments of both sides are expressed. I begin by considering the cases of Kirsty and Anna – individuals who, like Catrìona in the previous chapter, are in effect local 'front-line' Gaelic activists. These raise many more general issues about attitudes towards language and its contexts of use; and I then extend this to a discussion of the case of those women who resent the opening of the *cròileag*. Points raised here are then discussed in relation to other areas of linguistic use and contest – particularly the bilingual-medium primary education project – a discussion which returns us to questions of identity and ambivalence raised in previous chapters, as well as to questions about the nature of 'culture'.

Everyday Language Activists

Kirsty and Anna (who I visit in their own homes separately as well as at the playgroup itself) had both previously attended the old playgroup but felt that the children were just left 'to run riot while their mothers gossip'. Both had wanted something more structured and with a greater emphasis on Gaelic, though for different reasons. It is worth looking at their reasons for while both might be classified as 'activists' in that they are involved in establishing and running a pro-Gaelic development in Carnan, neither has the kind of strongly politicised vision of Gaelic that is characteristic of revivalist movements. They are, for example, very different from the 'militants' that Maryon McDonald writes of in Brittany (1989), who are mostly outsiders who have learned the language and who tie it in to a much broader radical, anti-state political vision. They are also unlike Duncan, with whom I began Chapter 2, for whom Gaelic is Scotland's language, a connection with other Celtic and minority countries, and a crucial marker of 'having an identity'. Here, I deal with Kirsty and Anna in turn.

Kirsty and her husband are both native Gaelic speakers born and brought up in Carnan. They attended the local school and then the Island High School. Their parents also live in the area and Gaelic is the everyday language of communication between them. Their children, the eldest of whom attends the playgroup (four-year-old Marsali), so far speak little English; and Marsali, who has spent a lot of time with her grandmother, is well-known for her charmingly old-fashioned Gaelic. Many of Kirsty's views on Gaelic are not those that we would expect of an activist. For example, she says that the use of Gaelic on signposts makes little differ-ence, that the use of Gaelic on official forms is not important and that it would be impractical and a waste of money to use Gaelic in courts. On the use of Gaelic at public meetings in the area she says that it should depend on who is there and that Gaelic should not be used if there are people present who do not speak Gaelic. Her own activism seems to be something of a surprise to her herself, and in talking about it she refers to the fact that she and her siblings always spoke Gaelic at home and were good at Gaelic at school. This was not something calculated or 'pushed' but simply a fact of life. Many other people locally, however, did not 'bother' and Kirsty thinks that this is a shame (*'Chan eil moran ann a seo a bodrigeadh – ach se 'shame' a th'ann'*). This theme of 'not bother-ing' is one that comes up repeatedly when I talk with Kirsty and is echoed by many others. The mothers at the old playgroup for the most part are said to be 'not bothering' with the Gaelic; and some of those who send their children to the Gaelic playgroup, she claims, do not 'bother' to back it up by using any Gaelic at home. She tells me of various people locally whose children might have spoken Gaelic and asks rhetorically why they do not do so. Her assumption seems to be that if children of Gaelic-speaking parents do not speak Gaelic then it is because the parents have not spoken to them in Gaelic. Kirsty is particularly critical of some of the school teachers who are supposed to be 'so strong on the Gaelic' but whose own children do not speak the language; and she says derogatorily of one of the women who has opposed the *cròileag* most vociferously, a woman who Kirsty claims has said that she will teach her children Gaelic when they are older, that she has 'fancy ideas' (*tha fancy ideas aice*). Kirsty also claims that the reason that so many local mothers are against the *cròileag* is because they fear 'being shown up'.

For Kirsty, a Gaelic playgroup provides a context in which her daughter will be able to speak her own first language. Kirsty is certainly not against her children learning English and assumes that they will do so, as she has done so herself, but she believes that unless they speak Gaelic first, this is extremely unlikely. The recent Gaelic revival developments and policies in the area are, she thinks, 'about time', though she is sceptical of some, such as the use of Gaelic in courts, which seem to her to be 'gimmicks'. And while she welcomes the increased national support and the establishment of the *cròileag* network in particular, she is also wary of outsiders' involvement at the local level and relieved, she says, that national Gaelic advisors have not been much in evidence in the locality: 'those from the cities don't always help'.

Kirsty's activism, then, is not especially politicised. Her own articulations of why Gaelic is important, and why there should be a Gaelic playgroup in the area, are not shaped in terms of the symbolic importance of a distinctive language. Her arguments are located in everyday social relations and evaluations. She talks not of the nation but of her family and of neighbours in the locality; she seems to regard non-local activists more as outsiders than as 'comrades'; and she is concerned not so much with Gaelic as a symbolic marker (e.g. the language of road signs) but with the social connotations of everyday language use and the contexts of learning (with 'bothering' and 'fancy ideas'). In this, she has more in common with Seumas, and even the women who oppose the *cròileag,* than she does with some aspects of the 'official' pro-Gaelic stance.

Let us, however, now turn to Anna for a somewhat different example of a local language activist. Anna comes from elsewhere in Skye and is trained as a Gaelic schoolteacher. Her husband, also from elsewhere on Skye (though with relatives in Carnan) had a Gaelic-speaking mother and a non-Gaelic-speaking father; and while he passively understands a good deal, has an A grade Higher in Gaelic, and does speak Gaelic at home 'a fair bit' according to Anna, he does not do so in my presence and most local people refer to him as a non-Gaelic-speaker. Like Kirsty, Anna has young children, though unlike Kirsty, her eldest, three-year-old Cailean, rarely speaks a word of Gaelic, though like his father is well able to understand the language. Indeed, one day I record a game played by Anna and Cailean in which Cailean is shop-keeper. In Gaelic, Anna asks him for various provisions – 'Do you have any potatoes today?' ('*A bheil buntata ann an diugh?*') – and Cailean invariably replies in English ('Sorry, no potatoes'). For Anna, Cailean's apparent 'refusal' to speak Gaelic is frustrating. She tells me that he used much more Gaelic until recently and that she thinks that a combination of English-language television and contact with predominantly English-speaking children at the 'old' Gaelic playgroup is the main cause. Her involvement in the Gaelic playgroup is partly a professional matter – she is a trained Gaelic teacher and was looking for some part-time work – and partly connected with her hope of inducing Cailean to use the language again. She also has a young baby who she does not want to 'go the same way as Cailean'.

In our conversations, Anna seems concerned that her status as a Gaelic teacher and more generally the way in which her family is regarded are at stake in her children's language use. 'What will folks be wondering what with me a Gaelic teacher and all?' she asks rhetorically. One thing that she seems to fear in particular is that people will regard her as somehow not having properly fostered Gaelic within the home – and worse, that they might even regard her as having *taught* Cailean English. The idea that she has purposefully taught Cailean anything is one which she repudiates in strong terms. She tells me that Cailean knows his alphabet and says that she suspects that neighbours think that she has taught him: 'But he just picked it up of his own accord – it was not that I was trying to get him to do it'. At one point she comments of her neighbours, in a remark that echoes some of Kirsty's castigations and which could be the reply to her own above rhetorical question, 'They'll be thinking that I am trying to be fancy'.

While Kirsty and Anna sometimes articulate their participation in Gaelic revival in revivalist language – e.g. Kirsty tells me 'Gaelic is our heritage and we should be proud of it' – much more prominent in their accounts are themes of autonomy and the avoidance of seeming pushy. For Kirsty and Anna, establishing a *cròileag* in Carnan was not entirely a political matter of 'saving the Gaelic'. It was also and at the same time a matter of positioning themselves in relation to local social values and changes that they perceived to be occurring. It was also a matter of distinguishing themselves from certain other women locally. In this, however, they were not unlike those from whom they wished to be distinguished.

'Why should we be made to feel like lepers?'

Most of the mothers who favoured a Gaelic-speaking playgroup in the days before it opened were,[3] with the partial exception of Anna and another mother of a child with 'lapsed' Gaelic, mothers of children who spoke at least some of the language. Those most against it were, perhaps not surprisingly, mothers of children with little or no Gaelic, many of whom had married into the area, though none of whom at that time were incomers with no Gaelic-speaking relatives. All of these children, then, might be expected to know more Gaelic than they seemed to and it was clear that many of the women felt, as Kirsty had said, that a Gaelic playgroup might make them 'look badly'. Some even implied that this was one of the motives for establishing the *cròileag* and that it stemmed from a personal animosity which was not connected with Gaelic at all. In voicing their reasons for not wanting a Gaelic playgroup, however, most of the women drew upon a cultural repertoire shared by those in favour of the *cròileag* and aspects of which we have seen in earlier chapters.

The following was a strongly voiced statement echoed by others: 'It's not that I mind things being done for the Gaelic but I don't see why we should be made to feel like lepers if our children don't speak it'. Here we see the notion that children simply do or do not speak Gaelic of their own accord and an unwillingness for parents to be judged on the basis of children's actions. Some mothers accused the *cròileag* of the kind of directed language learning which we have already seen seems to be disapproved of locally. They contrasted this with the situation at the 'old' Gaelic playgroup: 'They [children] can speak whatever language they want here. We don't try to force anything down their throats'. The metaphor used here, which was used on several occasions by different women, very vividly conveys the idea of an unpleasant coercion of children and an inversion of the usual notion of language emanating from the child.

The other theme which emerges in mothers' comments is annoyance over language being used to categorise and divide people. For example:

We already have a playgroup. It would be ridiculous to have two playgroups – one for Gaelic and one for English. That's not right.

It is hard enough to keep things going here as it is, without having Gaelic this and English that. And it just makes for, well, you know, dividing things up and people being against one another. And just on account of what language the children are speaking.

In part these women are referring to the practical difficulties of getting enough people together to run anything – particularly something restricted to young children – in a small and elderly community. In doing so, however, they are also mobilising an idea of community which ought not to manifest social divisions. As we have seen, linked conceptually with earlier notions of 'the people', this is rhetorically powerful. By accusing those setting up the new playgroup of dividing the community, these commentators also seem to be suggesting that language is being unnecessarily elevated to a position where it shapes social relations.

Just as with the autonomy of the child and the disapproval of strongly directing children linguistically, this dislike of language being used to effect social divisions is shared by women on 'both sides'. Whereas those in favour of an all-Gaelic playgroup suspected that children speaking English might be evidence of parents trying to gain social mobility through pushing their offspring to speak English, those against it suggest that it is Gaelic which is being used to create divisions within the community. Although mothers arguing against the establishment of a Gaelic playgroup clearly disagreed with those seeking to promote it, then, the cultural repertoire on which they drew to voice their arguments was not dissimilar from that of those wishing to promote it: both talked in terms of the autonomy of the child, of language as part of local social relations, and of disapproval of 'pushing' and 'forcing'. As I show below, these ideas can also be seen in relation to disagreements and ambivalence over other Gaelic developments in the local area.

Bilingual-medium Primary Education

Until the 1970s, primary education in the Highlands had officially been through the medium of English. In practice, a teacher might well use some Gaelic in the early weeks with Gaelic-monoglot children joining a school, but as one teacher told me: 'We tried to get English into them as fast as we could. We didn't want them speaking the Gaelic. We wanted to get them up to scratch as fast as we could. It was what the parents expected. I don't think we really stopped to think about it'. In doing so they were spurred on partly by the fact that children would have to sit examinations in English at the age of eleven to determine whether they would go to grammar school or not. Gaelic was usually taught as a special subject, most often in relation to music or religious education; but it was not the everyday language of instruction.

In Carnan, the first official attempts to introduce Gaelic as a medium of education – alongside rather than instead of English – were made in

1978 when the schools in the parish were designated as 'bilingual-medium primary schools'. The Bilingual Education Project had by then been running for three years in the Western Isles and its stated general aim was 'the introduction and development for children from a Gaelic-speaking background of a curriculum whereby they can learn through Gaelic as well as English' (Comhairle nan Eilean 1982; see also Murray and MacLeod 1981; Jackson 1983; Murray and Morrison 1984; Dunn and Boyd Robertson 1989; Mitchell 1992). The project was about far more, however, than merely increasing the amount of Gaelic that children would hear during the course of a school day, for it was also bound up with more extensive pedagogical changes which aimed to alter the ways in which children regarded both Gaelic and the school. In an article discussing the extension of the Project to Skye, Catherine Macdonald lists its broader aims as follows:

(a) To create a different image of the Gaelic language. The children had to be wooed. Gaelic had previously been a slotted subject where they were given a list of vocabulary and where there was little relevance to them in the wider scheme of things. It had to be made attractive. This feeling of Gaelic as a language study had to be erased. The main aim was the child's education and Gaelic was one of the many vehicles with which to attain this ideal.

(b) To make it personalised, beginning from their own surroundings.

(c) To make it immediately usable.

(d) To instil in them a feeling for their history and heritage. (Macdonald 1981: 22)

As is evident from the terms in which such aims are couched, the Bilingual Education Project was, at root, concerned with 're-claiming' Gaelic as an identity-language for children – that is, as a language which would be a deeply meaningful part of their self-conceptions, drawing on their own surroundings, history and heritage. However, according to the romantic discourse which permeates such notions of identity, formal schooling – especially that which has been controlled from outside – is generally regarded as not part of, and even as antithetical to, the meaningful contexts of identity-formation. Formal educational methods and teaching exclusively through the medium of English had been in danger of 'alienating children from their linguistic and cultural background' (Murray and Morrison 1984: 10). The problem was how to turn the school into a context in which children would be 'put in touch with' their cultural and linguistic identity. What the Project had to achieve, according to one pedagogue influential in its development, was to make the school 'part of psychological home, part of the "heart of the real" as Mircea Eliade has put it' (MacLeod 1984). The idea was to move from a 'didactic' to an 'experiential' model of education (Murray and Morrison 1984: xi). While 'child-centred' pedagogical ideas had to some extent been filtering in to mainstream education during the 1970s, the Bilingual Education Project was seen as an opportunity to bring in 'experiential' and 'relevant' education in a much more thoroughgoing way. There was to be 'an emphasis on the development of oral spontaneity' (Macdonald 1981: 21), and 'relevant' subjects which would bring education 'back home' (ibid.). There was to be 'exploration of the environment' (Macdonald 1981: 22) and 'close school-community ties were [to be] fostered' (ibid.) through the use of old photographs and life-histories with old people. In this way, it was hoped that children would both develop a sense of their own identities as part of a 'community' with a 'history' and a 'culture' – and, of course, a language.

As Maryon McDonald has argued in her study of Brittany, it is not surprising that 'alternative' pedagogical ideas should become especially bound up with minority languages for both are structured through similar sets of conceptual oppositions (1989). In both, the personal, the community, the meaningful, and qualities such as spontaneity, naturalness and freedom, are contrasted favourably with traditional formal education and with majority languages, which in turn are regarded as less amenable to individual expression and inherently alien to local and community values. However, drawing on such oppositions also implicitly reinforces the distinction between the 'majority' and the 'minority' language, and risks intensifying local perceptions of the latter as not thoroughly appropriate to 'normal' schooling and academic abstract subjects and, more generally, to the world beyond the local community. In the case of the Bilingual Project the fact that so many of the learning materials related to 'Highland' topics played a part in this, as noted by one teacher when he opened a new consignment of Project learning materials: *'a' chroit a rithist – se na space-rockets air a bheil feum againn'* ('the croft again – it's space-rockets we need'). While the great majority of those I interviewed in the mid-1980s were by then in favour of bilingual primary education, many made comments to the effect that Gaelic was not really suited to subjects such as mathematics and that children would need English for exams and getting on in life. Gaelic, it seemed, was welcomed as an 'extra' – the most common remark being that it was 'very nice' for children to learn some in school – rather than as a *medium* of teaching on a par with English.

Parents' Views

When the Project began in Carnan (prior to my fieldwork) there had been a good deal of concern expressed locally: 'Parents took bilingualism in its literal sense and feared that if children had no Gaelic their education in the basic skills would suffer' (Macdonald 1981: 22). It was not only the parents of children with no Gaelic who had been worried but also Gaelic-speaking parents who were concerned that time spent on Gaelic – especially if this had to be low-level in order to cope with children who were not fluent – would mean that the education of their children would suffer. Indeed, amongst those I interviewed, it was often parents in strongly Gaelic-speaking families who still expressed the most intense reservations about it. For example, the mother of children reputed to have very good Gaelic and to have started school with little English told me:

> I think that it is right that they speak Gaelic when they go to school but there's no need to do Gaelic at school. We don't pay money to do Gaelic at school – and it isn't at all right that learner teachers teach at the school. . . Gaelic is our native tongue but it is to learn English and other things that we pay. They can do Gaelic at [High] school or college. [trans. from Gaelic]

Another man, whose children had also begun school with little English, made a similar argument that school is the place where children learn to 'get on' and that Gaelic is not part of this:

> It's a daft thing to teach it in the school. They'll no want Gaelic when it comes to exams. It's English they'll be needing. Teaching the Gaelic is depriving them of more teaching of English, and it's English they'll be needing when they get away from here. They'll no get any Gaelic in Glasgow or London. What use is it? You can't go into a shop there and speak the Gaelic. No, it's a waste of money.

He, in common with the great majority of those I interviewed, was especially scathing of proposals then current to create an all-Gaelic-medium school in Carnan: 'No, no. It's more than daft'. At the same time, this man also emphasised the importance of Gaelic to himself and bemoaned the fact that so many children today seemed not to speak the language. For these strongly Gaelic-speaking families, the school was important as a means of providing English language and this did not detract at all from their conception of the home as properly a Gaelic domain. The most common view among Gaelic-speaking parents was that it was good for children to get some Gaelic in school but that this should not be allowed to detract from developing children's skills in English. As one mother, who expressed herself as being generally in favour of bilingual medium education put it:

> Well it's all right if they're going to sing at the Mòd. I wouldn't like to be quoted on it but I don't think that it will do the majority much good. It's nice to have the Gaelic and it's nice to have a second language but there's very few that will become fluent. And there's not many that will get jobs working with the Gaelic. There's more than there used to be, mind, but I think they'll be short-term – these things like at *Sabhal Mór Ostaig* [the Gaelic College].

Such local people clearly hold a view of the school as primarily a place for 'getting on'. Unlike the revivalist conception of school as an extension of 'home' – and as such as a key site for identity-formation – they seem more readily to regard it in contradistinction to the home and to the ideally egalitarian values of the locality. School is primarily about 'away', about social mobility, about English rather than the socialisation of children into a Gaelic identity. Nevertheless, as we have seen, there is a good deal of ambivalence about social mobility and the values of 'away' and this may have been one reason why the increase in Gaelic was in general widely accepted. Moreover, as we have also noted, the school was regarded as a context in which children's 'natural talents' could emerge, and the provision of *alternative* directions which children might autonomously choose fitted well with local ideas.

Also involved in the acceptance of the Project was the local mediation of the policies. As noted in earlier chapters, there is a widespread local distrust of policies which are seen to emanate from 'away' – from 'the powers-that-be'. In the case of bilingual primary education in Carnan, however, several of Carnan's teachers themselves had a longstanding interest in Gaelic and the Project provided them with a justification for expanding that interest. Their enthusiasm, coupled with their knowledge of local parents and their likely concerns, meant that participation in the Project was managed smoothly and that they assured parents that their children's English language education would not suffer (rather than, say, emphasising how children would become less alienated from their Gaelic identities, which would not necessarily have appealed so much to parents). In connection with this, was the fact that the 'new pedagogy' was not put fully into effect and much of the teaching remained in the formal style that many parents perceived as 'proper education'. Most teaching was carried out with children seated at their desks, through traditional subjects rather than through 'topics' (i.e. the curriculum was mostly ordered according to categories such as 'reading' and 'spelling' rather than 'fishing' or 'our community'), and children were usually required to raise their hands before answering questions. There was still emphasis on 'proper English' and 'good manners', concepts which are associated by some parents.[4] Children would invariably preface questions with 'Please Sir' or 'Please Miss', something which, even when the children were being exhorted to speak Gaelic, was not usually questioned by the teachers.

Moreover, although there was a substantial presence of Gaelic in class, it was certainly not the case that half of the curriculum was taught through the medium of Gaelic and this too may have reassured parents. Indeed, one mother told me that her initial concerns about the Project had been overcome when she found that 'ninety per cent of it is in English anyway'. Furthermore, despite the idea of Gaelic becoming a medium of education, it tended to be used in specific contexts – Gaelic reading, discussing Gaelic radio and television programmes, preparation for the Mòd and school concert, and religious education – and not for the most part in others, such as mathematics, so not really challenging current preconceptions.

Children's Views

The children themselves certainly seemed to perceive the domains of Gaelic use in the school as more defined than the teachers or Project leaders would have liked. For example, they would tell me at what times in the school week they 'did' Gaelic and what subjects were usually 'in' Gaelic. On the one hand, they associated Gaelic especially with religious education which, probably more consistently than any other subject, was held in Gaelic – and for some these seemed to be regarded as synonymous. Their perception here may also have been shaped by a common linking, especially among younger people, of the church with Gaelic, and even of both with 'old people' and old-fashioned-ness; and perhaps here too with the fact that their teacher was a church elder. On the other hand, children seemed to see Gaelic as belonging to a more 'recreational' sphere than English – with making pictures to send to radio programmes and learning songs for the Mòd. Their perception here, while influenced in part by the new emphasis on Gaelic as enjoyable and not just a 'study language', was not entirely that which those involved in the Project might have wished. This was particularly evident on the occasions when the visiting Project teacher came to the school (generally one or two mornings or afternoons each week). Groups of children would accompany her to the 'Art Room' to read, do project work or sing Gaelic songs. Here, where the desks were no longer in neat rows, these children, who were normally quiet and well-behaved in class, became noisy. They giggled behind their hands, sat on tables and swung their legs, looked blank when the teacher spoke to them in Gaelic and were generally far less cooperative than normal. The project leader often found herself having to threaten – in English – to send the children back to the classroom if they did not 'behave'. In part, the children's behaviour may have been due simply to the fact that they were outside their normal classroom and teacher situation, though they did not behave in this way with the visiting art or music teachers. Moreover, they had given impolite nicknames to both of their visiting Project teachers, though not to any other of their teachers. Their behaviour, it seemed to me, derived from a combination of the apparent informality of the context and the emphasis on self-expression – both of which they seemed to be uncomfortable with – and the fact that some of the children did not understand the instructions given to them, and other children seemed unwilling to let their friends be shown up.

The reception of the bilingual-medium project in Carnan illustrates the dynamic and sometimes subtle and contradictory meeting up of local and revivalist conceptions. It shows too, the important role that local mediators – in this case teachers – might play in accommodating policies to the local context. The project is, however, an important aspect of the increased politicisation of Gaelic in Carnan and, as I discuss in the final part of this chapter, this has significant consequences for the likely future directions of Gaelic language use.

The Politicisation of Gaelic

One consequence of Gaelic revival policies is that children not only learn more Gaelic in school, they also learn more about the language. Many of the revivalist language materials are designed to foster a sense of Gaelic, Celtic or minority identity. In Carnan primary school I witnessed children being told, either by teachers or on radio programmes, about how Gaelic was banned under the Statutes of Iona, about the prohibition on the plaid, about 'linguistic oppression' and 'revival' in Wales, Brittany and the Basque country, about linguistic similarities between Gaelic, Welsh and other Celtic languages; and I listened in class to music by Alain Stivell (a Breton folk-singer) alongside Run-Rig (Skye's nationally popular Gaelic rock group). It was pointed out to children that outsiders like myself were taking an interest in Gaelic, and that they were themselves fortunate to have two languages.

Not only children, but the local population in general was increasingly being presented with romantic nationalist notions of Gaelic and cultural identity. The Gaelic radio station regularly transmitted programmes about revivalist developments in Scotland and other countries, particularly Wales, Brittany, Ireland and the Basque country. The discourse used was one in which language was a central point in a constellation of notions such as 'heritage', 'identity', and 'culture'. For some local people, it seemed to me, these terms helped them articulate their own sense of the importance of Gaelic. For example, one elderly woman told me with very evident feeling:

> Sè an cànan againn – sin agad e. . . Tha mi 'n dòchas nach marbhrar e. Se, uill, it's our heritage mar a chanas iad

> [It's our language – that's it . . . .. I hope it won't die. It's, well, it's our heritage as they say]

Her manner of expression, however, also reveals the extent to which she is not entirely at home with the language which she is using – she uses English to express the idea of Gaelic as part of heritage and distances this still further by her use of 'as they say'. Nevertheless, to dismiss local expressions of attachment to the language – even where they are couched in language that is part of the revival – would be as unjustifiable as to dismiss local statements about Gaelic as a waste of public money. Both are part of the contemporary local repertoire and both, moreover, may at times be held by the same person as we have seen.

For most local people Gaelic use was not a strongly political matter. My survey results showed rather weak support, even among habitual Gaelic speakers, for many pro-Gaelic developments such as the use of Gaelic in courts of law, local meetings or even Gaelic on signposts. Indeed, white settlers were considerably more likely to support these than were local people. As I have argued, however, this is not to say that locals regard Gaelic as unimportant: on the contrary, the same people often regularly and even by preference spoke Gaelic among themselves and were very sad about the decline of Gaelic. Gaelic clearly did *mean* a great deal to them but what it meant was located more within local social relations than wider politicised developments. Gaelic was important to local people's sense of themselves and their relations with others, and it was embedded in local notions of proper behaviour, such as not being snobbish. To this extent, Gaelic was very much part of local identity. However, this was an identity rooted in everyday practice and everyday contrasts – between home and away, locals and incomers, older and younger people – rather than a politicised package of language, heritage and culture. Moreover, it was an identity in which Gaelic was not neces-sarily at the centre; and as we have seen some local people preferred to privilege other dimensions of that local identity (e.g. not being posh) over the speaking of Gaelic in itself.

We have here, then, two somewhat different models of identity at work: one, the romantic nationalist, which emphasises the expressive individuation of 'a culture' through certain features, particularly language; the other, a more fluid repertoire which might change over time. The potential within the local model for variety and for change is of particular importance for language revival, for it means that the future directions are not firmly determined but may be reshaped as part of a continuing dynamic between local notions and cultural developments.

Gaelic and Scottish Identity

One dimension of the politicisation of Gaelic – and also of a potential source of local ambivalence about it – is its increasing incorporation into Scottish identity and nationalism. In Gaelic renaissance literature, as described in Chapter 2, Gaelic is increasingly being cast as a language of *Scotland* and in some cases it is even implied or argued that the Highland/ Lowland divide is a myth created by the English (e.g. Ellis 1985: 29). In the Lowlands, Gaelic classes are flourishing and the Gaelic language is increasingly being used in the touristic marketing of Scotland as a whole.[5] Gaelic is becoming much more fashionable as witnessed perhaps most markedly by the success of the Gaelic rock group Run-Rig.

At the same time, while there was some small increase in the number of jobs specifically open to Gaelic speakers during the 1980s, the socio-economic world of young Highlanders is in many other respects a good deal less distinct from that of Lowlanders than that of their parents' generation. Today, they are unlikely to be called 'Teuchtars', and are more likely than their elders to inter-marry with Lowlanders, to wear the same clothes, to eat the same foods, to watch the same television programmes and to speak the same first language. Linguistic research on the English used by Skye teenagers shows a shift from a Highland towards a more Lowland accent (Shuken 1984: 153). I found that young people were more likely to support Scottish nationalism than were their parents; and they were also much more likely to refer to outsiders as 'Sasunnaich' (English) rather than 'strangers' or 'Goill' (Lowlanders/foreigners). For older people Gaelic was a given part of their experience and had they not spoken it they would have been outsiders in Carnan: Gaelic was the language of home, kin, neighbours, church, agricultural activities, and even for those who worked on the mainland, often of their friends and work mates as well. For younger people, however, a lack of Gaelic does not for the most part debar them from the world of their peers. Moreover, as Gaelic is increasingly politicised, there seems to be a shift from regarding language as primarily communicative and embedded in social relations, to regarding it as more of a *symbolic* matter. One young woman, Maggie, told me:

> Aye, Gaelic's our language right enough, and we ought to be trying to keep it up. But I don't think there's many today would be calling you an outsider just because you didn't have the Gaelic. A while back, yes, you'd be lost here without it. But now – well – it's just to know that it's there. You don't have to be speaking it every minute of the day.

Both older and younger local people may hold ambivalent views of Gaelic. For both, one aspect of their negative evaluation of Gaelic is its relative exclusion from 'opportunity' and the material advantages of 'away'. Yet where older people's more positive evaluation of the language derived primarily from its place in day-to-day social relations, for younger people positive evaluations are more likely to emanate from a politicised view of what it means to 'have a culture'.

At the same time, however, what it means to 'have the Gaelic' seems to be somewhat different for the generations. For older Gaelic speakers, those of Seumas' generation and above, 'having the Gaelic' entailed speaking the language fluently and using it regularly in social interactions in the locality. Gaelic was thoroughly bound up with other day-to-day social relations and evaluations: it was part of the 'banal' identity repertoire of everyday life. For younger people, such as Maggie, however, 'having the Gaelic' is not so much a matter of everyday practice. Instead, Gaelic has become objectified as part of a much more conspicuous package of 'culture' and 'identity' which can be drawn upon in those rather particular circumstances in which one may be called upon to express an identity. Instead of being inextricably bound up with other social relations and values (as it is for Seumas), Gaelic for Maggie seems to be much more like a folk costume which one might keep in the wardrobe to wear for special occasions. And while Seumas' way of 'having the Gaelic' requires fluency, Maggie's seems only to require what one of her contemporaries described to me (in describing his own level of competence) as 'enough to be convincing – providing it's not to have a long conversation with somebody who really knows the language, like [elderly Gaelic-speaking relative]'. Gaelic for these younger people is part of a politicised repertoire of what it means to 'have a culture' and 'to have an identity'; but this seems to be regarded as separate from everyday social relations within the locality. 'Culture' and 'identity' are regarded as separate 'objects' which can be disconnected from immediate relations.

It is important to note, however, that not all young people necessarily conceptualise Gaelic in this way. For the young men who go along to fanks, for example, Gaelic is very much bound up with their relations with other men and their identities not just as 'Highlanders' but as 'men'. In other words, for them, Gaelic will not be attached only to a romantic nationalist package of 'language and ethnicity', but to other identities, especially gender, which map partially onto one another and which bring identity 'home'.

The objectification of culture and identity and their separation from everyday social relations could be argued to be at odds with the romantic-nationalist conception of identity promoted by Herder and others, and with those involved in the contemporary Gaelic renaissance. Both, as we have seen, suppose an integration of community, identity and language, and in the case of, say, the bilingual education policies discussed in this chapter, have involved an attempt to promote the association between Gaelic and the local environment. However, at the same time, the romantic-nationalist conception and its more recent politicisation, particularly in ethnonationalist movements, has also demarcated 'culture' and 'identity' as specific phenomena *in themselves*; and this has made possible the separation from the social and the everyday which Maggie, for one, seems very easily to accept.

In this chapter we have looked at a number of Gaelic policies and I have argued that their reception – just as in the case of the reception of decades of earlier policies on the use of English in education – needs to be understood in relation to a repertoire of local notions of language use, social relations and identity. While language has been elevated by the Gaelic renaissance to the single most important aspect of identity, for local people it is part of a much wider range of ways of identifying. For this reason, together with the ambivalence manifest in relation to Gaelic, there is clearly a good deal of alternative potential over whether, to what extent, and in what ways, Gaelic will be 'saved.'

Notes

1. For a discussion of women's perceived role in the demise of East Sutherland Gaelic see Constantinidou 1994. McDonald 1994 shows a

similar association of women with social betterment in language-use patterns in Brittany.

2. The term 'semi-speaker' was coined by Nancy Dorian on the basis of her sociolinguistic research in East Sutherland (1978). While I use the labels 'Gaelic speaker' and 'non-Gaelic speaker' in this book – terms which are widely used locally – it should be noted that these are often far from clear-cut and there is a good deal of variation in Gaelic fluency in particular. Moreover, I have argued elsewhere that the notion of linguistic competence needs in the bilingual situation to be extended also to consider competence in knowing what language to use in what context and the codes for language switching (1987).

3. After the new playgroup had been running for a while, and the 'old' group had lapsed, several of those who had opposed it originally began to send their children. This was beyond the main period of my fieldwork but some of those involved told me that as there was nothing else running they felt that they 'might as well'. A similar phenomenon has occurred with Gaelic medium primary education in the area as I note in the following chapter.

4. For example, the mother of a mainly Gaelic-speaking two year old who used the English word 'thank you' told me, half-jokingly, *'Tha manners uabhasach math aice'* – 'she's got very good manners'.

5. This is a trend which has continued, most notably in the remarkable expansion of Gaelic broadcasting since 1993. See the next chapter for further discussion.

Reflections on Reimagining

'Happy were those who could talk of "the system"' (Edwin Ardener)

When I first came to write about my time in Skye I was for a long time frustrated that I could not seem to make the various practices and remarks that I had witnessed 'fit together'. Comments on the Gaelic language, on being a people, on the importance of crofting and tradition seemed to shift and to be marked by ambivalence. When were people *really* being Highlanders? Which statements and practices was I to privilege? And on what basis?

In the end I have tried to give voice to some of this ambivalence, and to give some sense of the complexities, overlaps and flexibility within classifications used to define 'who we are' and 'how we are'. I have also tried to highlight the kinds of semantic frames within which certain kinds of statements are likely to be privileged (because they speak of 'tradition' or 'community' for example). This is not, however, a picture of unpatterned ambivalence and complexity. For while I found the situation in Carnan daunting, I also came to be able to know what to expect to a certain extent, and to have a sense of what might be extraordinary or incomprehensible behaviour. At the same time, it was also clear to me that the preoccupations and assumptions of those living in Carnan, varied though they might be, were not all just the same as those of, say, members of the anthropology institute in Oxford. There were similarities certainly. And Carnan folk were not, I think, *more* ambivalent or given to diverse views than the academics or than others I knew (though perhaps I had not bothered to notice this before in some of my own more familiar contexts). But there were differences in ways of seeing and in expectations, in the kinds of collectivities that were invoked and regarded as important. Where the boundaries of these alternatives lies, however, is impossible to say. Even if anthropologists were to study every inhabited location along a line between Oxford and Skye it would, surely, still be impossible to point a finger and say 'Here is where one culture ends and another begins'. Something would happen on the England-Scotland border, certainly, but it would not be like shutting one door and finding a room furnished entirely differently. For all that the romantic-nationalist model of identity would suppose – and for all that anthropology has in the past seemed to substantiate – the world cannot readily be divided into distinct and bounded cultures. This is not to say, however, that there is no cultural difference or that anthropology has no task in the modern world.

Just because the world does not present itself in terms of neat packages of senses of peoplehood and distinctive practices, contained within a territory, does not mean that there are not alternative ways of seeing and doing. To think thus would be akin to refusing to accept a difference between yellow and blue because of all the possible shades of green. Edwin Ardener has emphasised the importance of what he calls 'semantic density' for anthropology (1982, 1989: ch.11): this is a statistical or frequential feature of meaning making. Categories, he argues (*contra* some interpretations of Saussure), are not simply defined by their place in an abstract system. Rather, they are also formed through the day-to-day experience of practice or 'materiality'; an experience in which some categories seem more or less 'empty' or meaningful than others, and in which there may be variations in the usages of categories. There may, for example, be a fuzziness over whether some particular shades will be referred to as 'blue' or 'green' but this does not throw into chaos the more frequent agreement over other usages of the terms. The task of anthropology, we might extrapolate, is not just about mapping boundaries but also about describing and accounting for both cultural alternatives and more elusive and fine-grained variations.

Alongside the widespread current perception that cultural difference is being eroded is an equally widespread manufacture of such difference. Peoples are being called upon to revive, maintain and express the cultural particularity that it is assumed that they have somehow lost touch with: they are being called upon to expressively individuate themselves as 'cultures'. The irony of this, however, is that the form that properly recognisable 'cultures' are supposed to take is in many respects rather invariant. Mostly, cultures are imagined in terms of what Richard Handler calls 'cultural objectifications' (1988): external markers of difference. A typical cultural 'identikit' includes distinctive language, food, music, dance, folklore, traditions (especially festivals), folk art and material culture (preferably housed in a folklife museum), and perhaps dress and literature. More ephemeral and everyday features, such as those that I have suggested seem important to the inhabitants of Carnan when they define who they are, are not part of this conception of what it means to be a culture and to have an identity. These are features which are neither so readily bounded, nor necessarily as 'safe', as the cultural objectifications in which peoplehood is preferably packaged. Negative views of authority or interfering outsiders, or evaluations which might in a politically correct world appear as 'chauvinism' or 'sexism', may be more politically problematic differences than those privileged by the romantic-nationalist model.

Nevertheless, the romantic-nationalist model of identity *is* one which is available to those living in Carnan. They are not, after all, outside modernity. Ontologies of being and of improvement, and a tension between the two (to develop or to remain true to oneself), are thoroughly part of their repertoire though, as we have seen, they are not necessarily manifest in the same ways, or accorded the same kind of weight, as they might be elsewhere. More than this, however, the romantic vocabulary of community, tradition and way of life is a very eloquent and persuasive one in which to express demands and it can certainly be imbued with personal resonance. At the same time, however, it is also one which is almost impossible to live up to; and so, romanticised on the one hand, Highlanders have too often found themselves cast as not having been quite true enough to their culture and as suffering from apathy and false-consciousness.

Here I have tried to give some sense of these alternatives by using the sociolinguistic notion of repertoire. While this is patterned, it is not 'a structure' or 'a system'. It deals in frequencies rather than static categories; and it is reckoned not in terms of a bounded whole but begins from a particular point and works outwards. Beginning from a different point will lead us to a different but overlapping set of possibilities. This way of thinking about the nature of culture, then, will lead us to be less concerned with 'the boundary' than with the many ways in which 'bounding' is performed. While there will, of course, be those who are keen to symbolically construct a distinct boundary between themselves and others – after all this is the dominant romantic-nationalist model – by ourselves using more flexible analytical frameworks we may be better able to perceive other ways of identifying. Moreover, because a repertoire is conceptualised as an assemblage of alternatives and variations and not as a set of pieces which fit together like a jigsaw, change – or process – is less problematic than it has been in structural models in the social sciences. Nor are we left with a vision of culture as an assemblage of random fragments as is the case in some post-modern anthropologies. Following the sociolinguistic analogy what we would expect is that the alternatives and variations within the repertoire would generate new possibilities, and that individuals would draw on the available repertoire in creative ways

Cultural reimagining is possible. We have, I think, seen something of this in the case of Carnan.

The Future of Gaelic Culture?

What, then, are the implications of this for those questions which are so central to the Gaelic renaissance: What future does Gaelic culture have? And will the Gaelic language be saved?

These are difficult questions and ones which it would be presumptuous to try to answer solely on the basis of my study here. However, it does, I think, have some relevant implications that can be noted. First, my research shows that although those living in the Highlands have been the object of numerous representations and policies emanating from elsewhere, they have not been passive in their responses. Rather, they have drawn on their own cultural preoccupations to challenge, make use of, or appropriate outside forms. Second, the fact of change, of divergence within a locality, or of ambivalence, does not mean that 'a culture' is somehow sick or pathological. These are, probably, the kind of cultural conditions which it is more usual to find; and indeed we might even suggest that they are evidence of a more extensive repertoire upon which peoples and individuals can draw and, therefore, act creatively. Third, identity does not seem to be located in any one single tradition or cultural practice; and although some, such as language, may be accorded great importance, they are not necessarily vital to a sense of peoplehood.

This having been said, however, there is clearly a danger of the loss of certain cultural practices and forms. How much this matters is an evaluative question likely to be answered in different ways depending upon the practice in question (e.g. violent clan feuding or Gaelic poetry). As an anthropologist I am, however, particularly aware of how much can be learnt from what Errington and Gewertz call 'cultural alternatives' (1987) – other ways of experiencing, classifying and evaluating – and would certainly rather see an enrichment than a shrinkage of the global cultural repertoire. This enrichment, however, needs to be more than a cultural identikit of standardised differences. As Richard Handler aptly puts it, the latter is like 'a row of ethnic restaurants in any North American city – all making use of a set of presuppositions that they share with their customers about what constitutes ethnic food, how, where, and when to eat it, how to pay for it, and what its value as nutrition and authentic experience is' (1988: 195). It is a production of differences that in effect 'makes them all the same' (ibid.; see also MacCannell 1992 and Ritzer 1996).

Codified Difference

Let me give an example of this. During my fieldwork in Skye, partly as a way of improving my own grasp of the Gaelic language, I explored the use of various Gaelic terminologies, including those of colour, parts of the body, and of time. I was inspired here by the work of my supervisor, the late Edwin Ardener. His account of colour classification showed on the basis of an analysis of dictionaries how in the case of Welsh there has been a shift in the usage of colour terms such that the referents of colour terms in Modern Colloquial Welsh, unlike in the older 'Standard Welsh', are the same as in English (see Figure 9.1) (1989: ch.1). Welsh colour terms are no longer distinctive in their classification of the world. A similar shift seems to be underway in the case of Scottish Gaelic. For example, according to older dictionaries, and in the unselfconscious speech of older Gaelic speakers, grass would be described by the term *gorm*. However, today the term *gorm* is thought of as a translation for 'blue', and 'green' is translated as *uaine*. In my experience children invariably referred to grass as *uaine* and more generally used Gaelic terms in the same way as the English terms for which they have become the 'official' equivalents. This is a shift which is also evident in dictionaries: the newer dictionaries being less likely to list what, even in the older dictionaries, were often perceived as 'anomalies' rather than a different classificatory pattern. For some Gaelic speakers the matter could be rather confusing. For example, one elderly Gaelic speaker, who I had noticed using *gorm* as a description of grass earlier, described it to me when I asked him for colour terms of various things as *uaine* (i.e. the 'official' translation). When I suggested *gorm* as an appropriate term he told me 'But that's blue rightly' and said that as grass was green the right term to use was *uaine*. English categories were being used to define the usage of Gaelic terms. In effect, Gaelic was being regarded as a kind of code for English. *Difference* was a matter of the words used, not of the harder to grasp and more culturally challenging matters of alternative cultural categories.

The increase of *codified difference* as opposed to *cultural alternatives* was evident in other domains too. Edwin Ardener (1989: ch.9) has shown well how Scottish Gaelic and Irish terms for times of the year – times which previously were not fixed according to date but varied according to such environmental factors as the weather – have come to be mapped on to a standardised European system of twelve months and four seasons. Figure 9.2 is Ardener's stylised depiction of the former Scottish Gaelic annual time terminology. The outer ring identifies two main seasons (*Samhradh* and *Gheamhradh*) and within this are a set of more flexible

ENGLISH	STANDARD WELSH	MODERN COLLOQUIAL WELSH
green	gwyrdd	gwyrdd
blue	glas	glas
grey	llwyd	llwyd
brown		brown
black	du	du

Figure 9.1. Certain English and Welsh colour categories (after E.W.Ardener)

temporal divisions. Now, however, *Samhradh* and *Gheamhraidh* have become identified as Summer and Winter and two other 'seasons' have been derived from the Gaelic annual cycle (*An t-Earrach* and *Am Foghar*). Most of the other terms listed here have come to be identified with the English months (represented in the diagram in the upper case letters at the centre).

In Carnan these 'new' usages were often unfamiliar to all but the younger Gaelic speakers who had recently learnt them in school. While some older speakers thought the new usages 'wrong' and explained to me their alternative understandings of them, there were others who saw their own lack of knowledge of the new terms as evidence of the inadequacy of their own grasp of the language. Even in discussions of alternative classifications there was an inclination to talk of the Gaelic usages as 'strange'. This tendency to regard Gaelic as a kind of exotic code for English is one which is also reinforced by dictionaries. Until the 1991 publication of *Brigh na Facal* (Cox 1991) (a dictionary aimed at children), there were *no* Gaelic dictionaries in which Gaelic words were explained by a Gaelic gloss. In other words, *all* Gaelic dictionaries explained Gaelic terms through reference to their English 'equivalents'. Clearly, this is a form of 'Anglicisation' but one more subtle than that of the forceful prevention of Gaelic speaking upon which Gaelic revivalist texts more frequently focus. Moreover, precisely because it is less immediately visible – and perhaps too because those promoting new Gaelic terms for the

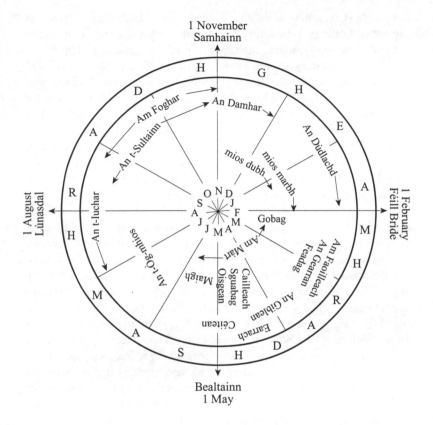

Figure 9.2. The Scottish Gaelic year (E.W. Ardener)

months and so forth come from those who are 'on the side of the Gaelic' – it may be that these forms of 'Anglicisation' are particularly 'insidious' (to use a term which has been used by Celtic nationalists).

The Expansion of the Gaelic Renaissance

Since the mid-1980s the Gaelic renaissance has expanded massively, and certainly beyond the expectations of the majority of those with whom I carried out research. In 1986 there were thirty-two Gaelic playgroups in Scotland operating under the auspices of Comhairle nan Sgoiltean Araich (the Gaelic Playgroup Association), whereas by 1994 there were almost 150 groups (Comunn na Gàidhlig, 1994a: 6). Likewise, in 1986 there were six Gaelic-medium primary school units, whereas by 1994 there were forty-eight (Comunn na Gàidhlig 1994a: 4). Since 1988 Carnan itself has had not just bilingual-medium primary schooling but a choice of Gaelic or English medium teaching in the primary school;[1] and since 1990 there has been at secondary level in Skye an optional 'Gaelic medium stream' in certain subjects (Maths, History, Domestic Science, Gaelic, and Personal and Social Education).[2] In both cases the number of children opting for Gaelic medium has grown steadily over the years. While only a few children initially opted for Gaelic medium, by 1996 this had grown to over half of the total school population, with each year showing a greater proportion of the new intake selecting Gaelic medium. At the secondary school in Portree, numbers opting for the Gaelic stream have more than doubled since its inception (to twenty in 1996).

So who is opting for Gaelic and why? And what might this indicate about views of Gaelic and identity? (I should note here that although I have returned to Carnan many times and have discussed the matter with various local people, I have not carried out the kind of detailed ethnographic research on which the account in this book is based.) According to teachers at the school, a few of those who opt for Gaelic medium are fluent Gaelic speakers or are from families with no Gaelic at all (indeed, one of the cases about which Carnan people particularly like to tell is of a child of white settler parents who now speaks Gaelic 'like a native'). The majority, however, come from homes where at least one parent is a Gaelic speaker but where children speak very little of the language on starting school. These are the families in which, in terms of my earlier analysis, children seem to have autonomously decided not to 'bother with the Gaelic'. That such families would choose Gaelic medium – providing they had become assured that it was not a 'gimmick'[3] or an educational disadvantage – illustrates that such families were not 'against' Gaelic, or somehow purposefully failing to provide it in the home. Given the possibility of Gaelic being available without it being part of a parental 'pushing' of children or a matter of social 'snobbishness', this is an option which they are comfortable to take. Indeed, we might say that providing the option allows them to draw on that strand in the local identity repertoire in which Gaelic is an important part of everyday social relations and connection with the locality. And as more take the option, the more it may become an 'unmarked' choice; and as the number falls of those deciding upon English medium – whose reasons are given as mainly educational (fear over whether children will be adequately prepared for secondary school) – the more difficult it becomes to classify the Gaelic option as a matter of 'being fancy'. Indeed, this kind of classification seemed not to be being used so often in relation to Gaelic use in the 1990s in Carnan as it was in the 1980s. More often it seemed to me, people remarked on how 'fashionable' Gaelic has become. Being fashionable, unlike being fancy, proud or snobbish, is not so morally dubious: it is more of an external evaluation rather than a personal quality. While the description of 'the upturn of Gaelic' (as the renaissance tends to be described locally) as 'fashionable' carries a connotation that this is an evaluation which might well change – indeed, several people suggested as much – it nevertheless also suggests that the behaviour which the term describes might continue.

The opportunity to draw on the idea of Gaelic as part of formerly important social relations is not, however, the only reason for opting for Gaelic medium. One consequence of the Gaelic renaissance is that the number of jobs available using Gaelic has expanded enormously;[4] and this has certainly helped to increase the attractiveness of Gaelic medium education. 'Jobs are part of it [the growth of uptake of Gaelic medium], there's no question about it', explained one teacher; 'If you have the Gaelic, you are almost promised a job today' commented a parent. This is a major change in the perception (and existence) of the job opportunities available for Gaelic speakers over the decade. Moreover, these are jobs which may mean that young people will not have to move so far away as they may in the search for jobs which do not require Gaelic, something which, as already noted, is attractive to many parents. Certainly in Carnan there are greater numbers of young people now choosing to remain in or return to the Island. Not all of these are directly employed in occupations requiring Gaelic (which are largely in the cultural industries) though there are increasing numbers of jobs indirectly related to it (for example, in tourism); and part of the attraction for some who choose to remain or return is that other people of their age are doing so. Even Robert (discussed in Chapter 4), who was making a good living as a solicitor on the mainland, told me that he was thinking of coming back to Carnan, not to croft, perhaps, but nevertheless 'coming home'. 'It's a bit livelier here than it was', he said, 'and a good place to bring up kids'.

Another consequence of this expansion of Gaelic-related jobs is that areas such as Carnan are experiencing a greater number of their educated young people following careers in which Gaelic, and the maintenance of Gaelic culture, is important to them. This group of young Gaels, who often hold strongly politicised views about their language, look likely to prove influential in the future of Gaelic in Scotland, and particularly within the Highlands themselves. Already there is evidence of the formation of a network of entrepreneurial young Gaels who are actively seeking to develop further Gaelic-related projects in areas such as Skye; and who are often reflexively engaged in trying to create new ways of 'being Gaels' (see Macdonald 1997). How they will be viewed by, and whether they will have any influence upon the speaking habits of, those such as Seumas and Maggie described in the last chapter of this book, is, however, a crucial question and one which remains to be seen.

Despite the revival, during the 1980s, alongside the flourishing of Gaelic promotion policies and projects, the number of Gaelic speakers in Scotland continued to fall. The 1991 Census reported 66,000 or 1.37 per cent of Scotland's resident population as 'able to speak Gaelic', a decline from the 80,000 or 1.71 per cent recorded in 1981, and continuing the general decline over the course of the century. However, the Census also contains figures which have been heralded as indicating the beginnings of an upturn in Gaelic speaking. In Skye, for example, the proportions of those reporting as Gaelic speaking in the younger age cohorts (up to 10 years) is greater in 1991 than it was in 1981;[5] and the Gaelic promotion agency Comunn na Gàidhlig projects 80,000 Gaelic speakers in Scotland by the year 2021, 40,000 of them under twenty-five years old (compared with less than 20,000 today) (Comunn na Gàidhlig 1994a: 2). What the Census and its question about Gaelic *ability* rather than *use* does not tell us, however, is the extent to which Gaelic is, and will be, part of the social and cultural world of these children. For this what is required is detailed and impartial research which, as yet, is not available.

How far the increase of Gaelic in education and the new opportunities to use Gaelic in the workplace will substantially affect the everyday use of Gaelic, and the overall number of Gaelic speakers, is then unclear. While in Carnan school playground Gaelic is now used as well as English, the latter still predominates. A teacher in Portree school observed that the children in the Gaelic stream seem not to talk to each other in Gaelic outside the classroom, and often within it (sometimes having to be reprimanded for this) and doubted that they used the language much outside school. Nevertheless, Gaelic-medium education and new jobs are providing a new *potential* for Gaelic use; and the greater number of younger people staying in the locality increases the likelihood that they will find Gaelic-speaking partners. Certainly at the level of individual families it seems to me that some children who would have had little ability in the language may do so now, and I have observed children who were once reluctant to use Gaelic speak it easily, and switch between English and Gaelic, with a lack of self-consciousness. Take Anna's children. As she hoped, her younger child has become fluent in Gaelic (to the extent that this was her first language and is still her preferred language). And even Calein, once so reluctant to speak Gaelic, now uses the language seemingly entirely comfortably with his mother and sister. Now on the brink of his teens, he tells me that he thinks that he will leave the Island when he is older and is looking forward to the opportunities of the mainland. This does not, however, mean that he feels that he needs to leave his Gaelic possibilities behind.

None of this is to say that ambivalence over Gaelic and its place in identity has disappeared; and nor that there are no longer those like Maggie for whom Gaelic is more of a symbolic object than a part of their everyday social relations. Neither is it to say that there are no longer any who would define themselves as 'locals' who would not speak Gaelic – though it is increasingly doubtful that they would choose to educate their children in English medium. And nor is it to say that language has now ousted other more everyday means of identifying as a 'local' or a 'Gael'; or that increasing numbers of Gaelic speakers alone will provide cultural alternatives rather than codified difference. It is, however, to suggest that Gaelic *may* find and maintain a place within a flexible identity repertoire in which it is more than an empty symbolic marker of symbolic difference in a global cultural identikit.

Gaelic and Scotland

One particularly important aspect of the development of the Gaelic renaissance over the past decade has been its expansion throughout Scotland. Gaelic-medium playgroups and primary education can now be found outside the area known as the *Fior Gàidhealtachd* (the Gaelic heartlands) – the Western Isles and Skye – in areas where Gaelic speaking is at very low levels (*A' Bhreac-Ghàidhealtachd* or 'Residual Gaelic area') as well as in urban locations such as Edinburgh and Glasgow. Bilingual place-names are now not only to be found in the Highlands but also in many other parts of Scotland, including as far South as the Borders. A Gaelic Learners Association, *Comunn an Luchd Ionnsachaidh*, for adult learners of Gaelic, established in the 1980s, now has nearly a thousand members; and Comunn na Gàidhlig claims that '8,000 adults in Scotland are now actively learning Gaelic and 1,000,000 would like to do so' (Comunn na Gàidhlig 1996: 9).[6] Perhaps of particular cultural significance, given the great importance with which it has been attributed in matters of cultural influence and language acquisition, is the major expansion of Gaelic broadcasting which began in 1993: from around one hundred hours per annum to three hundred hours. This includes a Gaelic soap-opera, *Machair* (set mainly at a Gaelic college), which is broadcast with English subtitles. Again, what is equally significant about this is the fact that much of this new television output has been at prime-time and throughout Scotland. Its imagined audience has been *Scots* rather than specifically Gaels.

In the 1990s, Gaelic has also gained a national and international visibility which it lacked a decade earlier. I now meet few people who are surprised to learn that Scottish Gaelic exists, whereas this was common, in England and abroad when I began my research. The success of Gaelic-singing groups such as Run-Rig and Capercaillie, and the attempts by Prince Charles to learn the language, have contributed to this, as has publicity given to Gaelic broadcasting and other developments. Now, at all party political conferences in Scotland, there is a motto in Gaelic as well as English. Gaelic has come to be accepted as a symbol of Scotland's distinctiveness.

The desire to symbolically mark Scotland's distinctiveness from England may also be, in part, a response to a growing political divide between Scotland and England, and also to the possibilities offered within a European framework – or more specifically a 'Europe of Peoples' or 'Europe of Regions' – for Scotland to act independently of England (see McCrone 1991, Harvie 1994a). Certainly, there are many now, not least in the Hebrides (which were among the most 'anti-Europe' regions in the 1975 referendum on joining the European Economic Community), who seem to be 'warming' to the opportunities for greater regional autonomy within a European framework (Hunter 1991, Parman 1993), though the increased levels of state support in the 1980s and into the 1990s (under a Conservative government) for cultural, and especially Gaelic, activities within Scotland may have been partly intended to indicate that cultural difference can be effectively pursued within a United Kingdom context. While a European framework offers the potential for greater Scottish autonomy, it may also, however, provide the possibility for certain regions within Scotland to differentiate themselves from Scotland as a whole. Indeed, the development of the Crofters Union, and an attempt in 1996 to define crofters as 'an indigenous people', are examples of an attempt to draw on more specific, historically sourced, identity possibilities: in this case an identity as 'crofters'.[7] What we see here, as we have seen in this book in relation to many earlier cases, is European and global definitions of peoplehood being drawn upon to help maintain and develop more local realisations. What we also see, however, as I have also argued here, is that we are not dealing with a single clear-cut identity or a single either-or pair of options: rather, there is available a more varied and changeable repertoire – informed but not constrained by the past – through which those living in places like Carnan can define what it means to be one of them. The future, I suggest, is open.

This book is a portrait of a community at a particular juncture in the process of cultural revitalisation. It has described some of the variations and ambivalences in views of Gaelic revival policies and more generally in ways of identifying. I am aware that there are those who will feel that to acknowledge that there are those who are less than wholeheartedly in favour of cultural revivalism, or that renaissance policies have not always been received as anticipated, is 'unhelpful'. (Indeed, Anthony Cohen (1996) has recently suggested that this may be a particular type of indigenous viewpoint.) However, to refuse to admit ambivalence, or dismiss as pathological those whose views do not conform to a renaissance ideal, is not only to silence those upon whom the success of the renaissance may depend, it is also to forgo the opportunity to come to understand better how cultural revitalisation might be best brought about. If Gaelic culture is to be reimagined, as it surely will be, then it is surely better that this is done in awareness of the widest repertoire of cultural alternatives available.

Notes

1. Both streams introduce some study of whichever is the 'other' language from Primary Three, so that children beginning secondary education will have a grasp of both.
2. Which subjects are available through the medium of Gaelic at secondary level depends upon which teachers are able and willing to teach through the medium. The subjects available in Gaelic medium in Portree, therefore, will not be the same as those available in, say, Stornoway.
3. As with the introduction of bilingual medium, discussed in Chapter 8, the fact that teachers with whom parents were already familiar were involved, and that an emphasis was still clearly placed upon educational achievement was important in convincing parents that Gaelic-medium education was not 'just a gimmick'. Nevertheless, several told me that they had not been keen on the idea in the early days as they did

not want their children to be 'guinea pigs'. Now that some children educated in Gaelic medium have gone on to secondary school with no evident educational problems, there is increasing confidence about taking the Gaelic option. Moreover, children educated in Gaelic medium are all also fluent in English while the converse does not hold for those who take English medium.

4. According to a report produced in 1993, 'the Gaelic industry' was estimated in 1991/2 to have 'directly created the equivalent of 450 full time jobs, with over 40% of jobs and output being created in the Gaelic-speaking "heartlands" of the Outer Isles and Skye' (Sproull 1993: ii). These jobs do not necessarily entail using Gaelic but are defined as relating to 'all those activities . . . whose principal purpose is the provision of Gaelic-related goods and services, including the promotion of Gaelic culture and language' (Sproull 1993: i). By 1992/3, with the impact of the expansion of Gaelic media being felt, there were estimated to be the equivalent of 280 more full-time jobs (1993: iii). In Skye and Lochalsh, such jobs were estimated to constitute the equivalent of 4.3 per cent of the areas' then total employment (ibid.).

5. In the Western Isles, however, there was a decline in Gaelic speaking, reading or writing at all ages. The pattern in the *Bhreac-Ghàidhealtachd* was generally similar to that for Skye, though the proportions involved are relatively small (Government Statistical Service 1994).

6. Information about membership of CLI was provided by them. The figures for those interested in learning Gaelic are much greater than the 15,000 quoted in 1994 (Comunn na Gàidhlig 1994a: 9).

7. This is not synonymous with 'Highlanders', 'Gaels' or 'Gaelic speakers' because the crofting areas include the Northern Isles, and of course, as discussed earlier not all those living in the 'crofting communities' are crofters legally defined.

Bibliography

Aitken, A.J. 1981 'Foreword', in E. Haugen, J.D. McClure and D.S. Thomson (eds) *Minority Languages Today*, pp. vii–xii, Edinburgh: Edinburgh University Press

Allan, D. 1993 *Virtue, Learning and the Scottish Enlightenment*, Edinburgh: Edinburgh University Press

American Ethnologist 1991 'Representations of Europe: transforming state, society, and identity' (special issue), Vol.18, no.3

An Account of the Present State of Religion throughout the Highlands of Scotland by a lay member of the Established Church 1827, Edinburgh

Anderson, B. 1983 *Imagined Communities. Reflections on the Origin and Spread of Nationalism*, London: Verso

Ardener, E. 1971 'Social anthropology and the historicity of historical linguistics', in E.Ardener (ed.) *Social Anthropology and Language*, pp. 209–42, London: Tavistock

—— 1982 'Social anthropology, language and reality', in D. Parkin (ed.) *Semantic Anthropology*, pp. 1–14, London: Academic Press

—— 1989 *The Voice of Prophecy and other essays*, ed. M. Chapman, Oxford: Blackwell

—— 1989a 'The construction of history: "vestiges of creation"', in E. Tonkin, M. McDonald and M. Chapman (eds) *History and Ethnicity*, pp.22–33, London: Routledge

Ardener, S. 1975 'Introduction', in S. Ardener (ed.) *Perceiving Women*, pp.vii–xxiii, London: J.M. Dent and Sons

Attridge, D. 1989 [1987] 'Language as history/history as language: Saussure and the romance of etymology', in D. Attridge, G. Bennington and R. Young (eds) *Post-structuralism and the Question of History*, pp. 183–211, Cambridge: Cambridge University Press

Badone, E. (ed.) 1990 *Religious Orthodoxy and Popular Faith in European Society*, New York: Princeton University Press

Bannerman, J. 1974 *Studies in the History of Dalriada*, Edinburgh: Scottish Academic Press

Barnard, F.M. 1969 *Herder on Social and Political Culture*, Cambridge: Cambridge University Press

Barth, F. 1969 'Introduction', in F. Barth (ed.) *Ethnic Groups and Boundaries. The Social Organization of Culture Difference*, pp. 9–38, London: George Allen and Unwin

Bauman, Z. 1991 *Modernity and Ambivalence*, Oxford: Polity Press

Bellin, W. 1984 'Welsh and English in Wales', in P. Trudgill (ed.) *Language in the British Isles*, pp. 449–79, Cambridge: Cambridge University Press

Berlin, I. 1976 *Vico and Herder*, London: Hogarth Press

Billig, M. 1995 *Banal Nationalism*, London: Sage

Blackadder, J. 1799 *Survey and Valuation of Lord MacDonald's Estates*, SRO, RH 2/8/24

Blackie, J.S. 1864 *The Gaelic Language: Its Affinities and Distinctive Character*, Edinburgh: Edmonston and Douglas

Blacklaw, B. 1978 *Bun-Chursa Gaidhlig. Scottish Gaelic. A Progressive Course*, Perth: Farquhar and Son Ltd.

Bogdanor, V. 1979 *Devolution*, Oxford: Oxford University Press

Boissevain, J. 1975 'Introduction', in J. Boissevain and J. Friedl (eds) *Beyond the Community: Social Process in Europe*, The Hague: Mouton

Boissevain, J. and J. Friedl (eds) 1975 *Beyond the Community: Social Process in Europe*, The Hague: Mouton

Bold, A. 1990 *MacDiarmid*, London: Paladin

Borland, J., R. Fevre and D. Denny 1992 'Nationalism and community in North West Wales', *Sociological Review* 40, pp.49–72

Bowie, F. 1993 'Wales from within: conflicting interpretations of Welsh identity', in S.Macdonald (ed.) *Inside European Identities*, pp. 167–93, Oxford and Providence: Berg

Brand, J. 1978 *The National Movement in Scotland*, London: Routledge and Kegan Paul

Breathnach, P. 1984 'Community participation in rural development. Examples of Scottish and Irish peripheries', paper presented to Institute of British Geographers annual conference, Durham

Breathnach, P., P. Duffy, K. MacKeogh and J. Walsh 1984 *Aspects of Rural Development in the Scottish Highlands and Islands*, occasional paper number 4, Geography Department, Maynooth College

Breuilly, J. 1982 *Nationalism and the State*, Manchester: Manchester University Press

Brown, C.G. 1988 'Religion and social change', in T.M.Devine and R.Mitchison (eds) *People and Society in Scotland, Vol.1, 1760–1830*, pp. 143–62, Edinburgh: Edinburgh University Press

Burleigh, J.H.S. 1960 *A Church History of Scotland*, Oxford: Oxford University Press

Caird, J. and H.A. Moisley 1961 'Leadership and innovation in the crofting communities of the Outer Hebrides', *Sociological Review*, 9 (1), pp. 85–102

Campbell, J.L. 1950 [1945] *Gaelic in Scottish Education and Life*, Edinburgh: W. and A.K.Johnston for the Saltire Society

Campbell, J.L. and D. Thomson 1963 *Edward Lhuyd in the Scottish Highlands 1699–1700*, Oxford: Oxford University Press

Campbell, R.H. and A. Skinner (eds) 1982 *The Origins and Nature of the Scottish Enlightenment*, Edinburgh: John Donald

Carter, I. 1974 'The Highlands of Scotland as an underdeveloped region', in
    E. de Kadt and G. Williams (eds) *Sociology and Development*, London:
    Tavistock
Celtic League Annual 1969–72, Dublin: The Celtic League
Chadwick, H.M. 1949 *Early Scotland*, Cambridge: Cambridge University Press
Chapman, M. 1978 *The Gaelic Vision in Scottish Culture*, London: Croom Helm
—— 1982 '"Semantics" and the "Celt"', in D.Parkin (ed.) *Semantic Anthropology*,
    pp.123–44, London: Academic Press
—— 1992 *The Celts. The Construction of a Myth*, Houndmills: Macmillan
Clifford, J. 1991 'Four Northwest coast museums: travel reflections', in I.Karp
    and S.D.Lavine (eds) *Exhibiting Cultures: The Poetics and Politics of Museum
    Display*, pp.212–54, Washington and London: Smithsonian Institution
Coghill, D. 1928 *The Elusive Gael*, Stirling: Eneas MacKay
Cohen, A.P. 1982 (ed.) *Belonging. Identity and Social Organisation in British
    Rural Cultures*, Manchester: Manchester University Press
—— 1982a 'A sense of time, a sense of place: the meaning of close social
    association in Whalsay, Shetland', in Cohen 1982 (ed.), pp. 21–49, *Belonging.
    Identity and Social Organisation in British Rural Cultures*, Manchester:
    Manchester University Press
—— 1985 *The Symbolic Construction of Community*, Chichester and London:
    Ellis Horwood Ltd and Tavistock
—— 1986 (ed.) *Symbolising the Boundary. Identity and Diversity in British Rural
    Cultures*, Manchester: Manchester University Press
—— 1987 *Whalsay. Symbol, Segment and Boundary in a Shetland Island Com-
    munity*, Manchester: Manchester University Press
—— 1996 'Owning the nation, and the personal nature of nationalism: locality
    and the rhetoric of nationhood in Scotland', in V.Amit-Talai and C.Knowles
    (eds) *Re-situating Identities: The Politics of Race, Ethnicity and Culture*, pp.
    267–82, Peterborough, Ontario: Broadview Press
Cohler, A. 1970 *Rousseau and Nationalism*, New York: Basic Books
Collier, A. 1953 *The Crofting Problem*, Cambridge: Cambridge University Press
Comhairle nan Eilean 1982 *Poileasaidh Da-Chananach (Bilingual Policy)*,
    Stornoway: Western Isles Council
Comunn na Gàidhlig 1994 *Gàidhlig 2000. A Strategy for Gaelic Development
    into the 21st Century*, Inverness: Comunn na Gàidhlig
—— 1994a *Ag obair dhuibhse*, Inverness: Comunn na Gàidhlig
—— 1996 *Fàilte. Welcome to Scotland's Gaelic Renaissance*, Inverness: Comunn
    na Gàidhlig
Condry, E. 1980 *Culture and Identity in the Scottish Highlands*, unpublished
    D.Phil. thesis, Oxford University
—— 1983 *Scottish Ethnography*, Edinburgh: Association for Scottish Ethnography
Connor, W. 1994 *Ethnonationalism: The Quest for Understanding*, Princeton,
    N.J.: Princeton University Press
Constantinidou, E. 1994 'The "death" of East Sutherland Gaelic: Death by
    women?', in P.Burton, K Kushari-Dyson and S.Ardener (eds) *Bilingual*

Women: Anthropological Approaches to Second Language Use, pp. 111–27, Oxford and Providence: Berg

Còr na Gàidhlig 1982 *Còr na Gàidhlig. Language and Community Development: The Gaelic Situation*, a report prepared for the Highlands and Islands Development Board

Cowan, J. 1990 *Dance and the Body Politic in Northern Greece*, Princeton: Princeton University Press

Cox, R. 1991 *Brigh na Facal*, Glasgow: Department of Celtic Studies

Craig, C. 1996 *Out of History. Narrative Paradigms in Scottish and British Culture*, Edinburgh: Polygon

Cranstone, M. 1994 *The Romantic Movement*, Oxford: Blackwell

Crofters Commission 1976 *Guide to the Crofting Acts*, Edinburgh: HMSO

—— 1986 *Information for Crofters*, Edinburgh: HMSO

Darling, F.F. 1955 *West Highland Survey*, Oxford: Oxford University Press

Davies, C.A. 1989 *Welsh Nationalism in the Twentieth Century: The Ethnic Option and the Modern State*, New York: Praeger

Davis, J. 1977 *People of the Mediterranean. An Essay in Comparative Social Anthropology*, London: Routledge and Kegan Paul

—— 1989 'The social relations of the production of history', in E. Tonkin, M. McDonald and M. Chapman (eds) *History and Ethnicity*, ASA Monograph 27, pp. 104–20, London: Routledge

Dawson, J. 1992 'The origins of the "Road to the Isles": trade, communications and Campbell power in Early Modern Scotland', in R. Mason and N. MacDougall (eds) *People and Power in Scotland: Essays in Honour of TC Smout*, Edinburgh: John Donald

Department of Agriculture and Fisheries (Scotland) 1986 *Scottish Agriculture. A ready reference to grants and services available to farmers in Scotland*, Edinburgh: HMSO

Devine, T.M. 1988 *The Great Highland Famine*, Edinburgh: John Donald

—— 1990 *Conflict and Stability in Scottish Society*, Edinburgh: John Donald

—— 1992 'Landlordism and Highland emigration', in T.M. Devine (ed.) *Scottish Emigration and Scottish Society*, pp. 84–103, Edinburgh: John Donald

—— 1994 *Clanship to Crofters War*, Manchester: Manchester University Press

Dodgshon, R. 1981 *Land and Society in Early Scotland*, Oxford: Oxford University Press

Dorian, N. 1970 'A substitute name-system in the Scottish Highlands', *American Anthropologist*, 72, pp. 303–19

—— 1978 *East Sutherland Gaelic: The Dialect of Brora, Golspie and Embo Fishing Communities*, Dublin: Dublin Institute for Advanced Studies

—— 1981 *Language Death. The Life Cycle of a Scottish Gaelic Dialect*, Philadelphia: University of Pennsylvania Press

Dorson, R.M. 1968 *The British Folklorists: A History*, Chicago: Chicago University Press

Dorst, J.D. 1989 *The Written Suburb: an American Site, an Ethnographic Dilemma*, Philadelphia: Pennsylvania University Press

Douglas, M. 1966 *Purity and Danger: An Analysis of Concepts of Pollution and Taboo*, London: Routledge and Kegan Paul

Duncan, J. and M. Savage (eds) 1991 'New Perspectives on the Locality Debate', special issue of *Environment and Planning A*, Vol.23, no.2.

Dunn, C.M. and A.G. Boyd Robertson 1989 'Gaelic in Education', in W. Gillies (ed.) *Gaelic and Scotland. Alba agus a' Ghàidhlig*, pp.45–55, Edinburgh: Edinburgh University Press

Durkacz, V. 1983 *The Decline of the Celtic Languages. A Study of Linguistic and Cultural Conflict in Scotland, Wales and Ireland from the Reformation to the Twentieth Century*, Edinburgh: John Donald

Dwelly, E. 1977 [1901–11] *Faclair Gaidhlig gu Beurla le Dealbhan. Dwelly's Illustrated Gaelic to English Dictionary*, Glasgow: Gairm

Edwards, Jeanette 1996 *Born and Bred* (unpub.MS)

Edwards, John 1985 *Language, Society and Identity*, Oxford: Blackwell

Ellis, P.B. 1969 *The Creed of the Celtic Revolution*, London: Medusa Press

—— 1985 *The Celtic Revolution. A Study in Anti-Imperialism*, Talybont, Ceredigion: Y Lolfa

Ellis, P.B. and S.Mac a' Ghobhainn 1971 *The Problem of Language Revival*, Inverness: Club Leabhar

Emmett, I. 1964 *A North Wales Parish*, London: Routledge and Kegan Paul

—— 1982 'Place, community and bilingualism in Blaenau Ffestiniog', in A.P. Cohen (ed.) *Belonging. Identity and Social Organisation in British Rural Cultures*, pp.202–21, Manchester: Manchester University Press

Ennew, J. 1980 *The Western Isles Today*, Cambridge: Cambridge University Press

Eriksen, T.H. 1993 *Ethnicity and Nationalism. Anthropological Perspectives*, London: Pluto

Erikson, E. 1968 *Identity: Youth and Crisis*, London: Faber and Faber

Errington, F. and D. Gewertz 1987 *Cultural Alternatives and a Feminist Anthropology: An Analysis of Culturally Constructed Gender Interests in Papua New Guinea*, Cambridge: Cambridge University Press

Evans, N. 1991 'Internal colonialism? Colonization, economic development and political mobilization in Wales, Scotland and Ireland', in G. Day and G. Rees (eds) *Regions, Nations and European Integration: Remaking the Celtic Periphery*, pp. 235–64, Cardiff: University of Wales Press

Fardon, R. (ed.) 1995 *Counterworks: Managing the Diversity of Knowledge*, London: Routledge

Fenton, A. and D.A.MacDonald (eds) 1994 *Studies in Scots and Gaelic* (Proceedings of the Third International Conference on the Languages of Scotland), Edinburgh: Edinburgh University Press

Fergusson, D.A., A.I. MacDhomhnuill and J.F. Gillespies London (eds) 1978 *Bho Na H-Innse Gall As Iomallaiche. From the Farthest Hebrides*, Toronto: Macmillan of Canada

Finlay, R. 1994 *Independent and Free: Scottish Politics and the Origins of the Scottish National Party, 1918–1945*, Edinburgh: John Donald

Fishman, J.A. 1989 *Language and Ethnicity in Minority Sociolinguistic Perspective*, Clevedon: Multilingual Matters

—— 1991 *Reversing Language Shift*, Clevedon: Multilingual Matters

Fordun, J. 1872 *John Fordun's Chronicle of the Scottish Nation*, W.Skene (ed.), trans from Latin by F.Skene, Edinburgh: Edmonston and Douglas

Forsythe, D. 1980 'Urban incomers and rural change. The impact of migrants from the city on life in an Orkney community', *Sociologia Ruralis*, XX.4, pp. 287–307

Foster, C.R. (ed.) 1980 *Nations without a State: Ethnic Minorities in Western Europe*, New York: Praeger

Fox, R. 1978 *The Tory Islanders. A People of the Celtic Fringe*, Cambridge: Cambridge University Press

Frankenberg, R. 1989 [1957] *Village on the Border*, Prospect Heights, Illinois: Waveland Press

—— 1966 *Communities in Britain. Social Life in Town and Country*, Harmondsworth: Penguin

Free Presbyterian Church 1974 *History of the Free Presbyterian Church of Scotland, 1893–1970*, Inverness: Publications Committee of the Free Presbyterian Church of Scotland

Friedman, J. 1994 *Cultural Identity and Global Process*, London: Sage

Gaskell, P. 1968 *Morvern Transformed*, Cambridge: Cambridge University Press

Gellner, E. 1983 *Nations and Nationalism*, Oxford: Blackwell

Gewertz, D. and F. Errington 1991 *Twisted Histories, Altered Contexts. Representing the Chambri in a World System*, Cambridge: Cambridge University Press

Giddens, A. 1990 *The Consequences of Modernity*, Oxford: Polity Press

—— 1991 *Modernity and Self-Identity*, Oxford: Polity

Godard, V.A., J.R. Llobera and C.Shore (eds) 1994 *The Anthropology of Europe: Identities and Boundaries in Conflict*, Oxford and Providence: Berg

Gordon, B. 1963 'Some Norse place-names in Trotternish, Isle of Skye', *Scottish Gaelic Studies* X.1, pp. 83–112

Government Statistical Service 1994 *1991 Census. Topic Monitor for Gaelic Language Scotland*, Edinburgh: General Register Office Scotland

Grant, A. 1988 'Scotland's "Celtic Fringe" in the late Middle Ages: the MacDonalds Lords of the Isles and the Kingdom of Scotland', in R.R. Davies (ed.) *The British Isles, 1100–1500*, Edinburgh

Gray, M. 1957 *The Highland Economy, 1750–1850*, Edinburgh: Oliver and Boyd

Grieve, M. and A. Scott (eds) 1972 *The Hugh MacDiarmid Anthology. Poems in Scots and English*, London: Routledge and Kegan Paul

Grigor, I.F. 1979 *Mightier than a Lord*, Stornoway: Acair

Grillo, R.D. (ed.) 1980 *"Nation" and "State" in Europe. Anthropological Perspectives*, London: Academic Press
—— 1989 *Dominant Languages*, Cambridge: Cambridge University Press
Grimble, I. 1962 *The Trial of Patrick Sellar. The Tragedy of the Highland Evictions*, London: Routledge and Kegan Paul
Hamilton, P. 1992 'The Enlightenment and the birth of social science', in S.Hall and B. Gieben (eds) *Formations of Modernity*, pp. 18–69, Oxford: Polity Press in association with the Open University
Handler, R. 1988 *Nationalism and the Politics of Culture in Quebec*, Madison: Wisconsin University Press
Handler, R. and J. Linnekin 1984 'Tradition, genuine or spurious', *Journal of American Folklore*, 97, pp. 273–90
Hanham, H.J. 1969 *Scottish Nationalism*, London: Faber and Faber
Hannerz, U. 1992 *Cultural Complexity: Studies in the Social Organization of Meaning*, New York: Columbia University Press
Hansen, M. 1952 'The third generation in America', *Commentary*, 14, pp. 492–500
Harris, R. 1980 *The Language Makers*, London: Duckworth
Harvie, C. 1994 [1977] *Scotland and Nationalism: Scottish Society and Politics, 1707–1994* (2nd. ed.), London: Routledge
—— 1994a *The Rise of Regional Europe*, London: Routledge
Hastrup, K. 1985 *Culture and History in Mediaeval Iceland. An Anthropological Analysis of Structure and Change*, Oxford: Oxford University Press
—— (ed.) 1992 *Other Histories*, London: Routledge
Haugen, E., J.D. McClure and D.S. Thomson (eds) 1981 *Minority Languages Today*, Edinburgh: Edinburgh University Press
Hechter, M. 1975 *Internal Colonialism: The Celtic Fringe in British National Development, 1530–1966*, London: Routledge and Kegan Paul
Heiberg, M. 1989 *The Making of the Basque Nation*, Cambridge: Cambridge University Press
Henson, H. 1974 *British Social Anthropologists and Language: A History of Separate Development*, Oxford: Oxford University Press
Herzfeld, M. 1987 *Anthropology Through the Looking-Glass: Critical Ethnography in the Margins of Europe*, Cambridge: Cambridge University Press
—— 1991 *A Place in History. Social and Monumental Time in a Cretan Town*, Princeton: Princeton University Press
Highet, J. 1950 *The Churches in Scotland To-day. A Survey of their Principles, Strength, Work and Statements*, Glasgow: Jackson Son and Co.
Hindley, R. 1990 *The Death of the Irish Language: A Qualified Obituary*, London: Routledge
Hobsbawm, E.J. 1990 *Nations and Nationalism since 1780. Programme, Myth, Reality*, Cambridge: Cambridge University Press
Hobsbawm, E.J. and T.Ranger (eds) 1983 *The Invention of Tradition*, Cambridge: Cambridge University Press

Hont, I. and M. Ignatieff (eds) 1983 *Wealth and Virtue. The Shaping of the Political Economy in the Scottish Enlightenment*, Cambridge: Cambridge University Press

Houston, R.A. 1985 *Scottish Literacy and the Scottish Identity. Illiteracy and Society in Scotland and Northern England, 1600–1800*, Cambridge: Cambridge University Press

Hudson, R.A. 1980 *Sociolinguistics*, Cambridge: Cambridge University Press

Hunter, J. 1976 *The Making of the Crofting Community*, Edinburgh: John Donald

—— 1986 'Introduction', in J. Murdoch *For the People's Cause*, pp. 9–40, Edinburgh: HMSO

—— 1991 *The Claim of Crofting. The Scottish Highlands and Islands, 1930–1990*, Edinburgh and London: Mainstream Publishing

—— 1992 *Scottish Highlanders: A People and their Place*, Edinburgh: Mainstream Publishing

Hunter, J. and C. MacLean 1987 *Skye: The Island*, Edinburgh and London: Mainstream Publishing

Hymes, D. 1974 *Foundations in Sociolinguistics. An Ethnographic Approach*, Philadelphia: University of Pennsylvania Press

Jackson, K. 1951 'Common Gaelic: the evolution of the Goidelic languages', Sir John Rhys Memorial Lecture, London: Geoffrey Cumberlege

—— 1953 *Language and History in Early Britain. A Chronological Survey of the Brittonic Languages, First to Twelfth Century AD*, Edinburgh: Edinburgh University Press

—— 1956 'The Pictish language', in F.T.Wainwright (ed.) *The Problem of the Picts*, pp. 129–66, London: Nelson

Jackson, M. 1983 'Skye Bilingual Project', *Aberdeen College of Education Gaelic Newsletter*, 3, pp. 15–19, Aberdeen: Aberdeen College of Education

Jedrej, C. and M.Nutall 1995 *White Settlers: The Impact of Rural Repopulation in Scotland*, Chur, Switzerland: Harwood Academic

Jenkins, R. 1995 'Nations and nationalisms: towards more open models', *Nations and Nationalism*, 1 (3), pp. 369–90

—— 1996 *Social Identity*, London: Routledge

Johnson, S. and J. Boswell 1924 [1775 and 1785] *A Journey to the Western Islands of Scotland. The Journal of a Tour to the Hebrides*, edited by R.W. Chapman, Oxford: Oxford University Press

Jones, B.L. 1981 'Welsh: linguistic conservatism and shifting bilingualism', in E. Haugen, J.D. McClure and D.S. Thomson (eds) *Minority Languages Today*, pp. 40–52, Edinburgh: Edinburgh University Press

Kapferer, B. 1988 *Legends of People, Myths of State*, Washington and London: Smithsonian Institution

Kedourie, E. 1993 [1961] *Nationalism*, Oxford: Blackwell

Kellas, J. 1980 [1968] *Modern Scotland*, London: George Allen and Unwin

—— 1989 [1984] *The Scottish Political System* (4th ed.), Cambridge: Cambridge University Press

Khlief, B.B. 1980 *Language, Ethnicity and Education in Wales*, The Hague: Mouton

Kidd, C. 1993 *Subverting Scotland's Past. Scottish Whig Historians and the Creation of an Anglo-British Identity, 1689–c.1830*, Cambridge: Cambridge University Press

King, A. (ed.) 1991 *Culture, Globalization and the World System*, Houndmills: Macmillan

Kuper, A. 1996 [1973] *Anthropology and Anthropologists: the Modern British School* 2nd.ed., London: Routledge

Lash, S. and J. Friedman (eds) 1992 *Modernity and Identity*, Oxford: Blackwell

Lash, S. and J. Urry 1994 *Economies of Signs and Space*, London: Sage

Lenman, B. 1980 *The Jacobite Risings in Britain, 1698–1746*, London: Methuen

Lerner, A.J. 1993 'Introduction', in M. Ringrose and A.J. Lerner (eds) *Reimagining the Nation*, pp. 1–5, Buckingham: Open University Press

Lhuyd, E. 1707 *Archeologia Britannica*, Vol. 1, Oxford

Llobera, J. 1994 *The God of Modernity: The Development of Nationalism in Western Europe*, Oxford and Providence: Berg

Lynch, M. 1992 [1991] *Scotland: a New History*, London: Pimlico

MacAlpine, N. 1831 *A Pronouncing Gaelic Dictionary*, Inverness

MacAulay, D. 1979 'The state of Gaelic language studies', in A.J. Aitken and T. MacArthur (eds) *Languages of Scotland*, pp. 120–36, Edinburgh: Chambers

MacBain, A. 1911 [1896] *An Etymological Dictionary of the Gaelic Language*, Stirling: MacBain

MacCannell, D. 1989 [1976] *The Tourist: A New Theory of the Leisure Class*, New York: Schocken Books

—— 1992 *Empty Meeting Grounds: The Tourist Papers*, London: Routledge

McClure, J.D. 1979 'Scots: its range of uses', in A.J. Aitken and T. McArthur (eds) *Languages of Scotland*, pp. 26–48, Edinburgh: Chambers

—— 1988 *Why Scots Matters*, Edinburgh: Saltire Society

MacColla, F. 1945 *And the Cock Crew*, Glasgow: William McLellan

MacCowan, R. 1902 *The Men of Skye*, Portree: John MacLaine

McCrone, D. 1991 'Politics and society in Modern Scotland', in G. Day and G. Rees (eds) *Regions, Nations and European Integration: Remaking the Celtic Periphery*, pp.89–102, Cardiff: University of Wales Press

—— 1992 *Understanding Scotland. The Sociology of a Stateless Nation*, London: Routledge

McCrone, D., A. Morris and R. Kiely 1995 *Scotland – the Brand. The Making of Scottish Heritage*, Edinburgh: Edinburgh University Press

MacDhòmhnaill, C.D. 1989 'Na marbhrann soisgeulach', in W. Gillies (ed.) *Gaelic and Scotland. Alba ague a' Ghàidhlig*, Edinburgh: Edinburgh University Press

MacDhòmhnaill, I.A. 1976 *Gàidhlig Bheò*, Cambridge: National Extension College

MacDiarmid, H. 1968 'Scotland', in O.D. Edwards, G. Evans and I. Rhys and H.MacDiarmid *Celtic Nationalism*, London: Routledge and Kegan Paul

MacDonald, A. 1741 *Leubhar a Theasgasc Ainminnin no a Nuadhfhoclair Gaoidheilg & Beurla*, Dun-Edin: Raibeard Fleming

Macdonald, C. 1981 'Bilingualism in education – the Scottish experience', *Education in the North* 18, pp. 21–3, Aberdeen: Aberdeen College of Education

McDonald, M. 1986 'Celtic ethnic kinship and the problem of being English', *Current Anthropology* 27 (4), pp. 333–47

—— 1986a 'Brittany: politics and women in a minority world', in R. Ridd and H. Callaway (eds) *Caught up in Conflict: Women's Responses to Political Strife*, pp. 163–92, Houndmills: Macmillan

—— 1987 'Tourism: chasing culture and tradition in Brittany', in M. Bouquet and M. Winter (eds) *Who from their Labours Rest? Conflict and Practice in Rural Tourism*, pp. 120–34, Aldershot: Avebury

—— 1989 *We are not French! Language, Culture and Identity in Brittany*, London: Routledge

—— 1993 'The construction of difference: an anthropological approach to stereotypes', in S. Macdonald (ed.) *Inside European Identities: Ethnography in Western Europe*, pp. 219–36, Oxford and Providence: Berg

—— 1994 'Women and linguistic innovation in Brittany', in P. Burton, K. Kushari-Dyson and S. Ardener (eds) *Bilingual Women: Anthropological Approaches to Second Language Use*, pp. 85–110, Oxford and Providence: Berg

—— 1996 '"Unity in diversity": Some tensions in the construction of Europe', *Social Anthropology*, 4.1, pp. 47–60

Macdonald, N. 1985 'Sabhal Mór Ostaig – College of Commitment', in J. Hulbert (ed.) *Gaelic. Looking to the Future*, Dundee: Andrew Fletcher Society

Macdonald, S. 1987 *Social and Linguistic Identity in the Scottish Gàidhealtachd*, unpublished D.Phil. thesis, Oxford University

—— 1993 (ed.) *Inside European Identities: Ethnography in Western Europe*, Oxford and Providence: Berg

—— 1994 'Whisky, women and the Scottish drink problem: a view from the Highlands', in M. McDonald (ed.) *Gender, Drink and Drugs*, pp.125–44, Oxford and Providence: Berg

—— 1997 'A people's story? Heritage, identity and authenticity', in C. Rojek and J. Urry (eds) *Touring Cultures. Transformations of Travel and Theory*, pp. 155–75, London: Routledge

McDyer, J. 1968 'Glencolumbkille report', *Donegal Democrat*

McFarlane, G. 1981 'Shetlanders and incomers: change, conflict and emphasis in social perceptions', in L. Holy and M. Stuchlik (eds) *The Structure of Folk Models*, pp. 119–136, London: Academic Press

Mac Gilleain, S. 1981 *Reothairt is Contraigh. Tagadh de Dhàin 1932–72. Spring Tide and Neap Tide. Selected Poems 1932–1972*, Edinburgh: Canongate

—— 1985 [1939] 'The poetry of the Clearances', in S. Mac Gilleain *Ris a Bhruthaich. The Criticism and Prose Writings of Sorley MacLean*, pp. 48–74, Stornoway: Acair

—— 1985a [1975] 'Màiri Mhór nan Oran', in S. MacGilleain *Ris a Bhruthaich. The Criticism and Prose Writings of Sorley MacLean*, pp. 250–7, Stornoway: Acair

McGrath, J. 1974 *The Cheviot, the Stag and the Black, Black Oil*, Kyleakin: West Highland Publishing Co.

—— 1986 'There are many truths', in M. MacLean and C. Carrell (eds) *As an Fhearann. From the Land. Clearance, Conflict and Crofting*, pp. 37–41, Edinburgh: Mainstream; Stornoway: An Lanntair; and Glasgow: Third Eye

MacInnes, J. 1951 *The Evangelical Movement of the Scottish Highlands, 1688– 1800*, Aberdeen: Aberdeen University Press

MacInnes, J. 1989 'The Gaelic perception of the Lowlands', in W. Gillies (ed.) *Gaelic and Scotland. Alba agus a 'Ghàidhlig*, pp. 89–100, Edinburgh: Edinburgh University Press

MacIntyre, D. 1865 *On the Antiquity of the Gaelic Languages*, Edinburgh: MacLachlan & Stewart

MacKay, I.R. 1966 *Who are the Highlanders?*, Inverness: An Comunn Gàidhealach

—— 1969 *Gaelic is . . .*, Inverness: An Comunn Gàidhealach

McKechnie, R. 1993 'Becoming Celtic in Corsica', in S. Macdonald (ed.) *Inside European Identities*, pp. 118–45, Oxford and Providence: Berg

MacKenzie, A. 1986 [1883] *History of the Highland Clearances*, Perth: Melven press

—— 1883a *The Isle of Skye, 1882–3*, Inverness: A & W MacKenzie

—— 1883b *The Trial of Patrick Sellar*, Inverness: A & W MacKenzie

—— 1884 *The Military Expedition to the Isle of Skye*, Inverness: A & W MacKenzie

MacKenzie, W. 1930 *Skye: Iochdar-Trotternish and District. Traditions, Reflections and Memories*, Glasgow: Alex. MacLaren and Sons

MacKinnon, K. 1974 *The Lion's Tongue: The Story of the Original and Continuing Language of the Scottish People*, Inverness: Club Leabhar

—— 1977 *Language, Education and Social Processes in a Gaelic Community*, London: Routledge and Kegan Paul

—— 1978 *Gaelic in Scotland 1971. Some Sociological and Demographic Considerations of the Census Report for Gaelic*, Hatfield: Hatfield Polytechnic

—— 1981 *Scottish Opinion on Gaelic. A report on a national attitude survey for An Comunn Gàidhealach undertaken in 1981*, Hatfield: Hatfield Polytechnic

—— 1991 *Gaelic: A Past and Future Prospect*, Edinburgh: Saltire Society

MacKinnon, R. 1971 *Gaelic. A Complete Course for Beginners in Scottish Gaelic*, Sevenoaks, Kent: Hodder & Stoughton Ltd

McLean, A.C. 1955 *The Hill of the Red Fox*, London: William Collins

—— 1962 *Ribbon of Fire*, London: Collins

MacLean, K. 1983 *Different Perceptions and Ideas of Skye. A Perception of Skye, through photographs of Gus Wylie and picture postcards*, BA thesis Glasgow School of Art

MacLean, M. 1986 'As an Fhearann', in M. MacLean and C. Carrell (eds), 1986 *As an Fhearann. From the Land. Clearance, Conflict and Crofting*, pp. 5–7, Edinburgh: Mainstream; Stornoway: An Lanntair; and Glasgow: Third Eye

MacLean, M. and C. Carrell (eds) 1986 *As an Fhearann. From the Land. Clearance, Conflict and Crofting*, Edinburgh: Mainstream; Stornoway: An Lanntair; and Glasgow: Third Eye

MacLean, S. 1986 'Vale of tears: a view of Highland history to 1886', in M. MacLean and C. Carrell (eds) *As an Fhearann. From the Land. Clearance, Conflict and Crofting*, pp. 9–18, Edinburgh: Mainstream; Stornoway: An Lanntair; and Glasgow: Third Eye

MacLennan, M. 1925 *Gaelic Dictionary*, Edinburgh: John Grant

MacLeod, D. 1856 *The Sutherlandshire Clearances*, Glasgow: Archibald Sinclair

—— 1892 [1883] *Gloomy Memories*, Glasgow: Archibald Sinclair

MacLeod, F. 1984 'School should be part of the "psychological home"', *West Highland Free Press*, 20.1.1984

McLeod, H. 1981 *Religion and the People of Western Europe 1789–1970*, Oxford: Oxford University Press

MacLeod, J. 1994 *No Great Mischief if You Fall: The Highland Experience*, Edinburgh: Mainstream Publishing Company

MacLeod, R. 1985 'The Bishop of Skye: the life and work of Rev. Roderick MacLeod (1794–1868) Minister of Bracadale and Snizort', *Transactions of the Gaelic Society of Inverness*, LIII, pp. 174–209

McLynn, F. 1996 'Charlie's last pretence', *Times Higher Education Supplement*, 12.4.1996, p.18

McNeill, W.J. 1986 *Polyethnicity and National Unity in World History*, Toronto: Toronto University Press

Malinowski, B. 1922 *Argonauts of the Western Pacific*, London: Routledge and Kegan Paul

Marcus, G. 1992 'Past, present and emergent identities: requirements for ethnographies of late twentieth-century modernity worldwide', in S. Lash and J. Friedman (eds) *Modernity and Identity*, pp. 309–30, Oxford: Blackwell

Marcus, G. and M. Fisher 1986 *Anthropology as Cultural Critique*, Chicago: Chicago University Press

Martin-Jones, M. 1989 'Language, power and linguistic minorities: the need for an alternative approach to bilingualism, language maintenance and shift', in R.D. Grillo (ed.) *Social Anthropology and the Politics of Language* (Sociological Review Monograph), pp. 106–25, London: Routledge

Mason, R. 1992 'Chivalry and citizenship: aspects of national identity in Renaissance Scotland', in R. Mason and N. MacDougall (eds) *People and Power in Scotland: Essays in Honour of TC Smout*, pp. 50–73, Edinburgh: John Donald

Melucci, A. 1989 *Nomads of the Present*, London: Hutchinson Radius

Mewett, P. 1977 'Occupational pluralism in crofting: the influence of non-croft work on patterns of crofting agriculture in the Isle of Lewis since about 1850', *Scottish Journal of Sociology* II, pp. 31–49

—— 1982 'Associational categories and the social location of relationships in a Lewis crofting community', in A.P. Cohen (ed.) *Belonging*, pp. 101–30, Manchester: Manchester University Press

—— 1982a 'Exiles, nicknames, social identities and the production of local consciousness in a Lewis crofting community', in A.P. Cohen (ed.) *Belonging*, pp. 222–46, Manchester: Manchester University Press

Miller, D. 1994 *Modernity: An Ethnographic Approach*, Oxford and Providence: Berg

Millman, R.N. 1975 *The Making of the Scottish Landscape*, London: BT Batsford

Mitchell, R. 1992 'The "independent" evaluation of bilingual primary education: a narrative account' (with editors' postscript), in J.C. Alderson and A. Beretta (eds) *Evaluating Second Language Education*, pp. 100–40, Cambridge: Cambridge University Press

Mitchison, R. (ed.) 1980 *The Roots of Nationalism*, Edinburgh: John Donald

Morgan, G.1966 *The Dragon's Tongue: the Fortunes of the Welsh Language*, Narbeth, Pembrokeshire, Wales: H.G. Walters

Morgan, P. 1983 'From a death to a view: the hunt for the Welsh past in the romantic period', in E. Hobsbawm and T. Ranger (eds) *The Invention of Tradition*, pp. 43–100, Cambridge: Cambridge University Press

Mulholland, G. 1984 [1980] *The Struggle for a Language. Gaelic in Education*, Edinburgh: Rank and File

Murdoch, J. 1986 *For the People's Cause. From the Writings of John Murdoch, Highland Land Reformer*, edited and introduced by J. Hunter, Edinburgh: HMSO

Murison, D. 1979 'The historical background', in A.J. Aitken and T. McArthur (eds) *Languages of Scotland*, pp. 2–13, Edinburgh: Chambers

Murray, J. and F.MacLeod 1981 'Sea change in the Western Isles of Scotland: the rise of locally relevant bilingual education', in J.P. Sher (ed.) *Rural Education in Urbanised Nations: Issues and Innovations*, Boulder and Oxford: Westview Press

Murray, J. and C.Morrison 1984 *Bilingual Primary Education in the Western Isles of Scotland*, Stornoway: Acair

Nadel, J.H. 1984 'Stigma and separation: pariah status and community persistence in a Scottish fishing village', *Ethnology*, XXIII (2), pp. 101–15

—— 1986 'Burning with the fire of God: Calvinism and community in a Scottish fishing village', *Ethnology*, XXV (1), pp. 46–60

Nadel-Klein, J. 1991 'Reweaving the fringe: localism, tradition, and representation in British ethnography', *American Ethnologist*, 18 (3), pp. 500–17

—— 1995 'Occidentalism as a cottage industry: representing the autochthonous "Other" in British and Irish rural studies', in J. Carrier (ed.) *Occidentalism: Images of the West*, pp. 109–34, Oxford: Clarendon

—— 1997 'Crossing a representational divide: from west to east in Scottish ethnography', in A. James, J. Hockey and A. Dawson (eds) *After Writing Culture: Epistemology and Praxis in Contemporary Anthropology*, pp. 86–102, London: Routledge

Nairn, T. 1981 [1977] *The Break-Up of Britain. Crisis and Neo-Nationalism*, London: Verso

Napier Commission 1883 *Royal Commission on the Highlands and Islands*, Scottish Record Office ref, AF 50

Neville, G.K. 1994 *The Mother Town. Civic Ritual, Symbol, and Experience in the Borders of Scotland*, Oxford: Oxford University Press

New Statistical Account (NSA) 1835–45 (15 volumes), Edinburgh: William Blackwood and Sons

Nicolaisen, W.F.H. 1976 *Scottish Place Names*, London: Batsford

Nicolson, A. 1930 *History of Skye*, Glasgow: Alex.MacLaren and Sons

Nisbet, J. 1963 'Bilingualism and the school', *Scottish Gaelic Studies*, X (1), pp. 44–52

Old Statistical Account (OSA) 1985 [1791–9] (21 volumes), Sir John Sinclair (ed.), Edinburgh: EP Publishing

O'Rahilly, T.F. 1946 *Early Irish History and Mythology*, Dublin: Dublin Institute for Advanced Studies

Owen, R. 1979 *Instant Gaelic*, Aberfeldy: Clò Chailleann

—— 1982 *Gàidhlig le Gaire: Gaelic with a Laugh*, Aberfeldy: Clò Chailleann

Owen, T. 1956 'The "Communion Season" and Presbyterianism in a Hebridean community', *Gwerin*, I (2), pp. 53–66

Parman, S. 1972 *Sociocultural Change in a Scottish Crofting Township*, unpub. PhD thesis, Rice University, Houston, Texas

—— 1976 'General properties of naming, and a specific case of nicknaming in the Scottish Outer Hebrides', *Ethnos*, 41, pp. 99–115

—— 1990 *Scottish Crofters. A Historical Ethnography of a Celtic Village*, Fort Worth, Texas: Holt, Rinehart and Winston

—— 1990a '*Orduighean*: a dominant symbol in the Free Church of the Scottish Highlands', *American Anthropologist*, 92 (2), pp. 295–305

—— 1993 'The future of European boundaries: a case study', in T.M.Wilson and M.E.Smith (eds) *Cultural Change and the New Europe: Perspectives on the European Community*, pp. 189–202, Boulder and Oxford: Westview Press

Payne, G. and A.MacLeod 1993 'The double gates: culture, interaction and experience in access to the "Exclusive Club"', *FASGNAG, proceedings of the second conference on research in the maintenance of Gaelic*, (ed.) K.MacKinnon, Hatfield: Hertfordshire University

Peristiany, J.G. (ed.) 1965 *Honour and Shame. The Values of Mediterranean Society*, London: Weidenfeld and Nicolson

Phillips, S.K. 1986 'Natives and incomers: the symbolism of belonging in Muker parish, north Yorkshire', in A.P. Cohen (ed.) *Symbolising Boundaries. Identity and Diversity in British Cultures*, pp. 141–54, Manchester: Manchester University Press

Piggott, S. 1968 *The Druids*, London: Thames and Hudson

Pittock, M. 1991 *The Invention of Scotland. The Stuart Myth and the Scottish Identity, 1638 to the Present*, London: Routledge

Prebble, J. 1961 *Culloden*, Harmondsworth: Penguin
—— 1963 *The Highland Clearances*, Harmondsworth: Penguin
—— 1966 *Glencoe*, Harmondsworth: Penguin
—— 1968 *The Darien Disaster*, Harmondsworth: Penguin
—— 1971 *The Lion in the North*, Harmondsworth: Penguin
Rapport, N. 1993 *Diverse World Views in an English Village*, Edinburgh: Edinburgh University Press
Richards, E. 1973 'How tame were the Highlanders during the Clearances?', *Scottish Studies*, XVII, pp. 35–50
—— 1982 *A History of the Highland Clearances. Agrarian Transformations and the Evictions, 1746–1886*, London: Croom Helm
—— 1985 *A History of the Highland Clearances, Vol. 2: Emigration, Protest, Reasons*, London: Croom Helm
Ringrose, M. and A.J. Lerner (eds) 1993 *Reimagining the Nation*, Buckingham: Open University Press
Ritzer, G. 1996 [1993] *The McDonaldization of Society*, Thousand Oaks: Pine Forge Press
Robertson, J.A. 1865 *Concise Historical Proofs respecting the Gael of Alban*, Edinburgh: William Nimmo
Rogers, S.C. 1991 *Shaping Modern Times in Rural France: The Transformation and Reproduction of an Aveyronnais Community*, Princeton: Princeton University Press
Rokkan, S. and D.W. Urwin (eds) 1982 *The Politics of Territorial Identity: Studies in European Regionalism*, London: Sage
Roosens, E. 1989 *Creating Ethnicity*, London: Sage
Ross, D. 1852 *The Scottish Highlanders: Their Present Sufferings and Future Prospects*, Glasgow: W.G. Blackie and Sons
—— 1854 *Real Scottish Grievances*, Glasgow: W.G. Blackie and Sons
Sabhal Mór Ostaig 1980 *A Two Year Course*, report prepared for the board of trustees of *Sabhal Mór Ostaig*
Sahlins, M. 1987 [1985] *Islands of History*, London and New York: Tavistock
Samuel, R. 1981 *People's History and Socialist Theory*, London: Routledge and Kegan Paul
—— 1994 *Theatres of Memory*, London: Verso
Saussure, F. de 1974 [1915] *Course in General Linguistics*, London: Collins
Seton-Watson, H. 1977 *Nations and States*, London: Methuen
—— 1981 *Language and National Consciousness*, London: British Academy
Shaw, W. 1778 *An Analysis of the Gaelic Language*, Edinburgh: W&T Ruddiman
—— 1780 *A Gaelic English Dictionary*, London: W&A Strahan
Sher, R. 1986 *Church and University in the Scottish Enlightenment: The Moderate Literati of Edinburgh*, Edinburgh: Edinburgh University Press
Shuken, C. 1984 'Highland and Island English', in P. Trudgill (ed.) *Language in the British Isles*, pp. 152–66, Cambridge: Cambridge University Press
Sillar, F.C. and R.Meyler 1973 *Skye*, Newton Abbot: David and Charles

Silverman, M. and P.H. Gulliver 1992 'Historical anthropology and the ethno-graphic tradition: a personal, historical, and intellectual account', in M. Silverman and P.H.Gulliver (eds) *Approaching the Past. Historical Anthropology through Irish case studies*, pp. 3–72, New York: Columbia University Press

Simpson, J.M.Y. 1981 'The challenge of minority languages', in E. Haugen, J.D. McClure and D.S. Thomson (eds) *Minority Languages Today*, pp. 235–41, Edinburgh: Edinburgh University Press

Skene, W. 1836 *The Highlanders of Scotland*, Stirling: MacBain

Smith, A.D. 1981 *The Ethnic Revival in the Modern World*, Cambridge: Cambridge University Press

—— 1986 *The Ethnic Origins of Nations*, Oxford: Blackwell

—— 1991 *National Identity*, Harmondsworth: Penguin

Smith, I.C. 1968 *Consider the Lilies*, London: Gollancz

Smith, Janet A. 1970 'Some eighteenth century ideas of Scotland', in N.T. Phillipson and R. Mitchison (eds) *Scotland in the Age of Improvement*, pp. 107–24, Edinburgh: Edinburgh University Press

Smith, John A. 1968 'The position of Gaelic and Gaelic culture in Scottish education', in D.S. Thomson and I. Grimble (eds) *The Future of the Highlands*, London: Routledge and Kegan Paul

Smout, T.C. 1972 [1969] *A History of the Scottish People, 1560–1830*, London: Fontana

—— 1986 *A Century of the Scottish People, 1830–1950*, London: Collins

Solomon, R. 1988 *Continental Philosophy since 1750*, Oxford: Oxford University Press

Sproull, A. 1993 *The Economics of Gaelic Language Development. A Research Report for Highlands and Islands Enterprise and the Gaelic Television Committee with Comunn na Gàidhlig*, with B. Ashcroft, Glasgow: Glasgow Caledonian University

Stacey, M. 1960 *Tradition and Change: a Study of Banbury*, Oxford: Oxford University Press

Stafford, F. 1988 *The Sublime Savage*, Edinburgh: Edinburgh University Press

Stephens, M. (ed.) 1976 *Linguistic Minorities in Western Europe*, Llandysul: Gomer Press

Stephenson, J. 1984 *Ford: A Village in the West Highlands*, Edinburgh: Paul Harris

Stewart, A. 1812 *Elements of Gaelic Grammar*, Edinburgh: Stewart

Stewart, K. 1996 *A Space on the Side of the Road. Cultural Poetics in an 'Other' America*, Princeton, N.J.: Princeton University Press

Storey, R.J. 1979 'Community co-operatives – a Highlands and Islands experiment', paper presented to the fifth International Seminar on Marginal Regions, Trinity College, Dublin

Strathern, M. 1981 *Kinship at the Core: An Anthropology of Elmdon, a Village in North-West Essex in the Nineteen-Sixties*, Cambridge: Cambridge University Press

—— 1982 'The place of kinship: kin, class and village status in Elmdon, Essex', in A.P. Cohen (ed.) *Belonging*, pp. 72–100, Manchester: Manchester University Press

—— 1982a 'The village as an idea: constructs of village-ness in Elmdon, Essex', in A.P. Cohen (ed.) *Belonging*, pp. 247–77, Manchester: Manchester University Press

—— 1987 'The limits of auto-anthropology', in A. Jackson (ed.) *Anthropology at Home*, pp. 16–37, London: Tavistock

—— 1991 *Partial Connections*, Savage, Maryland: Rowman and Littlefield

—— 1992 *After Nature. English Kinship in the Late Twentieth Century*, Cambridge: Cambridge University Press

Taylor, C. 1989 *Sources of the Self. The Making of the Modern Identity*, Cambridge: Cambridge University Press

Taylor, L.J. 1985 'The priest and the agent: social drama and class consciousness in the West of Ireland', *Comparative Studies in Society and History*, 27 (4), pp. 696–712

—— 1992 'The languages of belief: nineteenth century religious discourse in Southwest Donegal', in M. Silverman and P.H. Gulliver (eds) *Approaching the Past. Historical Anthropology through Irish case studies*, pp. 142–75, New York: Columbia University Press

Thompson, F. 1968 *Harris and Lewis: Outer Hebrides*

—— 1974 *The Highlands and Islands*, London: Robert Hale & Co.

—— 1984 *Crofting Years*, Barr, Ayrshire: Luath Press Ltd

Thomson, D. 1974 *An Introduction to Gaelic Poetry*, London: Gollancz

—— 1976 (ed.) *Gàidhlig ann an Albainn*, Glasgow: Gairm

—— 1979 'Gaelic: its range of uses', in A. Aitken and T. MacArthur (eds) *Languages of Scotland*, pp. 14–25, Edinburgh: Chambers

—— 1981 *The New English-Gaelic Dictionary*, Glasgow: Gairm

Tiryakian, E.A. and R. Rogowski (eds) 1985 *New Nationalisms of the Developed West: Toward Explanation*, Boston: Allen and Unwin

Tönnies, F. 1955 [1887] *Community and Association (Gemeinschaft and Gesellschaft)*, London: Routledge and Kegan Paul

Trevor-Roper, H. 1983 'The invention of tradition: the Highland tradition of Scotland', in E. Hobsbawm and T. Ranger (eds) *The Invention of Tradition*, pp. 15–42, Cambridge: Cambridge University Press

Urry, J. 1990 *The Tourist Gaze*, London: Sage

Wagner, R. 1991 [1975] *The Invention of Culture*, revised and expanded edition, Chicago: University of Chicago Press

Wainwright, F.T. (ed.) 1956 *The Problem of the Picts*, London: Nelson

Walker, M.K. 1973 *Social Constraints, Individuals, and Social Decisions in a Scottish Rural Community*, unpub. PhD thesis, University of Illinois, Urbana Champaign

Webb, K. 1978 [1977] *The Growth of Nationalism in Scotland*, Harmondsworth: Penguin

Weber, M. 1930 [1904–5] *The Protestant Ethic and the Spirit of Capitalism*, trans. Talcott Parsons, London: George Allen and Unwin

Williams, C. (ed.) 1991 *Linguistic Minorities, Society and Territory*, Clevedon: Multilingual Matters

Williams, C. 1991a 'Linguistic minorities:West European and Canadian perspectives', in C. Williams (ed.) *Linguistic Minorities, Society and Territory*, pp.1–43, Clevedon: Multilingual Matters

Williams, R. 1973 *The Country and the City*, London: Chatto and Windus

Wilson, T. and M. Estellie Smith (eds) 1993 *Cultural Change and the New Europe: Perspectives on the European Community*, Boulder: Westview

Withers, C. 1984 *Gaelic in Scotland, 1698–1981. The Geographical History of a Language*, Edinburgh: John Donald

—— 1988 *Gaelic Culture – The Transformation of a Culture Region*, London: Routledge

Author Index

Subject Index

ACAIR 58
acculturation xv
activism
in Land Wars 87–91 *passim*
see also Land Wars
local, 62, 140, 198–9, 203–7
local language, 227–30
pro-Gaelic, 56–61, 219
see also Gaelic renaissance
Adherents 168, 174–5, 185
Age of Improvement 44
Agricultural Development
Programme 25n16
Airigh Shamhraidh 59, 61, 107,
191, 195
see also shielings
Alba 40
alienation 10, 46, 48, 99, 219, 233
ambivalence
and identity 10, 11, 49, 135,
199
and modernity 4, 49
and the past 21, 69
and repertoire 13, 245, 248
see also repertoire
over Gaelic 23, 255
An Comunn Gàidhealach 35, 57,
60, 64n9
Anglicisation 47–9, 250–1
see also Gaelic, decline of
animals, attitudes towards
109–10, 118, 131
An Litreachadh Ur 58
annual cycle 249–51
anthropology
and community *see* community
and history 31–5

and ideas about language 11–13
and the individuation of
cultures 9, 246–8
nature of, xviii, 8–10, 20
of Britain 8–10, 25n11, 131
of Europe 8–10, 25n11 and 12,
196
of modernity and post-
modernity 24n1
of Scotland 8–10, 24n2, 25n12
post-modern 247
see also ethnography, fieldwork
apathy 138, 212, 247
Arnold, Matthew 42
authenticity
and identity 13, 38, 99, 197
and tradition 2–6, 110
see also tradition
authority
political, 204
religious, 176–7, 179–82
autonomy
of child 224–5, 230–2, 236
of Scotland 256
see also nationalism
away 118–20, 121, 132–5, 161n3,
168–9
see also home, localness

Basque 56, 65n18, 238–9
Battle of Culloden *see* Culloden
Being 50–1, 155, 247
see also ontology
belonging 13, 22, 130–59 *passim*
see also home, localness
best room 156, 158
Bible 46, 48, 82, 84

283

media
Gaelic 7, 133–4, 191, 256, 258n4
images of Highlands 71–2, 124, 131, 133–4, 197–9
see also Gaelic broadcasting, television
Member of Parliament 149
Members 168, 174–5
Men 83–5
men 120–5, 152–4, 185, 204–5
see also gender, identity
ministers 168, 174–6, 180–2
see also Highland churches
minorities 61, 238–9
minority languages *see* language
Moderates 82
modernity
and ambivalence *see* ambivalence
and community *see* community
and romanticism 25n9
and the Highlands 2
and tradition 3–6
as variable 8, 24n1
dissatisfaction with, 55, 134
modesty 185–6
mother tongue 219
Munro, Donald 82–3
Murdoch, John 88–9
museums 7, 71
music 81, 83, 163–4
muteness 13

naming 137, 161n6
see also surnames
Napier Commission 89–90
nation
conceptions of, xixn1, 11, 50–2
definition of, 24n6
see also culture, ethnicity,

identity, nationalism, nation-state
National Association of Gaelic Arts Festivals *see* Fèisean nan Gàidheal
National Gaelic Arts Council 59
nationalism
and language 37–9, 54–6
and philology 52–4
romantic, 38, 75, 88–90, 238
Scottish, 55–7, 64nn10 and 11, 240–2, 256
see also ethnonationalism
Nationality Act 58
National Mòd 35, 57, 60, 109
nation-state
and tradition-formation 3, 6
formation of, 6, 50–2
Scotland as, 5, 38, 54–7
see also nation, nationalism, state
natural ability 117–19, 124
naturalness 219–25
Nazism 55
Noble, Iain 7, 57, 217
Norse 40
North Sea oil 56, 71
nostalgia 133–4

oil *see* North Sea oil
ontology 49–50, 62, 155
of Being *see* Being
of improvement 155, 224, 247
see also expressive individuation, identity, improvement
ordùighean see communion
Ossian 49–53 *passim*

Parantan airson Foghlam Gàidhlig 59